MUEL LOUDON.

ade the twenty eighth Day of July

e Thousand Seven Hundred and Eighty four — Between Isaac Stoutenburgh and Philip Van Cortlandt, an Act of the Legislature of the said State, entitled, " An Act for the speedy Sale of the confiscated and forfeited Thousand Seven Hundred and Eighty-four, of the one Part, and Nathaniel Norton

---

mmissioners as aforesaid, by Virtue of the Power and Authority to them in and by the said Act granted; and for w York

— the Receipt whereof is hereby acknowledged, HAVE Granted, Bargained, Sold,

aid Nathaniel Norton
ituate in the Township of Southold in Suffolk County and State
ghway The Lands Northerly of the Highway is Bounded Westerly
reeve Northerly and Easterly by Lands of Dorothy Wells and
Lands of said Gooldsmith and Jennings
no Lands of James Tuthill a Division of Salt Meadow Lotts and the
and Thomas Wickham, Northerly by Lands of the aforesaid
dred and forty Acres more or less All which became forfeited to the People

---

in or to the said Premises, which in Consequence of any Conviction or Attainder is become forfeited, or attached ereby Granted, Bargained, Sold, Enfeoffed and Confirmed, with the Appurtenances unto the said to the only proper Use, Benefit and Behoof of the said Nathaniel Norton s to these Presents have hereunto interchangeably set their Hands and Seals, the Day and Year first above written.

Isaac Stoutenburgh

One Thousand Seven Hundred and

Esquires, and each of them respectively acknowledged that he s his voluntary Act and Deed, for the Uses and Purposes found no material Erazures or Interlineations therein

Ph. V. Cortlandt

SUFFOLK COUNTY HISTORICAL SOCIETY

Centennial Publication

THE OLD HOUSE. Built in 1649, this house in Cutchogue, New York, was the residence of three generations of Wickhams, the last of whom was Parker Wickham. The latter suffered the loss of all his property, including the house, at the close of the American Revolution. Today called the Old House, it became a national historic landmark in 1962. Photograph by Harvey Weber.

The Wickham Claim

being an inquiry into the
attainder of Parker Wickham

by Dwight Holbrook

1986 The Suffolk County Historical Society
Riverhead, New York

Library of Congress Cataloging in Publication Data

Holbrook, Dwight, 1941–
The Wickham claim.

Bibliography: p.
Includes index.
1. Wickham, Parker, 1727–1785. 2. Bill of attainder—New York (State). 3. American loyalists—New York (State)—Suffolk County. 4. New York (State)—History—Revolution, 1775–1783—Confiscations and contributions. I. Title.
KFN5078.W52H65 1986 346.74704′32 86-6040
ISBN 0-938769-00-6 347.4706432

The Suffolk County Historical Society
300 West Main Street
Riverhead, N.Y. 11901

Manufactured in the United States of America.

Type set by David Seham Associates; printed by Studley Press; binding by Publishers Book Bindery; production by Kenneth Milford

The Wickham Claim

The key to an ancient legacy
is found in an extraordinary punishment
enacted by the state of New York.

TO MY FAMILY

CONTENTS

ILLUSTRATIONS

ACKNOWLEDGMENTS

I WISH TO THANK the people who helped to make this book possible. These include, first of all, J. Parker Wickham, who sparked my long-term enthusiasm in this project by showing me some old papers of his ancestor, Parker Wickham. Then there were those who gave their time to read my manuscript and offer helpful suggestions. They include Professor J. Allen Smith, Robert Pike, Chris Holbrook, Professor Lowell Scheiner, Bert Hirsch, Myron Luke, Adrienne Mulholland, Edward Agbamu, Eileen Goble, Dr. David Yale, and an undisclosed reader for the *William and Mary Quarterly* who gave a valuable critique of my discussion of corruption of blood. I must also mention a recent reader, Professor Cyril C. Means Jr.

Then there were those who helped me in other ways. Liz Kirk and Harvey Weber labored painstakingly with the illustrations and photographs. The staff of the Long Island (now "Brooklyn") Historical Society and the Suffolk County Historical Society were helpful and assisting in many ways. I would like to mention in particular Alice Kappenberg and Diane Perry of SCHS, as well as its former librarian, Betty Carpenter. The Stirling Historical Society and the Southold Town Historian were also very helpful.

I would like to thank Margaret C. Mullen, John Wickham, and Evelyn Hale for their help with genealogy and local history. And among those who helped in other ways, I would like to mention Mrene and Kelben Holbrook, and for his patience in seeing the book production through, I want to mention yet one more person, Kenneth Milford.

Among the larger libraries which I am indebted to for their invaluable resources and assistance, three stand out: the New York Public Library, Columbia University Law Library, and New York University Law Library.

Finally, I want to thank the Suffolk County Historical Society for its support in taking on the publication of *The Wickham Claim*.

INTRODUCTION

ON THE AFTERNOON OF January 3, 1980, there was a public hearing at the Town Hall in Riverhead, Long Island. The subject of the public hearing was the Federal Estuarine Sanctuary Program, and it drew a large crowd. Inside the auditorium the seats were filled to capacity. I found my way to one side of the room and stood along an aisle with others, listening as a speaker at the podium discussed the ecological future of eastern Long Island. Behind me in the back of the hall there was a hum and whispering among dim-lit figures conferring in corners and near the doors.

The subject of the hearing was the sanctuary program, its guidelines, and the grant application to be drawn up by state officials from Coastal Management. Under the program the Peconic Bay was proposed to be made a sanctuary, within which a watchdog agency would function to oversee the ecology and uses of the bay. Tied into this proposal was another: the federal-state acquisition of Robins Island, a 445-acre undeveloped island in Peconic Bay, it being part of the proposed sanctuary. Reactions to the program were heard from a battery of speakers from the audience—residents, town officials, spokesmen for various interests—and as the afternoon wore on it became clear that opinion was sharply divided. There were the environmentalists at one end, development interests at the other. The two camps were pitted against each other in classic confrontation. Meanwhile on the stage in front of the audience, the Coastal Management officials sat impassively, taking occasional notes.

A number of speakers had been heard from. A range of issues covered. Opinions stated and repeated. And then this speaker, towering and patriarchal, began his testimony at the podium. His name was John Wickham. A farmer from Cutchogue, he was talking about Robins Island.

> . . . and again my background there is that uh not only did my family own it for 100 years, prior to 1780, but uh I went over every inch of it and because we operate a custom farming operation. . . .

Once there was a family that had an island and other land, an ancient legacy of land. This book takes up the story of how that legacy was lost, and whether it was lost.

THE ARGUMENT

REVOLUTION. A DIVIDING EMPIRE. The Thirteen Colonies declare themselves States, but one of them itself divides. New York becomes two entities: the state of New York to the north, the colony of New York to the south, each sector sealed off from the other by military lines across Westchester County.

With New York so divided, the legislature of the state sector, in the year 1779, enacts a judicial sentence. Known as an Act of Attainder, the legislative pronouncement accuses, convicts, and allegedly confiscates the estates of fifty-nine suspected enemies, inhabitants of New York. While some of these estates belong to persons living in the newly independent state, others belong to inhabitants of the colony of New York, a territory in the possession of the British army. The day after the Attainder Act, the state legislature passes "An Act to provide for the temporary government of the southern parts of this State, whenever the enemy shall abandon or be dispossessed of the same, and until the legislature can be convened." (Laws of New York, 3 sess. Ch. 28). The very title of this act recognizes that the state has no government or law in the British sector of New York, notwithstanding the Attainder.

Of the accused fifty-nine, one in particular is an inhabitant of Suffolk County, Long Island, a territory in the British sector. Though "declared" confiscated, his estate lies outside the state's jurisdiction and law, and so remains shielded from confiscation as long as the British are in control of that region. In 1783, his estate comes under the protection of the Provisional Treaty of Peace. Among other things, this treaty between the United States and England bars all future confiscations for the part which any person may have taken in the Revolution. It also protects from all lawful impediments anyone with interests in confiscated lands. In September of that year the Definitive Treaty (with virtually identical provisions) is signed, and two months later the British evacuate from Long Island and New York City.

Subsequently, the state of New York seizes and sells the estate of the Suffolk County resident, as it does others on Long Island and New York City, deeming them confiscated under the Act of Attainder.

Banished by the state of New York, the Suffolk County resident is kept forcibly out of possession of his property. His heirs also are kept out of possession, the state having sold "title" to the property to purchasers in 1784. In spite of their being kept out, the thesis is here proposed that the state's confiscation was void from the beginning, being in violation of the treaties; that title to this property has never transferred to the state; and that the Suffolk County resident's heirs and successors in interest are today the rightful owners of it.

AUTHOR'S NOTE

The American Revolution gave our nation birth and freedom. But revolutionary freedom never proceeds perfectly. The fact that this book is about a case involving a failure of revolutionary freedom should not be interpreted as a negative reflection on the patriotic cause as a whole and those who fought for it.

Guilty by Legislative Decree

KNOW THEN, That we consider ourselves, and do insist, that we are and ought to be, as free as our fellow-subjects in Britain, and that no power on earth has a right to take our property from us without our consent.

That we claim all the benefits secured to the subject by the English constitution, and particularly that inestimable one of trial by jury.

That we hold it essential to English Liberty, that no man be condemned unheard, or punished for supposed offences, without having an opportunity of making his defence.

Continental Congress, "Address to the People of Great Britain," September 5, 1774.[1]

CHAPTER 1

Guilty by Legislative Decree

On a March day of 1784, a year after the Provisional Treaty that marked the end of the American Revolution, a magistrate in exile writes back home to his family in Southold, Long Island. He gives his place of residence as "Roap Ferry," which on today's map puts his whereabouts in the vicinity of Rope Ferry Road, in New London, Connecticut. From Rope Ferry and New London, other letters come from the man in exile: one in August, one in December, another in April, 1785. Seven weeks after this he dies. The map reader, moving his finger four miles west of Rope Ferry Road, will sight Niantic. In that town is a little-noticed grave site off Oswegatchie Road, where the magistrate's tombstone is found to this day.

The letters of this Connecticut resident give scarcely a clue as to the nature of his punishment, or that he was being punished at all. In his March letter he speaks of the confiscations of property in Suffolk County, Long Island, and the little good that could be had by seeking relief from the authorities. Yet how was he affected by these circumstances? The magistrate keeps to the impersonal:

> I see no kind of propriety in applying to any power in York for any releaf respecting the interest of any individual of that state, for the legislative body has already made their law. Besides you may depend W^{m}~F and E^{a}~L were the cause of every confiscation in Suffolk County, and for any member (that is grieved) in that county to apply for releaf to the ruling members thereof, I think is as unnatral as snow in summer; however, to confer with them ant amiss, provided the conference is well seasoned with salt. . . .[2]

Later in his letter he makes passing reference to himself, speaking as if in answer to unknown accusations: "I flatter myself, I have acted consistantly and consianciously throughout my whole conduct, with a firm belief there is a future existance, and defie the state to produce one instance wherein I have acted rigidly, defrauded, or abused one member of it, altho twas in my power, tho had no right as an individual.'' But the matter of his past conduct ends there. His attention turns to other concerns, family and incidentals, which occupy most of his letters. His children Tommy and Parnel. He'd have Tommy shear sheep for a year, and wants him sent over, also the brown mare if she's not in foal. He mentions the payment owed him for repairing the county jail; the talk of a military call up in New York State; and local conditions, the scarcity of food—''Times are dreadfull hear''—but assures his readers that he is well provided for. Among these and other details, one in particular the magistrate brings up in his letter of August 2, 1784. It is an obscure reference to some property being auctioned off.

> I think just to in[form] you Owing [Orange?] Webb offered 700£ for the north Side. Ezekie[l] . . . offered 1000£ for the Roan Oaks to the middle Road. . . .

It would be the only clue the writer would give about his own personal misfortune, the heavy sentence that had been pronounced against him. For the property being auctioned was his own.

About the subject of his property we learn more by turning to certain public records of that day, where the name of Parker Wickham, the man in exile, comes up again. A public notice in the May 20, 1784, issue of a newspaper, the *New York Packet,* enumerates a list of landowners, among them Parker Wickham, whose estates have been confiscated by the state of New York. Later that summer, the state's Commissioners of Forfeiture record the sale of Wickham's lands, including his home and farm. As described in their official abstract, the property was disposed of in two installments. On July 28—five days before the August 2 letter—the state auctioned off Wickham's Neck, the magistrate's 160 acre homestead on the south side of the highway at Cutchogue, eastern Long Island. That, together with adjoining property north of the highway, sold for 900 pounds. The remainder of the estate consisted of two other tracts, which changed hands at the auction block on August 5, 1784. One of these tracts was called ''the River Head.'' Containing 800 acres, this parcel extended in a narrow band from the Long Island Sound to the Peconic River, through the present-day village of Riverhead. It sold for 1,030 pounds. The second parcel was Robins Island, an island in the Peconic Bay that looks much today the way it did at the time of its public sale. It fetched 1,250 pounds.[3]

But what wrongdoing had Parker Wickham committed? Why was his property being taken away from him? A clue to the reason for these proceedings and for Wickham's exile is found in the commissioners' abstract. These forfeitures, they write, came about by the ''attainder'' of Parker Wickham. An eighteenth century legal term, ''attainder'' signified that the magistrate had been pronounced guilty of a most serious crime: felony or treason. It meant that he had been deemed attainted under the law, adjudged stained or blackened by the infamy of his offense. Wickham's attainder would have led to the forfeiture, not only of his property, but of every right whatsoever. His civil liberties were extinguished. He could not seek the protection of the law. He had become a living nonentity—an outcast. And beyond this, there lay yet one further burden of his punishment, corruption of blood. His children and heirs were deemed contaminated by his evil blood. However innocent they may have been of his crime, they too must suffer by losing their inheritance even—as Blackstone, the legal commentator of that time writes—"to the twentieth generation."[4]

Given the attainder of Wickham, we would naturally suppose that a trial had taken place, that judgment against him had been rendered in a court of law by a jury of his peers. Trial by jury had been esteemed a basic American right in his day as in ours. It was an established right, staunchly defended by the Continental Congress. Yet in Wickham's case, though he was attainted he was not tried. Judicial proceedings never took place. Instead, something extraordinary happened, extra-ordinary in a very literal sense. He was attainted—not by a jury, not by the ordinary course of the law—but by a legislative act.

He did not know of the act until after it had been passed. By then it was too late. There was no summons, no witness to testify in open court, no opportunity for him to plead in his own defense, no right to counsel. There was no jury, no judge, no trial. The act, in a stroke, accused and convicted him of being "adherent" to the enemy. At one and the same instant, it declared him attainted, sentenced him to banishment, decreed all his estate, both real and personal, forfeited to the state of New York.

Made law by the legislature of the state of New York, it was called "An Act for the Forfeiture and Sale of the Estates of Persons Who Have Adhered to the Enemies of this State, and for Declaring the Sovereignty of the People of this State in Respect to All Property Within the Same."[5] It was commonly known as the Act of Attainder, or Confiscation Act, passed on October 22, 1779. Not the only object of this legislative decree, Wickham was one of fifty-nine alleged offenders, including the colonial governor of New York, supreme court justices, and prominent businessmen, to be sentenced in this way, their human rights and liberties snuffed out under the law of the state even as a Revolution was being fought for the "rights and liberties of America."

More than 200 years have elapsed since the passage of this act, yet even so it is not too late to raise a question about what this act did and what it failed to do. In particular, what legal effect did this extraordinary attainder have on the property of the banished magistrate?

A MAP OF NEW YORK PROVINCE by John Montressor. Paris: 1777. [section]. *Map Division, New York Public Library; Astor, Lenox and Tilden Foundations.*

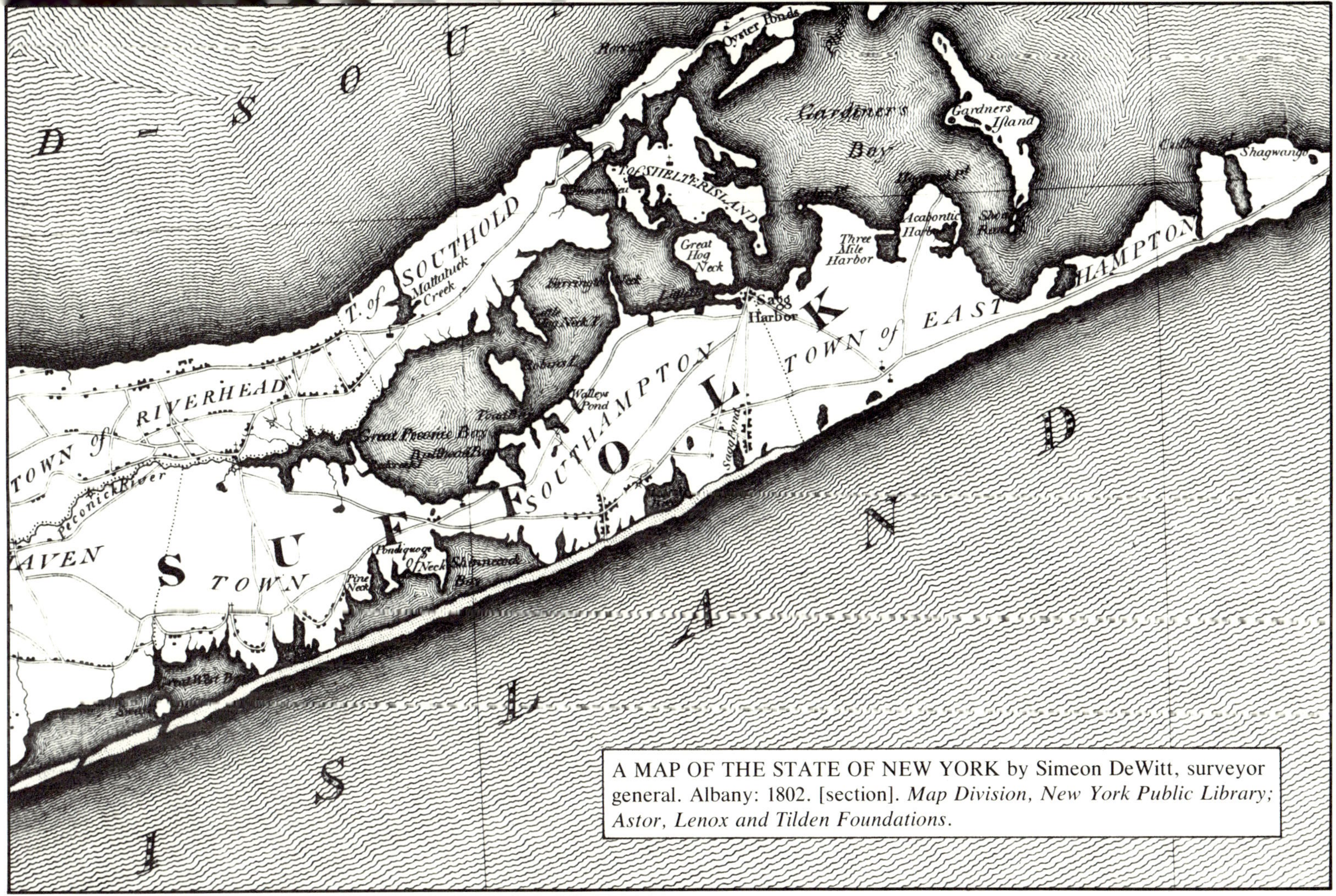

A MAP OF THE STATE OF NEW YORK by Simeon DeWitt, surveyor general. Albany: 1802. [section]. *Map Division, New York Public Library; Astor, Lenox and Tilden Foundations.*

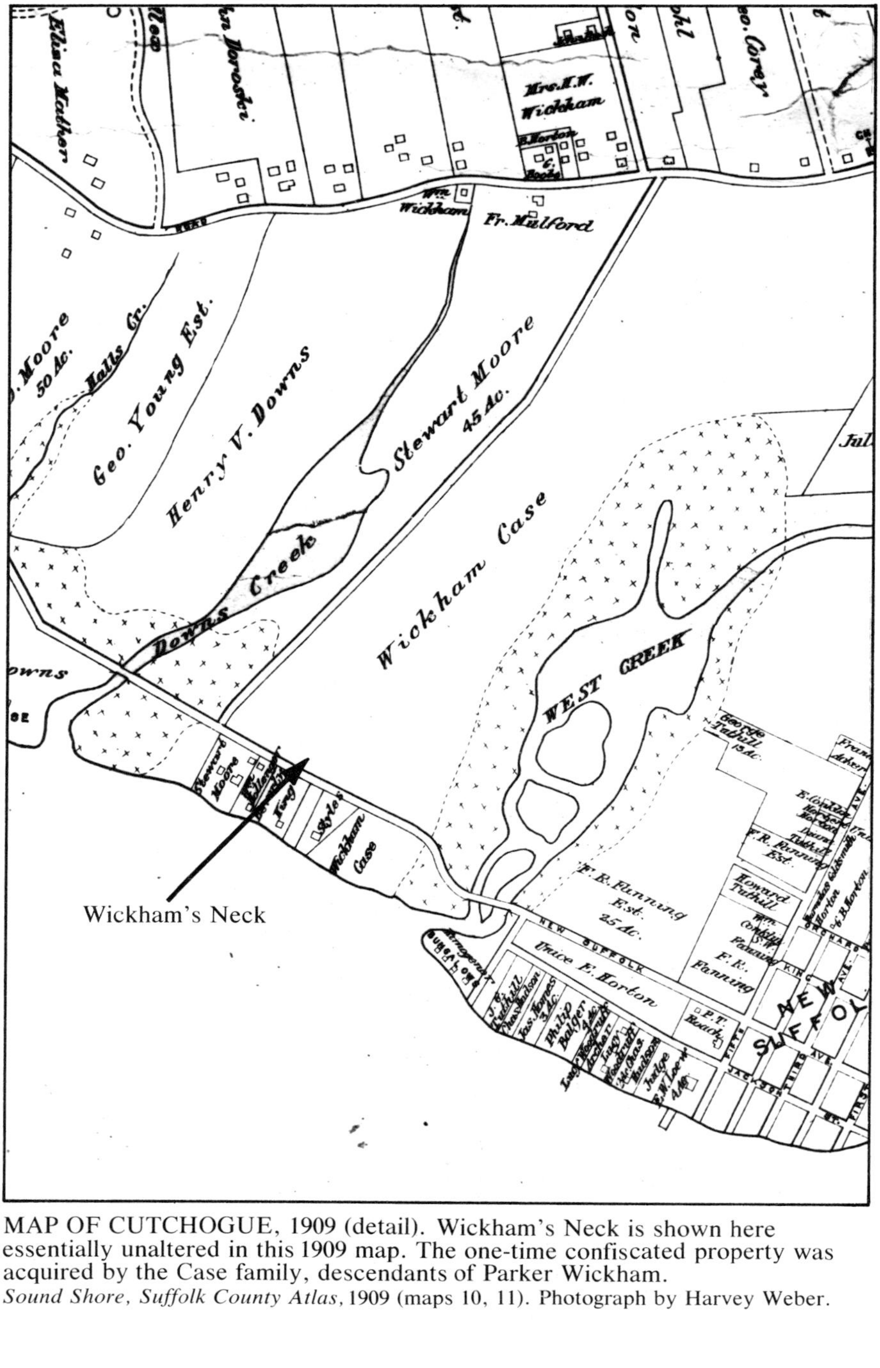

MAP OF CUTCHOGUE, 1909 (detail). Wickham's Neck is shown here essentially unaltered in this 1909 map. The one-time confiscated property was acquired by the Case family, descendants of Parker Wickham.
Sound Shore, Suffolk County Atlas, 1909 (maps 10, 11). Photograph by Harvey Weber.

Today on the North Fork of Long Island, many people inhabit the old estate of Parker Wickham, some living on these lands a short time, others for generations. At the north end of Wickham's Neck (now called Cutchogue Neck), near Route 25, one can still find the home of Wickham, known today as the Horton-Wickham-Landon Old House, and it is now a museum. The rest of the Neck is occupied by numerous landowners, the major one being the North Fork Country Club. Numerous landowners—farmers and other residents—also occupy the North Side, north of the highway in Cutchogue. At present a corporation holds title to Robins Island. It is the only one of Wickham's tracts that has not as yet been subdivided. Further west lies the River Head. Here, especially at the south end of the tract where the village of Riverhead is situated, one sees today a great multitude of homes and businesses, private lots and parcels, whose owners number in the hundreds.

All of the property owners on these tracts which were once the estate of Parker Wickham hold a singularly common origin of title to their property. That origin is the Commissioners of Forfeiture of the state of New York. The deeds of the current occupants derive, in each instance, from the sale and conveyances of Wickham's forfeited estate by the Comissioners of Forfeiture on July 25, 1784, and August 5, 1784.

Yet the question of what the Act of Attainder did and what it did not do to Wickham's property is not entirely answered.

In the vicinity of their ancestor's estate live many present-day descendants of Parker Wickham. Some still carry the Wickham name, like sixth generation descendant J. Parker Wickham of Mattituck, an airport proprietor, and farmer John Wickham of Cutchogue and his brother Henry Wickham. Their children are seventh generation descendants. Some are the married daughters of a Wickham, like Joan Silleck of Mattituck and Margaret Tooker of Riverhead. And some bear other surnames, like Ernest Wickham Case and Stanley Oliver Case; the family of Frank Case; the children of Annie W. Beebe; and Nancy Marschean of Southold. Still others, like Margaret Mullen of Hudson, Wisconsin, and her children, they and their forbears are long departed from their ancestral homestead and have only a vague notion at best that it ever existed.[6]

Diverse as they are in name and in some instances location, the descendants of Parker Wickham share a common origin by blood. They are all kin to a man whose fundamental rights—right to property, right to trial by jury—were snuffed out by the state of New York. Contemporary with Wickham's property losses, there occurred another, much greater loss of land suffered by the Oneida Indians of New York. In that same historical period, the Oneidas were deprived of a vast area of six million acres, or approximately 20 percent of the size of New York State. By unlawful treaties, the state had laid claim to this territory. Presently the Oneidas are suing for the recovery of their lands in federal court.[7]

The banished magistrate was never given the opportunity to be heard in a court of law. But what if, like the Oneidas, the heirs of Wickham were to sue in court for the recovery of their ancestral lands? What might be the foundation of their claim?

Part I: Wickham's Title to the Lands

In 1726, by deed of gift, John Parker conveyed to Joseph Wickham and Abigail Wickham, his daughter, all his land north of Peconic River, to the said Joseph for life and then to his daughter and her heirs. Her husband died in 1749. His widow died in 1780, and her oldest son, Parker, inherited her estate, which was confiscated after the war and purchased by Gen. Floyd, who sold the property to Mr. Jagger.

> *History of the Town of Riverhead, Suffolk County, N.Y.* Written by Hon. George Miller, and read by T.M. Griffing, Esq., at the Centennial Celebration, July 4, 1876. [n.p., 1876], p. 2.

Time Line of the

1715: Joseph Wickham Sr. buys Robins Island.

1720

1727: John Parker deeds his River Head land to daughter Abigail Wickham.

1734: Joseph Wickham wills Robins Island and Wickham's Neck to his oldest son Joseph Wickham Jr.

1740

1749: Joseph Jr. dies. His oldest son Parker Wickham is heir at law.

1768-1774, 1777: Parker Wickham is Southold Town's supervisor.

1776

July 4, 1776: The Declaration of Independence.

July 9, 1776: The Provincial Congress of the "state" of New York approves the Declaration of Independence.

July 16, 1776: The Provincial Congress resolves that all persons within the state of New York owe allegiance to its laws.

August 27, 1776: American forces evacuate from Long Island.

1777

April 20, 1777: New York State's first constitution is adopted.

Dec. 13, 1777: Parker Wickham is seized and made prisoner in Connecticut. He is back on Long Island, April 18, 1778.

1778

May 10, 1778: Parker Wickham quitclaims Robins Island and Wickham's Neck to oldest son Joseph.

August and Oct., 1778: 2,677 Suffolk County men swear allegiance to the king.

Period of the Wickham estates tail, which prevailed under British law until the British evacuation.

Wickham Claim

Oct. 22, 1779: The New York State legislature passes the Attainder Act.

April 4, 1780 (79?): Parker Wickham's mother Abigail dies.

July 12, 1782: The New York State legislature abolishes entailed estates.

July 12, 1782: Parker Wickham witnesses a will in Southold.

Jan. 20, 1783: The Provisional Treaty of Peace goes into effect.

Sept. 3, 1783: The Definitive Treaty of Peace is signed.

Nov. 1, 1783: Parker Wickham comes to New York City to draw up a power of attorney.

Nov. 21, 1783: British forces evacuate from Long Island.

Feb. 9, 1784: The New York State legislature considers a bill to revive the county courts in Suffolk, Queens, Kings, and Richmond counties.

May 12, 1784: The New York State legislature passes the Speedy Sales Act, expediting the sale of confiscated estates.

July 28, 1784: The Commissioners of Forfeiture sell Wickham's Neck.

August 5, 1784: The Commissioners of Forfeiture sell Robins Island and the River Head.

May 22, 1785: Parker Wickham dies in New London, Connecticut.

1789: The U.S. Constitution is adopted.

1791: Parker Wickham's oldest son, Joseph Parker Wickham, returns from England to Southold, Long Island.

No future confiscations under the Treaty of Peace.

Period of British occupation.

CHAPTER 2

The Legacy and How It Arose

THE STORY OF THAT legendary estate of inheritance comprising the River Head, Robins Island, and Wickham's Neck must begin with an occasion in the life of Parker Wickham's grandfather, two months before the magistrate was born.

His life drawing to a close, a sixty-nine-year-old fuller named John Parker sits down at his desk one winter day, takes pen in hand, and draws up a legal instrument called a deed of gift. It is January 4, 1727.

> To all Christian People to whom these presents Shall Come Greeting know ye that I John Parker of Southampton In the county of Suffolk and Colony of New York fuller for & in Consideration of the Natural Love & affection that I have and do bare unto my Daughter Abigail the wife of Joseph Wickham Junior. . . .[1]

The origins of Parker are a mystery. The only thing certain about his childhood is his date of birth, 1657. It is possible he knew of the Wickhams in England, but in any case he must have first met Joseph Wickham Sr. on Long Island, in a hamlet known today as Bridgehampton, east of Southampton. Wickham Sr. had been born in Wethersfield, Connecticut, and later settled on the island after being granted by the town of Southampton three acres of land to set up his trade of tanning for the benefit of the town. While Parker worked for the town as a fuller, treating wool in a fulling mill on Peconic Bay, his fellow tradesman was running his business of tanning, or leather making, off Sag Pond, seven miles to the south. Wickham continued his business here for thirteen years. In 1699 he bought a large house across the bay on the North Fork. It was situated on a neck of land in Cutchogue, called Horton's Neck, which was included with the purchase of the house. In time, the neck came to be known as Wickham's Neck.

A year after Wickham's relocation, the fuller was provided by Southampton Town with an acre of land at the Riverhead to build a house on. A wilderness in those days, the Riverhead was nevertheless important for its fording place on the Peconic River, where land traffic between the North and South Forks crossed. Prior to the granting of the acre lot, Southampton had granted Parker its rights to the "streame att the Riverhed" for him to operate his fulling mill there, upon condition that he full cloth for the town. Now with the acre allotment, he proceeded to construct a house at this site. Here he moved with his wife at about the time Wickham moved to Cutchogue.

John Parker's fulling operation at the Riverhead became a lucrative business. This we gather from his subsequent real estate acquisitions. One piece of land, a "first lot," he bought from Isaac Arnold in 1704. This tract, 5 miles long and with a width estimated at 50 rods or 825 feet, stretched from the Peconic River to the Sound. Another tract, abutting the first but slightly smaller in width, he bought from John Tucker in 1711. According to one historian, the south ends of the two tracts, taken together, encompass two-thirds of the present business district of Riverhead Village or, as a recent author put it, the "center of downtown Riverhead."[2]

In 1723, Parker's daughter Abigail married Wickham's oldest son, twenty-two-year-old "Justice" Joseph, and it is they—Abigail and this Joseph—who are named as recipients of the gift in John Parker's deed of 1727. The gift was a generous one, for by this deed all Parker's "Lands and Meadows Lying and being on the Northside the Great River Called Peoconnock River" were given to Joseph Wickham Jr. during his lifetime, and after his death to Abigail "and to the Heirs of her Body. . . ." And so it happened that the tract of land known as the River Head came into the possession of the Wickham family and would remain under their proprietorship for more than half a century.[3]

The River Head was not the only property that Joseph and his family inherited. In 1734 Wickham Sr. wrote out a will and in it devised to his namesake two tracts of his own. These were Wickham's Neck in Cutchogue and Robins Island, an island in the Peconic Bay that the testator had purchased in 1715. Both of these parcels were bequeathed in his will to "Son Joseph Wickham and to the male heirs of his body Lawfully begotten or to be begotten forever."[4] Both lands would remain in the Wickham family for close to half a century.

About the legacy that came by way of the tanner and the fuller, there was something of peculiar significance in all three bequests, raising, as we shall see, an important issue in the Wickham claim. What was peculiar about them was that they were bequests expressed in the form "to A and the heirs of his (her) body." During colonial times, a stipulation of this kind created a gift in tail or estate tail, as it was called in the law. Tail, from the French "tailler," to cut, defined the limited nature of the in-

THE RIVER HEAD.
Illustration A.
South detail showing east and west bounds.

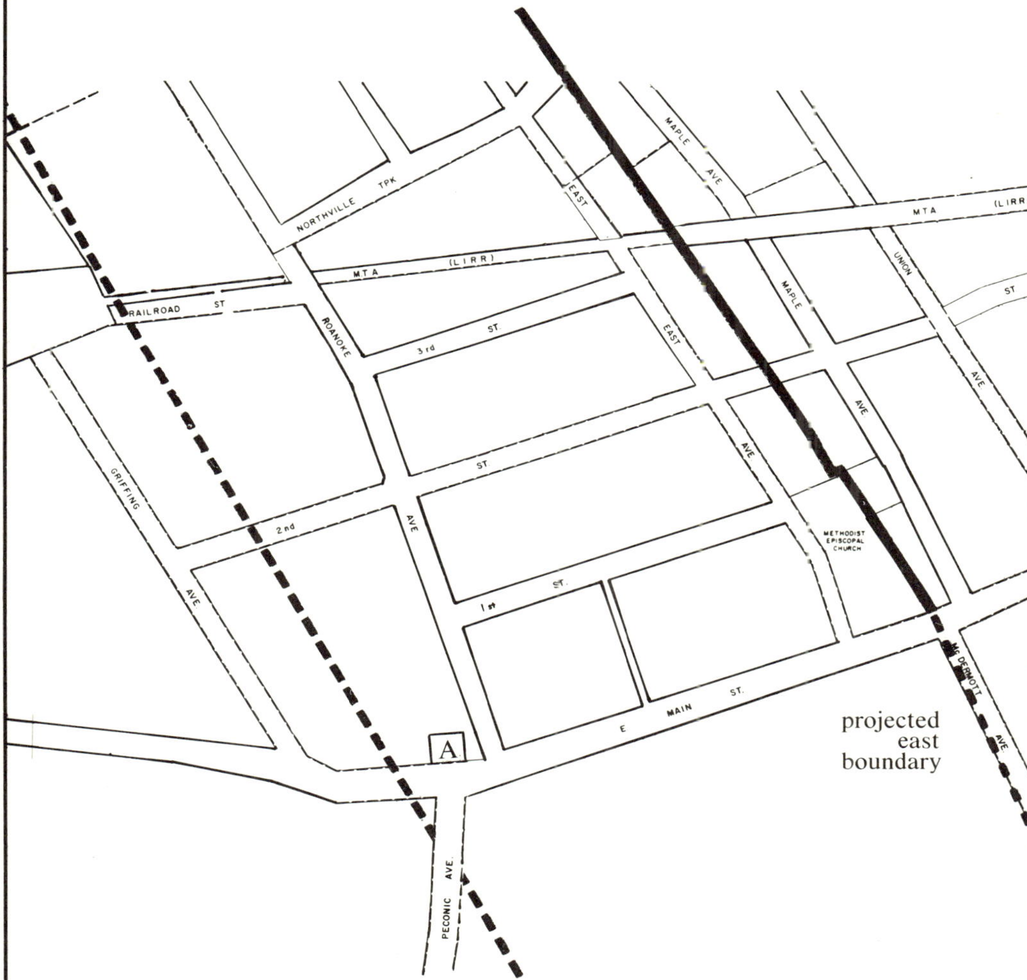

east boundary

projected west boundary at the time of the Revolution

[A] the old Court House

Note: Streets are added to show the boundaries in relation to the present village of Riverhead. The scale used is based on Riverhead tax maps 128 and 129.

THE RIVER HEAD.
Illustration B.
South detail showing east bounds.

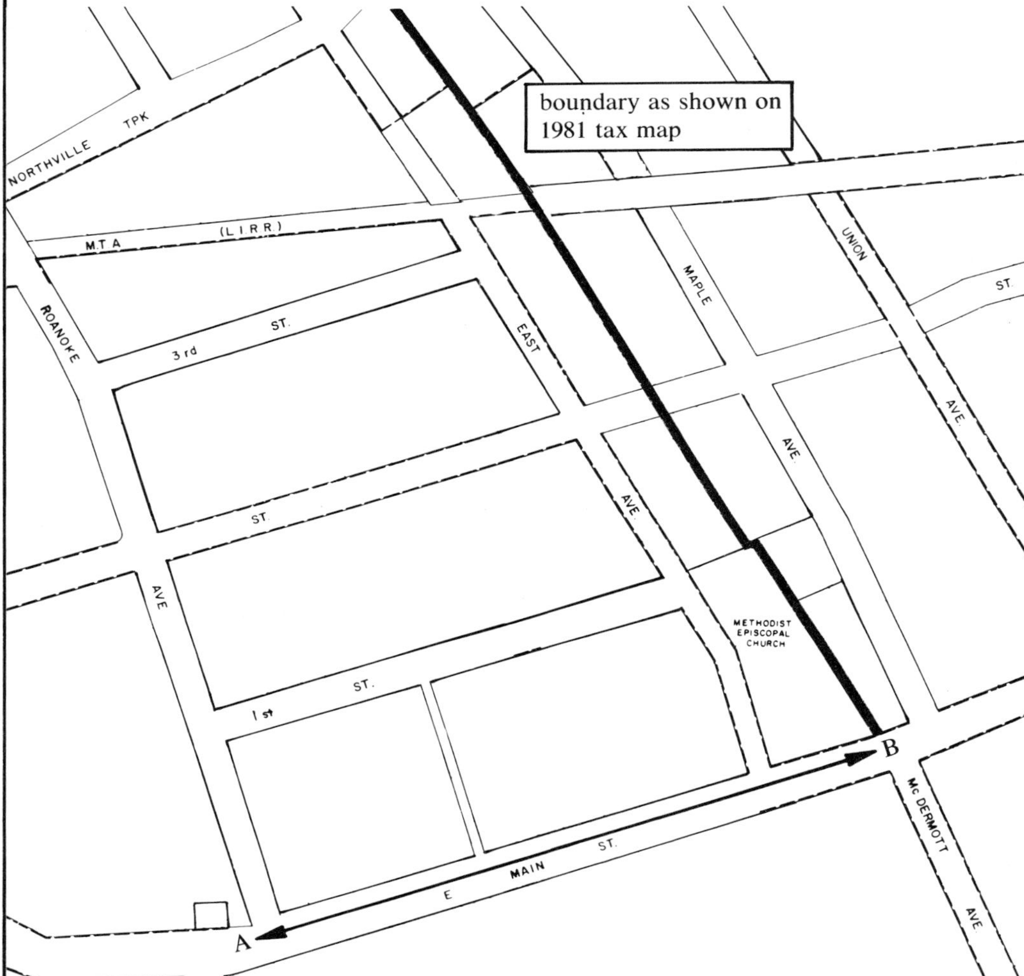

A ⟵⟶ B = 1067′ (1981 Riverhead Tax Maps 128, 129)
A ⟵⟶ B = 16 chains, 9 links; or 1062′ (1814 survey, *Riverhead Town Records,* pp. 271–272)

Explanatory notes:

Point A = the southeast corner of the old Court House. Its original location is computed from deeds L. 30/150 and L. D/101 as 41′ from Roanoke Avenue. In the 1814 survey the distance from B was measured not to the actual Court building but 1½ rods south, 11 degrees 45 minutes east from the southeast corner of the Court House.

Point B = the southeast corner of the Methodist Episcopal Church property.
In the 1814 survey this point is described as the Jagger-Howell boundary on the north side of the surveyed highway.

heritance, i.e., to the heirs born of the parent. These heirs of the body, unless otherwise specified, were further restricted by the laws of descent to include only the oldest son, that son's oldest son, and so on in an unending succession of inheritance from father to oldest son, which thereby ensured that the property entailed would remain within the same family.

Entailing property had been an accustomed right for centuries, its origins dating back in England to the enactment of *De Donis Conditionalibus* in the year 1285. Under that statute, an inheritance of land, if entailed, became secured to a family for generations. It could not be disposed of, but followed the hereditary course laid out by the donor or testator. As the statute explains: "So that they to whom the Land was given under such Condition, shall have no Power to aliene the Land so given, but that it shall remain unto the Issue of them to whom it was given after their Death."[5] In other words, a tenant in tail (the recipient of entailed property) could not sell this land, mortgage it, or do anything to deprive his posterity of it. His rights to the land could not infringe upon theirs. Consequently, the tenant in tail did not hold an absolute fee. His title was a limited one, equivalent in some ways to an estate for life. Later in England and in New York and the other colonies (before the Revolution), it became possible to "dock" the entail, or change it into an absolute fee, but this was a complicated procedure and rarely done, especially in such places as New York. The potential for docking did not alter the fact that the estate tail was looked upon as giving the recipient only a limited estate.[6]

What this meant in cases where a tenant in tail committed a serious crime, such as felony or certain categories of treason, was that the entailed property of the offender (as opposed to his unrestricted property) was generally not subject to forfeiture except during his lifetime. The property's immunity to more than limited forfeiture resulted from the nature of the fee tail itself. A tenant in tail's property was not absolutely his to the exclusion of others. It belonged to his heirs as well, in succession. The whole of what a tenant could relinquish was *his* title, his legal estate, his rights, but it was not in his power to give up more than was his. To forfeit an absolute fee would necessitate forfeiting not only his own but his heirs' rights and title to the property. That was not possible with an estate tail except by statute, in particular Henry VIII's Treason Act of 1535. This punitive act specifically directed that in cases of high treason all lands of which an offender had any inheritable title would be confiscated, regardless of the kind of estate. With the exception of a statute such as this one, *De Donis* prevailed and the conditional estate of which it spoke remained in the family.[7]

The early eighteenth century entailments of property by Parker and Wickham were not the first such transactions in Wickham history. We

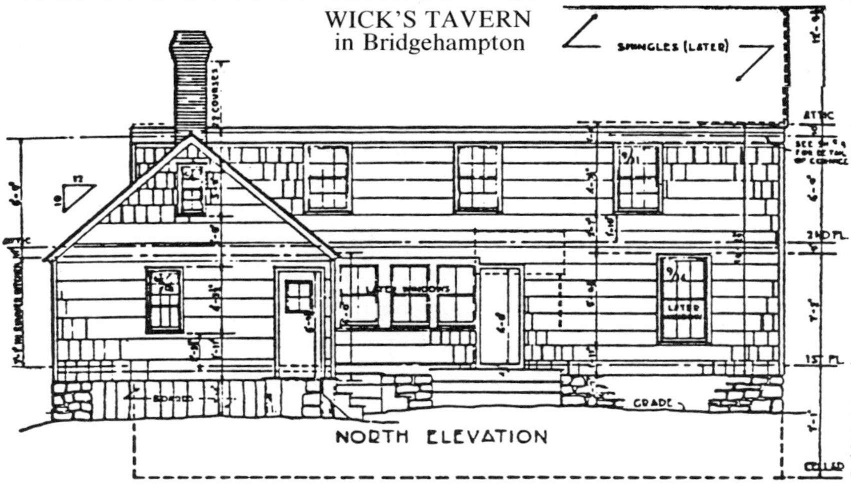

The Bull Head Tavern (Wick's Tavern) was built *circa* 1700 and demolished in 1940. Prior to the demolition, the Public Works Administration Program of the Department of Interior completed a Historic American Buildings Survey of it comprising ten sheets, one of them shown here. Survey NY5419, Jan. 1941. *Long Island Collection, East Hampton Public Library.*

can find record of an entailing act in this family as far back as the year 1397. Written by Bishop William of Wykeham, Chancellor of England, it is in Latin:

> Maneria de Burnham & Brene cum suis pertinent, integra remaneant Wilhelmo Wikeham consanguineo dicti Domini Episcopi & Aliciae Uvedale, & haeredibus masculis de corpore ipsius Wilhelmi. . . .[8]

''The manors of Burnham and Brene with their entire appurtenances,'' he writes, ''will remain unto William Wikeham, cousin of the said master Bishop, and to Alicia Uvedale [his wife], and to the male heirs of William's body. . . .'' Three centuries later, John Wickham of Chipping Sodbury, England, devises in his will a meadow to ''my Grandson John Wickham (Son of my Son Henry Wickham) and the heirs Males of his body Lawfully issuing.'' Then there was John Wick, who was a son of this testator. Wick made the crossing to America in his youth, changing his surname to Wick possibly to avoid old creditors.[9] He settled in Bridgehampton, Long Island, about a mile from where the tanner Joseph Wickham lived, and pursued a merchantile business that had connections in Antigua and back home in England. He prospered, was appointed sheriff of Suffolk County—the highest county post at the time—and after his death became the subject of legends in local Bridgehampton history. As some of these legends relate to a disenchantment over an entailment, they deserve a moment's consideration.

One story tells of Wick's Tavern on Main Street, where peddlers were on occasion said to have gone in but never come out. Other folklore speaks of the merchant's wizardry. Some men of the village, fishing off the coast at the moment of his death, "saw the devil carrying his black soul through the air, seaward." Still another legend tells of how his body was brought to the cemetery for burial, but there swarms of ants, the story goes, so infested the newly prepared grave that the gravediggers were forced to remove his corpse from the cemetery grounds. Curiously, most of the folklore about Wick has to do with his death, and in particular his will. C.H. Hildreth's version of the will story is perhaps the best known. Wick, he says, made a provision in his will to be buried in the middle of a lot that never was to be sold but entailed forever. That was the lot in Bridgehampton, north of Main Street, where in fact he was buried. The story then relates how Wick's son, wishing to sell the property, got out a summons and read it over the grave. "If anyone had objections to the sale of this property," the summons declared, such person was "to appear in court and make it known." (Another version has it that Wick's heirs, piqued by his will, read a summons calling *him* to appear in court to show cause why the will should not be broken.) What happened next, according to Hildreth, is that

> No one appearing to object, they put it [Wick's property] up at auction, but people appeared to be afraid to bid. Capt. Edmund Topping, coming out of the woods on horseback, hearing the cry and not knowing what was up, sung out in fun "a penny more," when down came the stick and he got all this property, as they said, for almost nothing (including the Augustus Corwith place which Wick owned). Capt. Topping did not know what to do with the property as no one would buy it, so he sold his own farm and went to live at the Corwith place.[10]

Sure enough, a perusal of Wick's will confirms that he had in fact made an entailment of property. The fourth proviso reads: "I give to My Son Henry and to his heirs Male Lawfully Begotten of his Body My New [*sic*] Dwelling House and Barn and Home Lot of Land with My Right in the Lot Number One and ffourteen. . . ."[11] This explains why nobody wanted to buy Wick's land. And who knows? The yarn about Captain Edmund Topping coming out of the woods on horseback and singing out, "A penny more!" might not have been far from the truth. Whatever the property went for was probably far lower than its real value. There must have been bitter feelings among some Wick descendants, Henry in particular, after the auction was over, a circumstance which might explain how the other unflattering legends about the merchant of Bridgehampton arose.

Born on February 7, 1727, was another recipient of entailed land, inheriting a legacy that was not his alone but his to share with other generations of heirs. The first son of Joseph and Abigail Wickham, he was given as his name the names of his two benefactors: Parker Wickham.

CHAPTER 3

Parker Wickham

ABOUT PARKER WICKHAM'S YOUTH there is scarcely any surviving information. In an undated memorandum, written sometime in his adult years, the magistrate recalls some particulars about a property feud when he was a child and makes passing reference to his grandfather and father. The feud, we learn, arose over a land patent for Robins Island made out on April 1, 1734, to two land venturers, Charles Williams and Frederick Morris, the latter being Deputy Secretary of the Province of New York. What was peculiar about the patent, which was issued by the governor of New York, was that it concerned property belonging to Joseph Wickham Sr. It was he who had bought Robins Island from William Nicoll in 1715, and in his will of April 20, 1734, Joseph mentions the livestock and farming on the island, stipulating that the property itself be entailed to son Joseph and the heirs of his body. Grandson Parker Wickham, in his memorandum, recounts the story of the Williams and Morris patent and how it was eventually resolved:

Memorandom

April in the Year 1735 [1734] ~~April~~ my grandfather was sent for to New York by Governor Clark [Cosby], who Informed him that he had Made out a patten for Robins Island to Charles Williams and Frederick Morris ~~two of his bookkeepers~~, Dated 1st April 1734 - and advised him to take it and Said he Should have it for £ 60 - 0 - 0. My Grandfather applyed to Mr. Smith new York, who advised him not [to] Except the Patten. My Grandfather Died Soon after, [and] about in the year 174 [?] in march My father was also Sent for Mr. Clark, (that was within My Memory), my father waited upon him, who likewise advised him to take the said Patten for the above Sum of £ 60 - 0 - 0. My Father Told me he waited upon Mr. Smith and he advised him not to Accept it as agift as the Island was beyond Doubt Pattened. My Father went back to Mr. Clark and told him that he Should not take the patten. he [Cosby] answered he Should go Soon to England, and when he Returned he Should have atryal for the Island. my father Returned to Mr Smith and told him as above, who Replyd, "apoor goutey Creature if he goes to England he will Never Return. he said that to Scare you." . . . Note after this Daniel Miller of East ampton, was Repo[rt]edly with my father and in his Sly way Moved to

> my father to have the affair of the Island Settled between Mr. Sylves[ter] and him, and Said he Should Git the above patten for Mr. Sylvester, and he Could git it for a pistole, and it was afterwards Said he obtained it for that Sum. Note also Mr. Nicoll all along advised to have Nothing to Do with them. This Relation is as near the matter as I Can Remember and Since before now, have heard nothing about the matter.[1]

Parker Wickham grew up in a family of nine children, five boys and four girls. As the oldest son, he alone was heir to the prestigious estate of his grandparents, after his father's death. Of those in a position to shape young Parker's character, there was of course his father. The nature of his influence can be conjectured from what we know about this man. Like his father before him, Justice Joseph was proprietor of the family farm at Wickham's Neck and, like Joseph Sr., kept up civic interests as well. He was the elected town assessor in 1743 and 1745, and a commissioner of roads for Southold in 1745 and 1746. Judging, however, from the title given him, it was in another public role that he became best known—that of justice.

In Suffolk County during colonial times, there were two county courts holding sessions in October and March of each year. One of these, the Court of Common Pleas, was a civil court; the other, the Court of General Sessions of the Peace, was a criminal court. Early in the century both courts met alternately in Southold and Southampton, but beginning in 1729 they found a permanent home on John Parker's estate, at the newly constructed Suffolk County Court House, 300 feet north of the fording place at the Riverhead. Here, the young Parker Wickham's father served as justice in the criminal court, a position he would hold for twenty-two years.

On Sunday, August 22, 1742, a judge from New London, Joshua Hempstead, crossed the Sound and went visiting in Cutchogue, Long Island. The entry in his diary for that day reads:

> Sund 22 fair. I went with Brother & Sister Salmon to Cutchauge Meetting. no minister at Town. wee heard Mr Gold pr al Day & Dined att Justice Wickhams & Lodged at Son Hempsteds.

Another entry is dated March 22, 1749.

> Wednsd. Wind NE & Snow. Brother Salmon & I went to visit Justice Wickham at his house who is in a very poor State of health p haps Consumption.[2]

The forty-eight-year-old justice died shortly thereafter, leaving his oldest son, now twenty-two, master of the farmstead at Wickham's Neck.

THE FIRST SUFFOLK COUNTY COURT HOUSE seen at left in photograph of Riverhead Village taken before 1911. *Suffolk County Historical Society.* Photograph of original print by Harvey Weber.

Besides his father and others in his immediate family, there may have been a more remote source of influence on young Parker. A tenuous link can be detected between the Wickhams of Long Island and the Wickhams of Antigua. It was on that British island in the Caribbean that a political struggle had taken place earlier in the century, involving Parker's kinsmen by the same name.

At the beginning of the seventeenth century there were four Wickham brothers living on Antigua. What exactly their connection was with the Wickhams of Long Island is uncertain. In any case, there is evidence of correspondence between at least one Long Island Wickham—John Wick—and the Antigua clan, as we shall see shortly.

We know that three, and probably all four, of the Antigua Wickhams were planters, that is, owners of plantations. In all likelihood they belonged to that class known as merchant planters, running sugar plantations and at the same time engaging in trade with England and the British colonies of North America. One of the brothers, Benjamin, owned a 420-acre plantation in 1720, utilizing as all the plantations did a great number of slaves. In 1713, this Benjamin writes a letter to John Wick of Bridgehampton, Long Island, and in it we see his mercantile connections with that part of the world.[3]

Antigua Sept : the 4th 1713

Sir

This moment I have red the goods you consigned me of the Sloop I & Ann Cap Harrison & by the hands of Mr. Rip Van dams whose amt th charges is £ 50″ 59/11 they being charged very high at this present won't Sell for the prime Cost nor indeed the Time of the year won't afford any Sort of goods we having a very great glutt of rain & storm has hindred our grinding. the sloop being bound to Corroso can't attend the makeing any goods; but when Sold will remitt you the Noete proceeds of yr Effects by the first vessel in the Spring. all sorts of fleshly provisions are adeugg [adoing?]. the prizes are Sett down underneath & what sells best from yr parts. I am hearty Sorry cant follow orders but will come as high as in my power. In the Interim must conclude wth: my hearty respects to yr: Self wth: out complement am yr friend and Kinsman at Command:

Benj: Wickham

candles sells at 12d upf by the box
hoops in Time of year + yer M 100s
pease & bread & flower sells very well here
hams and honey in bottles & setts of twp hoops
all those above rarely fails these prices
Beef sells here now for 30s barrel
& pork in full barrels at £ 12
the Dearies [dairies] & butter & cheese from 6d to 9d

verso: Benj Wickham
Sept 4 1713
Dated in Antgua

~~Capt Harison~~ These

To
M^: J n Wick ____
: In Long Island
to be left at
Mr: Rip Van dam's
In New York

A few years before the time of this letter a political struggle unfolded on the island of Antigua, and the Wickham brothers were a part of it. In April 1706, Colonel Daniel Parke was appointed by England the new captain-general and governor of the Leeward Caribbee Islands. Taking up residence in Antigua, Parke would find his first two years as governor relatively tranquil. But in the third year trouble began. Disfavor toward his policies had spread among several factions on the island, and a petition was drawn up accusing the governor of browbeating, infringing on local custom, overextending judicial prerogatives, encouraging hooliganism, questioning Christopher Codrington's title to the island of Barbuda, taking extravagant fees, and so on. The document was circulated clandestinely among local inhabitants for signatures, after which it would be sent to England with the request that Parke be replaced by a new royal governor. Before the document left the island, however, Major Samuel Wickham, another of the Wickham brothers, got wind of it. A member of the legislative assembly, Samuel belonged to the party loyal to the governor. Immediately Parke was apprised of what was going on, and a counter-petition to the queen of England was prepared. It was signed by seventy-eight of the island's inhabitants, including Samuel and his brother Captain John Wickham, the latter of whom the governor once lauded as "a gentleman that has a very good Estate and Wind-mill [sugar mill] on the Island, and who has neither Place nor Dependance on one of the Government." Bearing the title

> The humble Address of several of the most considerable Freeholders, Merchants, Planters, and Inhabitants of the Island of Antegoa

the counter-petition begins:

> We your Majesty's most loyal, dutiful and obedient Subjects, do with utmost Transports of Joy, receive the several Relations of the Success of your Majesty's Armies, and those of your Allies, all over Europe; and should think our selves as happy as any other your Majesty's Subjects whatsoever, under your most auspicious Reign, if a Spirit of Division (which of long time has been brewing) had not at this Time broke out into a Flame in this Island, begun and carry'd on by the restless Malice of some few Persons, who . . . have . . . endeavour'd to alienate the Affections of your Majesty's Liege People of this Island, from Daniel Parke, Esq. . . .[4]

A MAP OF THE ISLAND OF ANTIGUA by Robert Baker. London: 1748–9. Details show names of Wickham kin and their plantation (windmill) sites.
Map Division, New York Public Library; Astor, Lenox and Tilden Foundations.
Photograph by Harvey Weber.

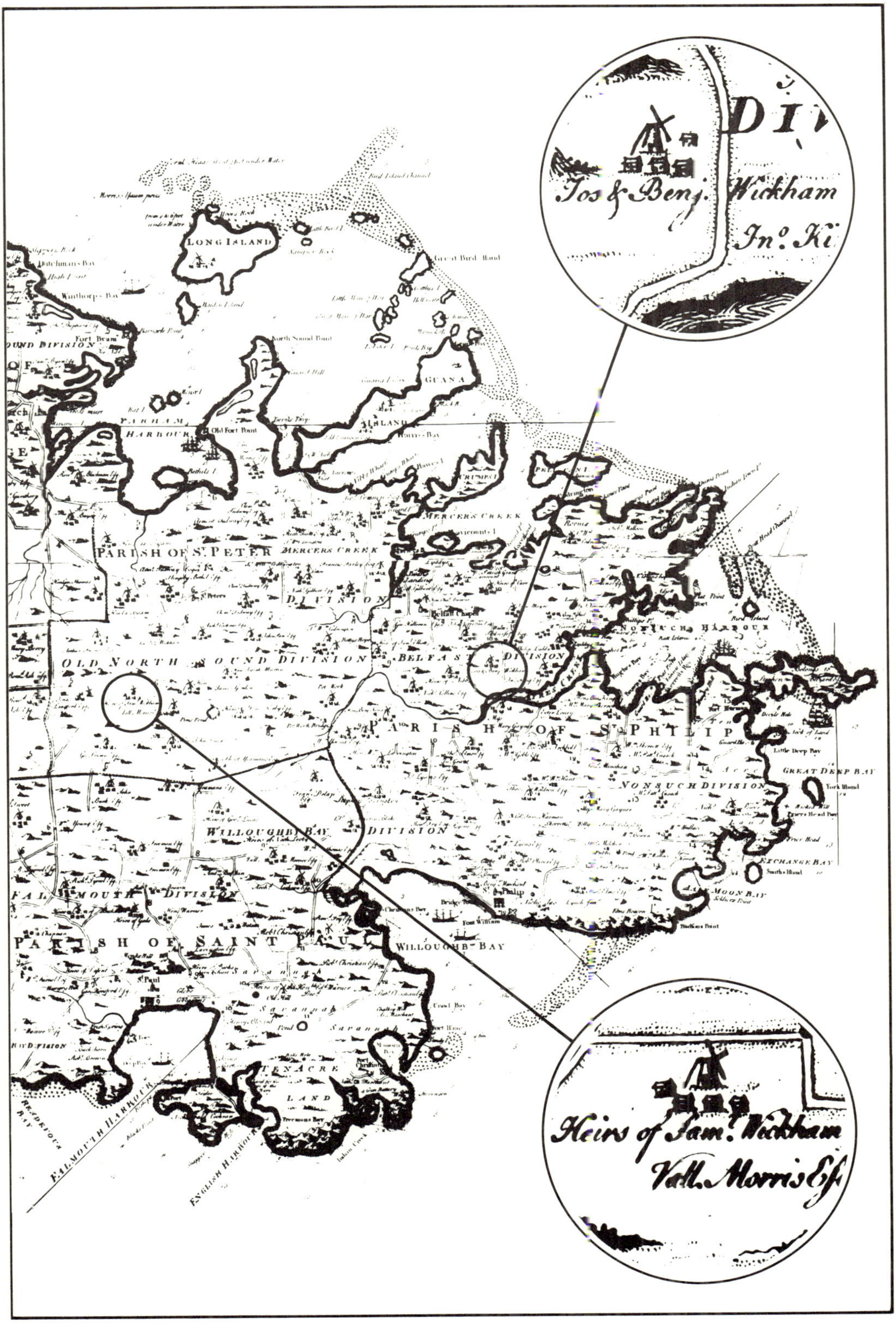

LONG ISLAND
PARHAM HARBOUR
GUANA ISLAND
MERCERS CREEK
PARISH OF S.T PETER
MERCERS CREEK DIVISION
OLD NORTH SOUND DIVISION
BELFAST DIVISION
NORTH HARBOUR
PARISH OF S.T PHILIP
GREAT DEEP BAY
NONSUCH DIVISION
WILLOUGHBY BAY DIVISION
EXCHANGE BAY
FALMOUTH DIVISION
PARISH OF SAINT PAU
WILLOUGHBY BAY
TENACRE LAND
FALMOUTH HARBOUR
ENGLISH HARBOUR
Jos & Benj. Wickham
Jn.o Ki
Heirs of Sam.l Wickham
Vall. Morris Esq

The petition was sent to London in May 1709, where it was received along with the original complaint.

Meanwhile the loyal party on the island suffered a major defeat in the assembly. Samuel Wickham died in 1709, reason unknown. Opposition to Governor Parke was growing, but despite it he refused to step down. Finally, on December 7, 1710, violence broke out and the struggle came to a head.

There were many people that morning in the market place of St. John's, the main port of Antigua. They were all armed or fetching arms from a stack of guns heaped against stocks. One of the leaders, a man by the name of Smyth, was dressed in a white waistcoat and carried a cartridge box on his belt and a sword by his side. He was later heard to say he would have gone twenty miles on his head to do it.

The governor knew about their preparations and summoned fifty soldiers uphill for his defense. The provost-marshall read a proclamation to the crowd ordering them to disperse, but the crowd, already above 500 strong, responded by ordering him to take it back to the general and tell him to "wipe his arse with it." They then issued a proclamation of their own declaring in the name of the assembly "that the general was a Traytor, and all those who would not take up Arms against him, are deem'd Traytors and Rebels to their Country; are to be banished off the Islands, and their Estates confiscated."

They divided themselves into two parties, one led by Captain John Piggot, the other by Captain John Painter, a rich planter, and in two paths began the march uphill to the governor's home. A promontory above the house, guarded by a sergeant and six of the general's soldiers, was easily overtaken, the soldiers dropping their guns and deserting at the approach of the men from below. Reaching the promontory, the one group entrenched itself and began shooting at the house. Piggot's group, stationed in another position, opened up a second volley. There was a brief exchange of gunfire; then Piggot's group staged an assault. His men made it to the door, entered, Piggot fell, but the governor, shot in the thigh, was taken. Surrounded by his enemies, Colonel Parke was laid out on the floor and stripped. His captors then proceeded to beat him with the butts of their rifles until dead.

Panic struck those who had been loyal to the governor. A new appeal went out overseas to the queen, signed by John Wickham and others in the loyal camp.

> Most Gracious Sovereign,
>
> A Few of your Majesty's dejected, but loyal Subjects of this Island, privately meeting together, do by this our most humble Address, lay our Selves prostrate at your royal Feet for Protection of Lives and Interests, for adhering to that late loyal Gentleman, Col. Parke. . . .

How the queen responded to this plea is not recorded. There was an investigation, at any rate, into the assassination, and some action was taken. Smyth, one of those allegedly involved in the governor's death, was brought to England, where he was indicted for high treason, levying war against Her Majesty on the island of Antigua, and murdering Colonel Parke. But as the trial proceeded, the evidence against him was found wanting and he was acquitted.

The events of 1710 gradually retreated into the past, though in some families the account of what had happened may have traveled afar, like ripples from an epicenter. Perhaps hearing of it from kinsfolk, even Parker Wickham in Cutchogue, Long Island, may have known the story of that political uprising. In any event, surviving Wickhams on Antigua appear not to have lost their lands or fortunes. John Wickham became a justice of the peace in 1712, a major, a member of the assembly in 1717 and again in 1721. He died in 1723 at the age of forty-one. Benjamin was elected to the assembly in 1714; another brother, Nathaniel, in 1717. After these years references to them and their families are scattered and few. A 1748 map of Antigua shows the estates of the Wickham brothers, but there was probably a younger generation living on them now. Older Wickhams may have returned to England and retired. Some may have migrated to other parts of the New World. For example, later in the century we come across another John Wickham in nearby Barbados. A rum shipper, "John Wickham & Sons" has business dealings with such prominent New Yorkers as John Watts, and a record of their correspondence is found in Watts's letterbook.[5] Watts was a merchant, a member of the Governor's Council of New York, and a former assemblyman of the colony. He would be among the fifty-nine to be one day attainted by the legislature of the state of New York.

The state of New York was of course still a British colony at the time of Justice Joseph Wickham's death in Cutchogue, Long Island. After his death, there was a gradual exodus of his sons and daughters from Wickham's Neck, leaving only one son, Parker, the sole proprietor of the ancestral estate. Parker's brothers settled on other lands, while his sisters, those that married, moved to their husbands' farms. In 1752 the new master of the Wickham farm married Mary Goldsmith. Her father, like almost every man in the region, was a farmer, and her family was one of the oldest in Cutchogue. Soon after their marriage, a new generation of Wickhams would grow up on the family estate, beginning with Parker's first son, Joseph Parker Wickham.

Parker, like his father and granddad, also served in public office, but

FAMILY PORTRAITS. Painted by "R. Earl" (i.e., Ralph Earl), an American portrait painter and loyalist during the Revolutionary War.

These family portraits are believed to be of Parker Wickham and his wife Mary Goldsmith Wickham. *J. Parker Wickham*. Photographs by Harvey Weber.

unlike them he achieved local prominence not so much for the appointed positions he would hold as for those he was elected to. His political career began in 1751 when he was elected Fence Viewer and Prisor of Damage, posts which probably went together. The duty of a Fence Viewer was to supervise the erection and maintenance of fences and boundaries. In the years 1754 and 1755 he was elected Overseer of the Poor. Numbering eight, these officials provided for the paupers of the town. In the first of those two years, Parker was also one of eight townsmen to sign a petition addressed to James DeLancey, Lieutenant Governor of New York. The petition requested that they, the subscribers, be allowed to form themselves into "a compleat organized company of Troopers" for the town of Southold. Nothing is known of the answer they received, but in 1765 Parker is referred to as "Major" Wickham in the town records, suggesting that he had been commissioned a militia officer at some time in the intervening years.

Meanwhile another turn in Wickham's public career had taken place, his judicial appointment. On August 3, 1763, he and two other justices were named Commissioners for the County of Suffolk, empowered to take affidavits for the supreme court of the province. The following year we come across Parker's first known court appearance as a justice of the peace. With him on the bench was another justice, Robert Hempstead, son of the Joshua Hempstead who had kept the diary we spoke of earlier. The case brought before them on this occasion concerned "amail Bastard Child Lately Born in the Town Ship of Southold."[6] By chance the deliberations of Wickham and Hempstead in this case have been preserved—the only instance where this has happened—giving us a glimpse into the manner of justice dispensed by these men.

The facts of the case as told by the justices are these: On January 18, 1764, Mary Baley, a single woman, gave birth to a male child at the house of one Isaac Liscum in the township of Southold. The child became chargeable to the town and was likely, as the court believed, to continue so. Testimony was heard from the Overseers of the Poor, from Mary Baley, and other sources, to determine who the child's father was. The evidence pointed to Jonathan Dickinson. One of the justices then proceeded to Jonathan's home. When he got there, the youth's father answered the door, but Jonathan was nowhere to be found. It appeared that the young man "was now absconded so that the Constables as Usal Could not take his body." The court proceeded to adjudge Jonathan the father of the child, and Justices Wickham and Hempstead issued an order that he immediately pay the Overseers fifty shillings for the maintaining of the child and the "lying in" of Mary Baley. Official notice of this order was put out, but whether the notice ever caught up with Jonathan we are not told. As for the unwed mother, the court ruled that she pay a weekly expense to the

Overseers as long as the child continued in their charge, and that was the extent of the judgment against her. For a woman in her circumstances, the decision seems surprisingly mild, considering the time in which it was made.

That there was something more to Parker Wickham's sense of justice than a mere right or wrong according to the law is suggested in an undated letter he writes, addressed to his brother Hull Wickham, a merchant in New York.

> One Parmenas Horton, formerly of this Town, moved to North Carolina & there became wealthy. His only sister Elisabeth, *a Pauper,* has by the mere compassion of Lieut. Jonathan Horton, our Friend & Neighbour, been fed & Supported through her long Illness of fourteen Years last past. This Spring past She died, & a few Days after her Death a Letter arrived from Messr John Tomlinson & Jacob Shepard of or near Newbern in North Carolina, stiling Themselves Exrs to the last will & Testament of Parmenas Horton. . . . By their Letter, directed to Sd. Elisabeth, Parmenas's Sister, Sd. Lieut was informed of Sd. Parmenas's Death, & that he [Parmenas] had bequeathed to his Sd. Sister Elisabeth one Hundred Pounds equal to York Money, & they desire her to impower Some Person to recieve the Legacy. Now She was dead just before the Letter arrived, & we all are agreed that in Equity the Legacy falls to Sd. Lieut. But as he cant properly be Said to be Heir at Law So he cant give a Power, & yet tis allowed He ought to have the Mony.[7]

The writer then goes on to mention he is enclosing letters for the executors which are left unsealed "that you may know the whole affair," and asks his brother to negotiate on Horton's behalf.

Beginning in the 1770's, the county courts at the River Head had as one of their justices Parker Wickham. In General Sessions, Parker Wickham Esq. first appears in the minutes book in 1773, then again in 1774. The last entry for this court is dated 1775, the year Southold, at its town meeting on April 4, chose "a Commitee to meete att the River head with the other Comities for the County to Consult upon affairs Relating the Congress." In Common Pleas, Parker's name appears as justice first in March 1773, then in October of that year, then in October of 1774, and finally on March 28, 1775. The last entry of the Common Pleas minutes is of that date too. It reads:

> The Sheriff protests the County Goal [i.e., jail] is insufficient to secure his prisoners.[8]

Meanwhile in the local township of Southold, whose jurisdiction included at that time the present township of Riverhead, Wickham's political importance had grown. He was elected town assessor in 1765 and again in 1766, when he is referred to in the records as "Parker Wickham, Esq." Then in 1767 he became supervisor, the highest elected official of the town. He was reelected supervisor each year for the next seven straight years. During the tumultuous period of 1775 and 1776, the magistrate was out of office. But then in 1777 he appears in public life again. On April 10 of that year, at a meeting of supervisors at the County Hall, he was appointed a commissioner for collecting excise duties, presumably those referred to in colonial and state laws as the duties of excise "from retailers of strong liquors." Nine days earlier, at a public meeting in Mattituck, he had been once again elected Southold supervisor for the ninth time. Parker's tenure in this office was one of the longest the town had known up to that time and probably would have continued longer were it not cut short by a raid on Southold December 13, 1777. It was a raid conducted by Americans from the mainland, people fighting a war of independence.

The next we hear of Wickham is on the twenty-eighth of December. General Parsons writes from Lyme, Connecticut, to Governor Clinton of New York State:

Lyme in Connec'tt 28th Dec. 1777

Dear Sir,

Several Persons have been bro't from Long Island who have been exceedingly active in distressing the well affected there;

Among these are Major Wickham, Major Hudson, Orange Webb, & Matt'w Wells of Southold Township, John Ireland of Huntington & sundry others. None of these act under military Commissions except Hudson; the others must be considered as State Prisoners & fall within your Direction being Subjects of your State: they are now with the Commissary of Prisoners at Hartford; if you think it necessary to give any Particular Orders respecting them the Commissary will doubtless comply with any Directions you give.

The well affected Inhabitants of Suffolk County are anxious to have Wickham, Hudson & Ireland kept upon the main. they much fear their Return, they are now all upon their Parole. I am y'r Excellency's Obed't Serv.

Sam'l. H. Parsons[9]

To be on the wrong side of the law, that was a novel turn of events for the man who had been an officer of the law. But what country's law had Wickham broken? And why was he being carted off to the state of Connecticut?

CHAPTER 4

A Family Connection

PARKER HAD AN IMPORTANT contact in New York City, a cousin named William Wickham. An attorney, William was the son of a Newport, Rhode Island, merchant, who in turn had been one of the sons of Joseph Sr. of Cutchogue, Parker's grandfather.[1] William had been orphaned as a child and grew up first at Brookhaven, Long Island, and then in Orange County. After graduating from Yale, he became a lawyer, setting up his practice both in Goshen, where he lived, and in New York City, at that time the capital of the province.

The attorney made periodic trips on Long Island to the county courts of Suffolk, representing clients in that region. On occasion clients came to him in the city, where he represented them in cases before the Supreme Court of New York. William kept a record of cases he argued before this court, what he called his "Supream Court Register," and in it are found several notations concerning Parker Wickham's legal matters. Three cases are entered where Parker is named plaintiff, these all within the five years 1764–9. In one, involving a suit of ejectment for lands in Suffolk County, the disposition is not given. In another, the cause is not given, but Parker appears to have paid costs. And in the third, *Parker Wickham* v. *Samuel Landon Esq.*, the issue was one of debt, but the disposition of the case is not stated.[2] The defendant in this instance, Samuel Landon, was a prominent judge of Suffolk County, a former supervisor of Southold whose son Jared became surrogate of the county in 1768. More about him at another time. *Wickham* v. *Landon* is an unusual case by the very fact of its existence. For a justice and a judge, reputable men of their community, to be engaged in a suit, for the one to find it necessary to resort to the supreme court to settle his differences with the other, suggests a degree of ill-feeling that may have extended to more than just the issue over a debt. Samuel's name comes up again in the entry *Thomas Fanning* v. *Samuel Landon*, under which is the notation "P. Wickham & Nicoll Havens on 28 March 1764 desired me to prosecute this suit." The cause here was a debt of eighty-eight pounds, less sundries, leaving an amount due of forty-four pounds. Noted below the due figure is the memo: "June 9, 1764 Rec'd this sum of J. Landon in the presence of Mr. Rich Morris." And so Landon's son Jared, twenty-four years old, had made the journey to New York that day—with what feelings we do not know—to pay Parker Wickham's cousin a disputed debt that had been extracted from the boy's father.

In 1770 an exclusive society was formed in New York City called the Moot. Here we meet up with William again, finding him among impressive company. "Moots" in the jargon of English law meant exercises using formal arguments on points of law raised by students, and this explains the name of the society, whose purpose was to give its members an opportunity to debate, over wine and hors d'oeuvres, various refinements of the law. However, the gentlemen of the Moot were no students. Quite the contrary. Numbering twenty, they were an elite group, distinguished lawyers of the colony, many of whom were to become even more distinguished in the years ahead, while others with a different political persuasion would meet an opposite fate. There was David Mathews, Princeton '54, destined to become the last crown-appointed mayor of the city, and one of those later attainted by the state of New York; he was a Moot member. There was John Jay, the state's first chief justice, president of the Continental Congress and first Chief Justice of the United States Supreme Court; he was a Moot member. There was the attorney general of the colony John Tabor Kempe, later attainted by the state. And Richard Morris, a future chief justice of New York, and his half brother Gouverneur. There was Robert R. Livingston, Jr., the state's first chancellor, and his cousin William Livingston, the first governor of the state of New Jersey. There were John Morin Scott, James Duane, and Egbert Benson, future members of the legislature of New York State. And William Smith, Yale '46, the last chief justice under the crown. He would be banished by the state. And there were two gentlemen who, not espousing the cause of independence, managed to hang on to their property despite their beliefs: William Wickham, Yale '53, and Peter Van Schaack, the latter the founder of the first law school in New York.[3]

The subscribing members of the Moot drew up their charter. The rules provided for the election of officers, time and place of meetings, the manner of proposing a question that would then be debated at the next convening of the society. Article 5 of the charter expressly forbade members "upon any Pretence, to introduce any Discourse about the Party Politics of this Province"—on pain of expulsion.

The minutes tell us that the first meeting was held on November 23, 1770, at Barden's, that is Edward Bardin's, who ran the King's Arms

Tavern on Broadway, now Whitehall Street. The Moot elected its officers there, and the president-elect, William Livingston, proposed a question for the next meeting, at which time that question would be discussed and decided, and a new question proposed, and so on. Sometimes at these sessions the topic of discussion stirred minor differences of opinion, as on a night at Fraunces Tavern when the issue was one of two debts and which had priority. Members could all agree on the priority but not on the collateral issue of a suit. At other times the discussions were more heated as on the night of July 5, 1771, at Bolton's. On this occasion there were but five members attending, and William Wickham was chosen president, *pro tempore*. The issue before them was also one of legal priority, but now it concerned land and mortgages. Debate ensued. Members fell into opposing camps. Wickham, Samuel Jones, and Rudolphus Ritzema—a new member—took one side, Jay and Benson another. And the night ended that way, a three-two decision. There were still other times too when the problem before them brought complete unanimity of opinion, as on April 5, 1771, at Bolton's. Present were John Tabor Kempe, Samuel Jones, John Jay, Peter Van Schaack, Egbert Benson, Robert R. Livingston, and Rudolphus Ritzema. The question before them was as follows:

> A being seized in Fee of certain Lands devises them to his Son B, and to his Heirs and Assigns forever; And if B dies without Issue [then] to C in Fee. The Devisor dies, and B enters. What Estate has he by the Devise?

It was the same sort of question that in actuality was put to Edmund Pendleton by George Washington in a letter of 1769, concerning his Mount Vernon estate.[4] The matter was now taken up, and the Moot debated, and on this occasion reached consensus. Its answer—have you guessed?—"All the members present are of Opinion that B has an Estate Tail."

The last gathering of the Moot occurred on April 7, 1775. But there were few members present. Most had long since gone their separate ways, preoccupied with matters of greater import. Wickham's last date of attendance was December 10, 1773, six days before the Boston Tea Party.

CHAPTER 5

The Magistrate Makes a Decision

THE DUMPING OF BRITISH tea into Boston harbor on the evening of December 16, 1773, aroused from across the seas a storm of anger in Parliament, which determined upon harsh reprisals. Boston harbor was, by Parliamentary decree, ordered closed. The town was garrisoned with British troops. The Massachusetts assembly was dissolved. The colony's charter revoked. And that cherished right of trial by peers of one's vicinage was now rescinded at will by the new governor, the British commander General Gage.

Alarm spread through the colonies. "American liberties" became a rallying cry. Boston's Committee of Correspondence, writing to committees in sister colonies, appealed for united action.

New York's reply was given by Isaac Low, chairman of that colony's Committee of Correspondence. He wrote back on May 23, 1774, declaring that "the alarming Measures of the British Parliament relative to your ancient and Respectable Town, which has so long been the Seat of Freedom, fills the Inhabitants of this City with inexpressible Concern." Boston's injuries were a common cause, Low assured his correspondents, and he underscored the need for joint action by proposing "a Congress of Deputies from the Colonies in General."[1] Broadly supported, the idea of a congress took hold. Plans were laid out over the summer, and on September 5 they met: A congress of deputies from the twelve colonies gathered at Smith's Tavern in Philadelphia at ten o'clock, and then walked to Carpenter's Hall, their place of assembly. Here the opening session was held of the First Continental Congress.

As deputy himself, Low and the other delegates from New York had the initial task of approving the credentials of their colleagues, fellow deputies from the province. His colony's delegation included first of all those from the capital: Jay, Duane, Philip Livingston, and later John Alsop. Then there were a few from outside New York City: Kings County delegate Simon Boerum, William Floyd of Suffolk County, and John Haring and

Henry Wisner—a staunch patriot—from Orange. The latter two had been elected at a meeting of committeemen in Orange County on August 16, where out of a county of 1,000 freeholders less than 20 were said to have been in attendance at the meeting to vote.[2] To strengthen Wisner's credentials, he was elected a second time at a meeting in Chester on September 3. Here a decision to send a delegate to Congress won by a majority of two votes.

Attorneys William Wickham and David Mathews, residents in Orange County, were uneasy about these election proceedings. William wrote a first letter to Isaac Low on September 2, and then both composed a second after the election at Chester. Though their letters have not survived, Low's answers have. His first response was to Wickham's letter.[3]

Philadelphia Sept 6th 1774

Dear Sir

I did not arrive here untill Saturday Evening after the Return of the Post which brought me your Favor of 2nd Inst. or you would have had an Answer to it as requested.

The different Members of the Congress, a very few Individuals only excepted) met yesterday Morning at Carpenters Hall. Mr. Randolph was chosen President, Mr. Charles Thompson Secretary without opposition. I shall be happy if the same Unanimity prevails in their future Proceedings.

On producing our Credentials with a Short account of the peculiar Circumstances of our Election it was unanimously resolved to receive us and such other County Delegates as might hereafter appear as Representatives for the Colony of New York. Mr. Harring [Haring] having no Credentials to produce retired without offering himself as a Delegate tho' he had constantly appeared amongst them as such — He said he was going Home, but as I saw him still in this City last Evening I suspect he means to pluck up Courage and depend on the Support of his Friends this Day. I suspect he will have a majority if he can produce a Certificate of his having become duely elected, signed by only half a dozen Freeholders of his County which I suppose he may easily obtain. Seek further Information therefore as you can give relative to his Election I beg to [be] favoured with as soon as possible.

Coll: Floyd produced a Certificate of his Election signed by about Seven or Eight Committee Men which was thought by my Colleagues to be too authentic and formidable to be overset by any Thing we could produce to the Contrary, and thus he passed duely qualified Mem. Con [gress].

Shallow Politicians have we been since [w]ith a little Pains, we might have procured Certificates signed by ten or a doz. reputable Freeholders in each County deputing us their Delegates which to all appearance had been deemed a sufficient Qualification to arrogate to ourselves their entire Confidence.

Mrs. Low joins in best Compliments to Mrs. Wickham and you, heartily wishing her well over her Trouble.

I am Dr Sir
Your Most Hbl Servant
Isaac Low

verso: To William Wickham Esq.
New York

Low's second letter of September 20, written this time jointly to Wickham and Mathews, comments that Haring had not made a second appearance (the *Journals of the Continental Congress* indicate he was admitted a delegate on the twenty-sixth). As to the other delegate, based on the certificates he produced from the Orange County elections, it was "our unanimous opinion that we could not with any Prospect of Success oppose Mr. Wisner's Qualifications."

Whatever the electoral qualification in any one case, it was undoubtedly true that some delegates enjoyed a far broader base of support within their respective counties than others. The delegation from New York City, in fact, had been chosen by several counties to represent them, and among these—the city delegates—Isaac Low, for one, stood equal to any in terms of popular backing at this time. A wealthy merchant, Low became chairman of the New York Chamber of Commerce in 1775, a post he was reelected to every year thereafter until 1783. In 1774 and '75, he held the chairmanship of the colony's Correspondence Committee, and was voted into the New York Provincial Congress in May of 1775. However, he resigned from that congress shortly afterward, declining as well the opportunity to serve in the Second Continental Congress. Both congresses were moving in a direction he was not prepared to accept. Politically conservative, Low refused to align with the growing revolutionary ferment, "the violence of a party," as he explained it, "whose zeal and Designs extended far beyond what they professed."[4] And so his fortunes changed. The Revolution once in progress, he came to be looked upon suspiciously, perhaps because of the following he had had. He was imprisoned in 1776 and released. Then on October 22, 1779, his lot fell in with fifty-eight others, accused and at once condemned by the Act of Attainder of the state of New York.

One of the initial tasks attended to by the First Continental Congress was the drawing up of the Association. Adopted on October 20, 1774, the revolutionary Association was a bold document for its time. It begins on a conciliatory note—"We, His Majesty's Most Loyal Subjects, the delegates of the several colonies" avow their "allegiance to His Majesty. . ."—and proceeds to a recitation of Parliament's oppressive measures. Then follows a declaration announcing a united course of action to oppose these measures. They, the Congress, for themselves and the inhabitants of the several colonies whom they represent, agree not to import, consume, or export products from, of, or to Great Britain. In short, a commercial boycott is proclaimed against the mother country. Specifics are laid out and rules set down by which enforcement is to be sought. Committees are to be created in every county, city, and town, chosen by those who are qualified to vote for representatives in the legislature. The "business" of these committees will be "to observe the conduct of all persons touching this association." And as for any transgressor, anyone who should violate this Association, the committee is to publish an account of his action in the newspaper "to the end that all such foes to the rights of British America may be publicly known and universally contemned as the enemies of American liberty; and thenceforth we respectively will break off all dealings with him or her." Beyond this quasi-judicial authority, the committees are to be endowed with another one, a rather broad quasi-legislative function: They are, in addition, "to establish such further regulations as they may think proper, for carrying into execution this association."[5]

The common grievances notwithstanding, these steps which the delegates subscribed to gave considerable, unrestrained authority to what were technically extra-governmental, extra-legal bodies of men, these newly created city, county, and town committees. The vast majority of people were no doubt behind the resolutions of Congress. Yet while this was true, it can also be said that a minority in America would sooner or later discover, perhaps in their own experience, that in the cause of liberty the Association was encouraging a situation in which liberty was in danger of being lost.

The Association of Congress was followed up in subsequent months by a slew of general associations on the local level, subscribed to by the populace where each association was drawn up. It was from their signatures, and the lists of those refusing to sign, that judgments were to be made about loyalties: what members of the community were "well-affected," which ones "disaffected." In New York the bulk of the local associations were subscribed to in the months of May and June of 1775, at which time a new revolutionary body, the Provincial Congress, was formed in the city, its membership elected from the different counties. In that respect it was similar to the former legislative assembly of the colony, composed also of delegates elected by the county constituencies. The assembly, however, had refused to approve the resolutions of the Continental Congress, despite the persistent efforts of a number of delegates. Part of the old government, the assembly adjourned on April 4, never to reconvene. In the wake of its demise the new Provincial Congress took power, meeting for the first time on May 22. By week's end this congress had passed resolutions respecting the local committees and the handling of the associations. Counties which had not already done so were advised to appoint county committees and subcommittees to carry out the resolutions of the Continental and Provincial Congresses. They were also instructed about the associations, which were to be tendered to every inhabitant—limited to adult free males—by committees within the county, and these associations and the names of those not signing were to be returned to the revolutionary body in New York. The instructions, drafted in a letter, also noted that "it is the sense of this Congress that no coercive steps ought to be used to induce any person to sign the Association."[6]

In upstate New York large numbers of people turned out to subscribe to the association. Orange, Ulster, and Dutchess counties all had long lists of subscribers and comparatively few dissenters. In the southern part of the province, however—Long Island, Westchester, and New York, including Kings and Richmond—the situation was diametrically opposite. Richmond County, for example, refrained from any response at all until February 1776, when a Jersey contingent of troops under the command of Colonel Herd advanced upon Staten Island, whereupon "seven-eighths" of the county's menfolk were reported to have subscribed. In Queens, the same procrastination: no response until the troops were ordered in by Congress, at which time the dissidents in the county were obliged to sign an oath of obedience to the Continental and Provincial bodies. Kings has no record of any association. Nor does Westchester, except one of a different kind, a declaration of support for the king and the constitution, subscribed to by over 300 inhabitants, their names included in the published pledge.[7] New York County had an association in support of the congresses, but its subscribers—ninety-eight—were all deputies to the Provincial Congress. Of the five southern counties, it was only in Suffolk where the association made headway. Several townships in Suffolk, East Hampton and Southampton, had all or practically all male inhabitants subscribing to the association. Other towns like Brookhaven and Southold had subscriber lists as well as a list of inhabitants not agreeing to the association. Still other towns like Islip had noticeably small subscriber lists.

In Southold's association, curious symbols are found next to certain names.[8] These marks bear two distinct shapes depending on their meanings, which are explained as "Not Signed" or "Not Appearing." In addition, sometimes the word "Signed" is written in to mean signed after previously refusing to sign. Southold's association begins with Captain Josiah Lupton's militia company. From the explanatory marks we learn that twenty-nine in this company signed, fourteen did not, twelve didn't appear, and four signed after previously not signing. A postscript informs us that most of Captain Lupton's company "will sign," and that the captain himself has been down and signed. In the list's second group, Captain Hallock's company, eighteen are shown to have signed, two weren't at home, and a third "if at home would be full in signing." Then comes Captain Goldsmith's company: three signed. Captain Horton's: two. Captain Barnabas Wines's: two. Captain Barnabas himself appears in the "Not agreeing" group, but apparently had a change of mind as there is no "Not signed" mark next to his name. Following these companies we come to three more, captains without any signers at all. Finally, below them, we arrive at the "Not agreeing to the association" group, a category by itself. Under this heading are listed thirty-four persons, but eighteen of them are also indicated as having a change of heart, there being no "Not agreeing" symbol next to their names. That leaves us with the rest of the lot, the hardcore sixteen. These are not only labeled with the "Not agreeing" mark (+), but in some cases are saddled with it two or three times in repetition, as if to underscore the intransigence of the non-associator. Ezekiel Petty Jr., for example, is spiked with two of these marks next to his name (+ +) coupled with the words "verry bad man." Another, Thomas Overton, has three. Jonathan Terry has as many as six. Exceeding Terry and all the others is Parker Wickham's name, tagged with seven. His name comes up again in a remark appearing on the association document. Written by Colonel Phineas Fanning, the compiler of this list, it is addressed as a postscript to Ezra L'Hommedieu, delegate of the Provincial Congress. Fanning writes:

> I likewise hear that the toryes at matatuck had a meeting and signed or did something. But I fear they are all Like Majer Wickham only to deceive.

Whatever the basis for Fanning's personal judgments, it is clear as much from the derogatory marks as from the message which follows that the compiler of this pledge list had turned it into a vehicle for publicly branding people. The association had become more than an association. Wickham and other dissenters were not just being listed. They were being labeled, condemned behind their backs. There was nothing, of course, Wickham could do about Fanning's notations or about the record of his own dissent. The pledge list would go before the Provincial Congress, where it would be kept on permanent file. The verdict had been reached, and there would be no opportunity offered for the accused to speak in defense of his action. History would condemn him without having heard him.

Still we know that Wickham must have had his reasons for dissenting. Why did he abstain from the association? What thoughts and feelings led to his decision? History has made no record of them, and so we can only propose a fictional account of his preoccupations, giving his side of the story as best we can.

It would have been a day shortly before July 1, 1775, the time of Colonel Fanning's document. Before dawn that day, Major Wickham is already up and out of the house. We find him taking a solitary ride on his horse, a sorrel, out to Little Hog Neck Point, a journey of a few miles from his home. It is still dark, moonless, but the way over Dam Meadow is known to horse and rider. Listening to the cadence of his horse's hoofbeats through the brush, the major peers up at the dark, arching shapes of trees, sinister in their darkness yet so familiar in the light of day. His thoughts move to the troubles in New England, the fighting at Lexington and Concord. And now at Bunker Hill. "In New York our governor returns from England," the rider muses. "But what is left of his authority? The assembly is closed. The courts of justice are disregarded. Congress and the committees tell everybody what to do." Horse and rider move across an open field, the air dank with the smell of manure. Wickham ponders in his mind the local talk about bringing in powder and cannon to guard the livestock, as they say, from the enemy. "I sometimes wonder who the enemy are," he thinks. "Crown officers? The governor? Myself?"

They stop as if by habit at a wateringhole on Robins Island Neck, now called New Suffolk. Ahead to the east, in an opening between the foliage, the first pink crows feet of the dawn crease the horizon.

"Where lies a man's duty? I have sworn an oath of allegiance to the king, as every crown officer has done. An oath of obedience, binding me to my given duty. Now I'm asked to subscribe to this association, turn my allegiance to the Congress. Take part in this general revolt. Even as I, a justice, am supposed to defend the law, I am asked to usurp the law." He looks down at the drinking sound of his horse. "Parliamentary taxation. Oppressive regulations. It is true," he thinks. "The blame falls heavily on England's shoulders for this state of affairs. But we cannot throw off our obligations either. Can allegiance be broken at will? The law disregarded? Government insulted and trampled upon? Others seem fit to do this with a free conscience; I cannot. Nor can it be forced on me. There must be law. Respect for a higher authority. If treason becomes the law, then authority, allegiance, and the law become empty words."

The sorrel lifts her head and turns an eye into the forming dawn. Wickham, his gaze also that way, cannot stop brooding.

"Even were I to resign my commission," he thinks, "I am not by that action above the law. I am still a subject of the king. 'But no,' they say, 'we are no longer subjects of the king. We have thrown off our allegiance to him.' And how, may I ask, can subjects transform themselves into nonsubjects, aliens, by taking part against the realm to which they belong? Such an idea is inadmissible in law and contrary even to what these Whigs propose as the social compact."[9]

He coaxes his horse on. They travel some distance, then follow a deer

DETAIL FROM "MAP OF THE TOWN OF SOUTHOLD TAKEN BY THO. MOORE, SUPERVISOR, 1797." Part shown is a section of Cutchogue. Rolled Map #394, *New York State Archives, Albany, N.Y.*

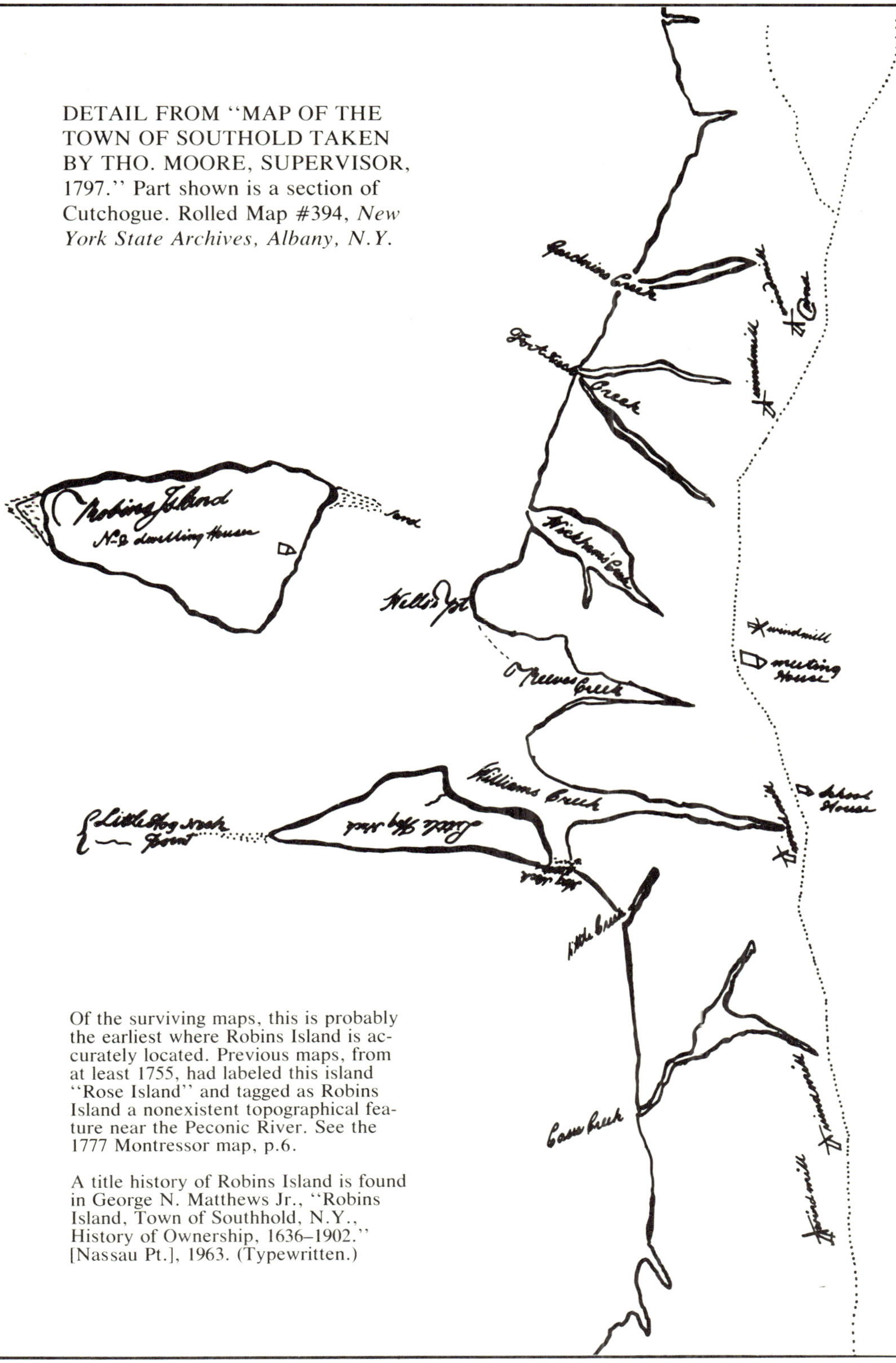

Of the surviving maps, this is probably the earliest where Robins Island is accurately located. Previous maps, from at least 1755, had labeled this island "Rose Island" and tagged as Robins Island a nonexistent topographical feature near the Peconic River. See the 1777 Montressor map, p.6.

A title history of Robins Island is found in George N. Matthews Jr., "Robins Island, Town of Southhold, N.Y., History of Ownership, 1636–1902." [Nassau Pt.], 1963. (Typewritten.)

path along a broad inlet, an estuary called Wickham Creek on maps today, but known to the rider as Reeves Creek. The pallid light of the dawn, mistlike, seems to hover over the water, the ghostly surface opening its arms into Great Peconic Bay. Wickham watches a mallard fly over the surface, feels the liberty of its vibrant wings. "Liberty." The word causes a new unsettling of his soul. He wrestles with a web of feelings. "Liberty belongs to everyone," he thinks, "not just to the Whigs, though they'd engross it all upon themselves. How did that writer put it in the gazette? 'They allow not to others who differ from them the same liberty of thinking and acting that they claim themselves.' "[10] Trodding under the bough of a tree, the major's horse gives a downward lurch of his head, avoiding a specter of bees near a hive. "This liberty," Wickham asks his horse, "what do you know about it?" As if in answer, a quotation comes to the justice's mind: " 'The enjoyment of liberty, even its support and preservation, consists in every man's being allowed to speak his thoughts, and lay open his sentiments.' Certainly there is truth in that," he thinks, "though I wouldn't doubt there are limits to the rule."

Wickham pulls on the reins, turning down a trail in Little Hog Neck. His memory, meanwhile, is busy recollecting where that came from, those words about liberty of speech. "It was a declaration of Congress," he recalls, "an address to the inhabitants of the Province of Quebec, published last year, October sometime."[11] In a flash, the whole of the declaration sweeps across his mind. The principles of liberty. The "great rights," as they were called, and how they were explained. He remembers that first great right: people sharing in their government, representational government. And the second great right? "Trial by jury," he thinks. "The right of the accused, as Congress tells it, to be tried by 'twelve of his unexceptionable countrymen and peers of his vicinage, who from that neighborhood may reasonably be supposed to be acquainted with his character, and the characters of the witnesses, upon a fair trial, face to face, in open Court' without which 'neither life, liberty nor property, can be taken from the possessor.' " He marvels at how vividly the words come back and thinks about the rest of the declaration. The third great right, habeas corpus, and that part about separation of powers. " 'There is no liberty if the power of judging be not separated from the legislative and executive powers.' " He muses. "Well spoken, all of it. Truly great words about liberty written by men of great learning." The magistrate peers at a spit of land in the sea. "These gentlemen of Congress," he thinks, "they cannot be wrong in their ideals. I grant as much. No, not in their ideals."

His horse stops. The vista of Peconic Bay stands before Wickham, the first gleams of the sun pouring freely across the outstretched expanse of sea. In the midst of this bay, southwest, a mound of about a mile and a half in dimension protrudes like a whale's back. Now, as the sun gleams, the whale's back begins to take on features of dune and treescape. The major admires it as if for the first time, as always he did from this vantage point. A proud island, his island, this whale's back in the sea, commanding the notice of all who gaze out here. His Robins.

But soon his attention withdraws itself. Preoccupations move back upon their old track. Gazing out to Robins, he thinks: "It is not their ideals I am afraid of, but dangers we all fear. The loss of liberty. Oppression. Persecution. Bloodshed. What will be the cost if there is no reconciliation? What new tyranny awaits us?" Another newspaper article comes to his mind, an editorial signed "Suffolk County." Excerpts from it will illustrate its slant.

> The Association . . . takes the Government out of the hands of the Governour, Council, and General Assembly; and the execution of the law out of the hands of the Civil Magistrates and Juries. The Congress exercises the Legislative, the Committees the Executive Powers.
>
> . . . .
>
> Their [the Committees'] power is arbitrary and unlimited; they may judge by appearances, and condemn unseen and unheard; they are under no check, there is no appeal to another Court; they are not accountable to any power.[12]

Opinions like these may have struck a responsive note in the justice, who we now imagine thinking about that article, undoubtedly with questions of his own about the county and town committees. Were their executive powers unlimited? Were they free to judge? Was there no longer a judicial system? Could they condemn a man unseen and unheard?

The major dismounts from his horse and ties her to a post. He gives her a little rub on the nose, then turns and walks over to the pebbly beach, where he starts out upon the spit of land called Little Hog Neck Point. Once by a protective shelf of dune, a breeze whips into life and simultaneously a burst of low-flying terns, alarmed by his intrusion upon their grounds. He watches them but is not deterred by their aerobatics and keeps on his way. Further out, the terns leave him, satisfied by his distance. Wickham keeps walking and at length arrives at the end of the point. Here there is nothing to disturb him. To the southwest, the long almond eye of dune on Robins Island gleams gold in the sun. Wickham looks at the eye and thinks about a possibility. "Suppose," he thinks, "I should be taken by one of these committees. Suppose one day I stand accused of a crime, accused before their tribunals of breaking a law. What will their rules of the game be?" he wonders. "What constitutional rights will I be allowed? Habeas corpus? Trial by jury? The charges brought against me—will I be informed of them? See my accusers? Call my witnesses? Plead my defense? Will my liberties, my rights be honored as much as those they claim for themselves?"

The breeze dies. The sky is a cloudless blue. The bay and the island's eye sparkle in the sun. But Wickham, despite the tranquil scene, is not at peace.

Of the revolutionary committees in Suffolk County, it is only Brookhaven's whose minutes have survived essentially intact. No records of minutes from the other towns are known of, and perhaps they did not keep them, at least not in any formal sense.

There were actually two committees in Brookhaven, and they met at different times. The Committee of Observation convened at Coram, Long Island, for the first time on June 27, 1775.[13] On that occasion several resolutions were passed. One expressed loyalty to King George, acknowledging him rightful lord and sovereign. Another declared opposition to various acts of Parliament. Support for the Continental Congress and Provincial Congress was affirmed, and the need for watchful observation that no provisions fall into the hands "of our Enemies." An official apology was also made at this time "for comeing so late into Congressional measures," the reason being that "opposission ran so high heretofore in some parts of this Town that an attempt of this kind would perhaps have answered no valuable purpose." Some of the resistance, and perhaps the most serious, was led by Brookhaven's supervisor, Major Benjamin Floyd. He and his cousin William Floyd stood on opposing sides in the struggle with England. William was a delegate to the Continental Congress, and by summer's end he had become chairman of Brookhaven's Committee of Observation. This committee, at its meetings, took up various concerns, among them the procurement of gunpowder and lead, the association lists, the conduct of certain persons about whom the Provincial Congress was to be notified, election of militia officers, and so on. One of these matters, the third mentioned, had an important follow-up in New York City, where the Provincial body was meeting. On August 3, the Brookhaven committee wrote to that congress about Benjamin Floyd, his brother Colonel Richard Floyd, and others who were opposing the measures of the Continental Congress. "They damn all congresses and committees," the committeemen write, adding that the persons named had publicly served notice that they intended to furnish the enemy men-of-war and cutters with provisions. The letter concludes with a request that they, the petitioners, be directed as to what actions should be taken against these transgressors. In response, the Provincial Congress passed several resolutions on September 1 having to do with the general question of political dissidents.[14] Any person found guilty before a committee of attempting to furnish provisions to the British army was to be punished by up to three months in confinement. A person

FLOYD FAMILY[15]

Richard Floyd II (1653-1738)
Col. of Suffolk Militia;
proprietor of Mastic farm

Nicoll Floyd (1705-55)
marries Tabitha Smith;
inherits Mastic farm;
children:

Ruth = Gen. Nathaniel Woodhull
President of Provincial Congress; Commander of Long Island militia

William Floyd
delegate to Continental Congress; signer of Declaration of Independence

Charity = Ezra L'Hommedieu
delegate to Provincial Congress; later state assemblyman and state senator

Anna = Hugh Smith
son of Josiah Smith, Col. of the 1st Suffolk Regiment

Richard Floyd III (1703-71)
marries Elizabeth Hutchinson;
Suffolk judge; proprietor of Pattersquash farm;
sons:

Richard IV (attainted)
marries Arrabella Jones, sister of Judge Thomas Jones (attainted); inherits Pattersquash estate; commander of loyalist Suffolk militia;
son:
David Richard Floyd-Jones

Benjamin Floyd
Brookhaven supervisor

FANNING FAMILY

Captain James Fanning (1695-1779)
marries Hannah Smith;
Southhold supervisor, 1760-66.
Among his sons:

James Fanning Jr. (b. 1719)
His grandson James Aldrich marries Hellen, daughter of Parker Wickham, in 1800.

Thomas Fanning (b. 1722)
His Lebanon farm in Connecticut is confiscated in 1781.

Phineas Fanning (b. 1724)
Colonel of Suffolk Militia; attends Provincial Congress on April 20, 1775.

Edmund Fanning (b. 1739)
Governor Tryon's Secretary; is attainted in North Carolina in 1781; his sister, presumably a twin, marries John Wickham, brother of Parker Wickham, in 1762.

denying the authority of a congress or committee was to be disarmed. A second such offense would lead to arrest and confinement at the perpetrator's expense.

Following these instructions, the Brookhaven committee took a bolder step in asserting its own authority. On September 21 it issued a resolution ordering that anyone complained of for threatening or disturbing the peace of others "shall be cited before us, and punished according to the Judgment of us on hearing their Crime."

The election of members to Brookhaven's second committee, the Committee of Safety, was held April 16, 1776, and on May 13 this newly elected body met for the first time. Unlike the earlier group, Brookhaven's Committee of Safety was a much more aggressive judicial instrument, an inquisitorial board that interrogated, heard testimony of informers, and the like. A typical entry in the minutes describes a witness's sworn statement about what he heard somebody else say. On May 13 Daniel Nash testified "that he heard Andrew Patchin say (as he was going home from General training) the congress goes on as they ought not to and Dam^{ed} the Congress in all their unlawful proceedings." Nathaniel Finch testified that Patchin "particularly Dam'd Colonel William Floyd, saying he came home from the Congress on purpose to make Disturbance and the Divil would have him." On May 20, John Allabeen gave information on a person suspected of communicating with the British fleet. Allabeen testified that at the house of John Bayles, Innkeeper, he heard Daniel Rose say "I have more half Johannises [gold coins] in my Chest, that I brought from on Board the Ship, than all the Town can produce beside. . . . I can have the Ship come ashore anytime when I please, & can sell them my produce of any kind & not be beholden to your Committee nor Congress: and I can go on board the Ship any time when I please, & live a Gentleman all my Days." Sometimes alarmist news was given as evidence. On June 20 James Smith reported that William Longbottom said "there was Twelve Thousand to Land at Rockaway . . . and at the same time the Shiping to attack New York." On other occasions the committee was busy apprehending fugitives and suspects, persons "dangerous to the Liberties of America." Captain Jonathan Baker and Stephen Fountain, for example, were ordered on June 4 to be brought to New Haven and secured there in confinement until "legally" discharged. One of the fiercest sessions occurred with Thomas Fanning. A fifty-four-year-old farmer, Fanning had been a member of the previous Committee of Observation. He was two years older than his brother Phineas, the compiler of the Southold pledge list, and seventeen years older than his much younger brother, the notable Edmund Fanning, surrogate of the province and Governor Tryon's private secretary. The committee's complaint against Thomas, served May 13, arose over several of his activities, including his correspondence with his brother Edmund "and other our Enemies." He was ordered to bring all mail he had received in the last three months relating to the political crisis with England. Thomas refused to comply. Appearing before the committee, he declared he had such "but would not shew them if he had his flesh all pul'd off with hot pinchers. He Deny'd the Authority and Legality of this Committee: Used them with Contempt and abusive Language," according to the minutes. The committee then offered him "a fair hearing & Tryal," but Thomas refused. He was given the alternative of posting bond for his future good behavior, but that too he refused. The committee then resolved to take him before the Provincial Congress for them to deal with. Whether Fanning actually was taken is questionable as the *Journals of the Provincial Congress* do not mention him.

A graduate of Yale in 1757, Edmund Fanning settled in Orange County, North Carolina, and received his license to practice law in the colony in 1769. In Orange he became a colonel of the militia, a county register, and a judge of the superior court. He acquired a formidable estate in these years and became a protege of William Tryon, who was then lieutenant governor of North Carolina. In 1771 Tryon was appointed the governorship of New York, and when he left for his new post Edmund went with him, becoming the governor's personal secretary and surrogate of the province. In 1774 Edmund accompanied the governor on his journey to England and returned later that year to North Carolina. A letter to William Eden, a British peace negotiator in 1778, describes the governor's secretary this way: "A plausible good natured Gentleman: but of shallow Understanding & held for his affectation in contempt by those in Congress who are acquainted with him." When news reached Fanning of the Battle of Lexington and Concord, he moved back to New York, where he was appointed surveyor general of the province. This position he held until February 12, 1776, at which time he was forced to "fly for refuge," as he says in later testimony, on board the British *Asia,* a man-of-war. Soon after, the governor joined him on board the *Dutchess of Gordon,* moored in New York harbor under the *Asia*'s protection.

The governor, meanwhile, had returned from England on the 25th of June, 1775. The event, somewhat incidental to another, was noted in the diary of a Moravian pastor in New York.

> June 25th Sunday.—Considerable excitement in Town. Our Governor, William Tryon, was expected today from England; and also General Washington of the Provincials, who has been appointed Commander-in-chief of all the troops by the Continental Congress. Some regard would be shown to the governor, but the chief attention was paid to Gen Washington. The Governor arrived late in the evening.[16]

Already as Governor Tryon arrives, there are others preparing to evacuate. Merchant John Watts, a member of the Governor's Council, considered it advisable to embark for England in May, "all government being dissolved." It was that spring also when the attorney general, John Tabor Kempe, took the precaution of removing his family into the country. Soon after arriving in New York, the governor dispatched a letter back to the English secretary of the colonies, describing the situation in which he now found himself as one of "diminished authority." He goes on to explain: "The General Revolt that has taken place in the Colonies has put his Majestys civil Governors in the most degraded situation. . . . If it were the wish, it is not in the Power of any one Province to accommodate with Great Britain, being overawed and controuled by the General confederacy."[17] In New York, his own province, the governor saw firsthand how serious the state of affairs was. Five thousand men were being enlisted throughout the region, in "defense as it is said of the liberties of America." Detachments of troops were filing in and out of the colony, the governor helplessly looking on. In the city the king's military stores were being sacked and plundered; crown officers found themselves beseiged by mobs. "Moving out of the city continues," the Moravian pastor jots down on a day in late August 1775. "Some of the Streets look plague-stricken, so many houses are closed." Not long thereafter, the time had come for yet another resident, the prestigious James DeLancey, to pack up. A member of the former legislative assembly, DeLancey was a consummate landowner, one of whose properties was the 343-acre farm "in the Bowry near the City of New York," as he describes it. Departing first to Fort Stanwix, this refugee went on to Canada and from there journeyed to England later that fall.

By the middle of October Tryon's time had arrived. Earlier that month the Continental Congress had formally recommended that the provincial conventions and committees of safety "arrest and secure every person in their respective colonies, whose going at large may, in their opinion, endanger the safety of the colony, or the liberties of America."[18] What precisely the word "may" would mean, in the opinion of the committees, was a question that Governor Tryon, for one, was not about to wait around to learn the answer to. Moving offshore, he took up residence on the *Asia* in New York harbor, and soon after changed his quarters to the *Dutchess of Gordon*. Here he met up with the attorney general of the province, John Tabor Kempe, and in the spring with another of his ministers, Edmund Fanning.

In early December 1775, Tryon received aboard ship some encouraging reports suggesting that political opinion, at least in his province, was not as overawed and controlled by the general confederacy as he had thought. The exiled governor discerned a ray of hope on the horizon, and his gloomy assessment began to change. Writing to the Earl of Dartmouth, he points to the loyal conduct demonstrated by the inhabitants of Queens, and surmises that "the rage of the populace in this province for Committees and Congresses seems to have greatly abated." He goes on to note that several counties had refused to send delegates to the Provincial Congress. There were in fact two such counties, both situated in what was then the southern district of New York. One was Richmond. It had refused to subscribe to the association, but its resistance on that score ended in February 1776, after the Revolutionary authorities ordered a detachment of soldiers to Staten Island "to call the people to account." The other county, Queens, which included today's Nassau County, was a more serious matter.

Queens's defection from the American cause put the Provincial Congress in an embarrassing position. What was more, the spirit of resistance in this county was in danger of spreading elsewhere. Provincial Congressman Alexander McDougall to John Jay, delegate to the Continental Congress:

> The majority of the County are not against the Public measures, yet a majority of those who are active are against them; and therefore if Delegates should be sent by these, if the measures are to have this for their end, they would only be spies on our Conduct. . . . I know of no steps that have not many objections. If you suffer them to continue in their present state, Kings will follow their example as Richmond has done.[19]

The recalcitrant spirit of Queens became a concern of the Continental Congress, which took up the question of how to deal with the county. On January 3, 1776, stern measures were decided upon. The report of that date in the *Journals of the Continental Congress* begins as follows:

> Whereas a majority of the inhabitants of Queen's County, in the colony of New York, being incapable of resolving to live and die freemen . . . have deserted the American cause, by refusing to send deputies. . . .

Attributing their conduct to a fainthearted wait-and-see-who-wins attitude, the report then announced what steps Congress was taking. All persons in Queens who had voted against sending delegates were to be "put out of the protection of the United Colonies, and that all trade and intercourse with them cease." Attorneys were prohibited from defending any of the county's dissenters in any action at law. The New York Convention (i.e., Provincial Congress) was instructed to publish the dissenters' names in the local newspapers for a month. And any inhabitant of Queens who traveled into another colony had to carry a certificate attesting his support of the American cause. Along with these measures, a military action was taken as well. Continental units were ordered into Queens to disarm the dissenters and round up the principals among the disaffected population. In a letter of February 7, Governor Tryon gave his account of the events that followed: "The latter end of last month twelve hundred men from New Jersey, under the command of Col. Hard went over to Long Island, and after ten days marauding disarmed upwards of six hundred inhabitants

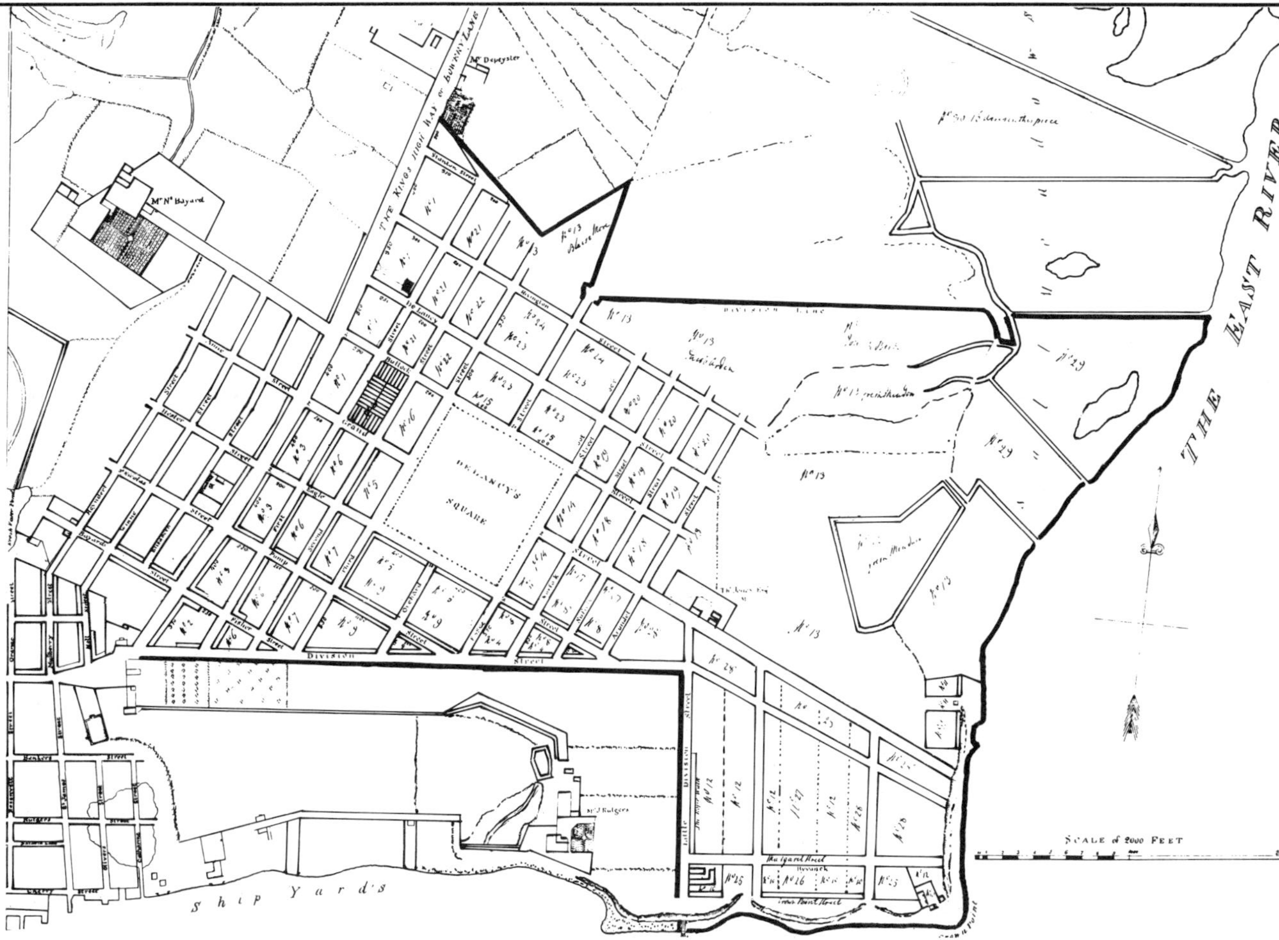

DELANCEY FARM BEFORE THE BRITISH EVACUATION.
Sources: Thomas James, *History of New York During the Revolutionary War*, Vol. 2, map opposite p. 558.

DELANCEY FARM AFTER THE BRITISH EVACUATION, drawn from file maps 492a, 492b. Office of the Register, New York Co.

Date of Sale.	Loyalist Owner.	Purchaser.	Price.	Description and Remarks.
Aug. 16, 1787	James De Lancey, attainted.	John Delafield, merchant.	£810	Lots No. 11 and 12 in Out Ward. W. by Bowery Lane, N. by lots No. 13 and 14, E. by lots No. 17 and 18, S. by lots No. 9 and 10.
" "	" " "	Cornelius C. Roosevelt, merchant.	1,120	Messuage and 2 lots in Out Ward. W. by Bowery Lane, N. by lots No. 97 and 126, E. by First St., S. by Eagle St.
" "	" " "	William Beekman, gentleman.	570	Lots No. 673 to 675 and 682 to 684 in Out Ward. W. by Third St., N. by lots No. 676 and 681, E. by Fourth St., S. by lots No. 672 and 685.
" "	" " "	Edward Dunscomb, Esq.	400	E. half of lots No. 714 to 721 in Out Ward. S. by Pump St., E. by Fourth St., N. by lot No. 713, W. by half lots No. 714 to 721.
" "	" " "	Daniel Williams, of Westchester co., farmer.	190	Lot No. 878 in Out Ward. W. by Fourth St., N. by lots No. 879, E. by lot No. 885, S. by lots No. 874 to 877.
" "	" " "	John Delafield.	560	Lots No. 1578 and 1579 in Out Ward. S. by Division St., W. by Norfolk St., N. by Eagle St., E. by John Egberts.
" "	" " "	James Beekman.	2,760	Lots No. 132 to 135 in Out Ward. W. by Bowery Lane, N. by lot No. 136, E. by lots No. 144 to 147, S. by lot No. 131. Lots No. 140 to 157 in Out Ward. E. by First St., S. by Grand St., W. by lots No. 128 to 139, N. by Bullock St.
" "	" " "	Jacob Reed.	2,000	Lots No. 128 to 131 in Out Ward. S. by Grand St., W. by Bowery Lane, N. by lot No. 132, E. by lots No. 136 to 139. Lots No. 136 to 139 in Out Ward. W. by Bowery Lane, N. by Bullock St., E. by lots from 140 to 143.
" "	" " "	Ebenezer Young.	1,800	Lots No. 212 to 215 in Out Ward. S. by Rivington St., W. by Bowery Lane, N. by lot No. 216, E. by lots No. 240 to 243.
" "	" " "	James Saidler.	480	Lots No. 236 to 239 in Out Ward. E. by First St., S. by lot No. 240, W. by lots No. 216 to 219, N. by lot No. 235.

Portion of sales records taken from Alexander Flick, *Loyalism in New York During the American Revolution*, p. 246. Sales of Delancey's property spanned the years 1784–1787.

of Queen's County, and took seventeen of the principal gentlemen prisoners, who have since been marched under guard to Philadelphia.''[20]

To what extent the opposition in Queens was spreading to its neighbor to the east, Suffolk County, is difficult to judge. One assessment at this time, made by General Washington, suggests that the loyalty of Long Island as a whole had come under a cloud of suspicion. On January 8, 1776, the general sent an urgent message to the New York Committee of Safety, copies of which were also dispatched to General Lee and Governor Trumbull of Connecticut, who supported the American cause. Informing the committee of a British war fleet on sail from Boston for an unknown destination south, Washington remarks:

> Having such information as I can rely on, that the inhabitants of Long Island in your Government, (or a greater part of them,) are not only inimical to the rights and liberties of America, but by their conduct and public professions have discovered an apparent inclination to lend a helping hand to subjugate their fellow citizens to ministerial [i.e., British] tyranny, there is a great reason to believe that this armament, if not designed immediately against the city of New York, is nevertheless intended for Long Island.[21]

On May 25, 1776, the Provincial Congress issued new instructions to the local committees on how to proceed against suspected persons. Crown officers who refused to associate and persons of ''equivocal neutrality'' were to be summoned and interrogated before the committees. The committees would have the responsibility of deciding whom to release and whom to confine or parole. Persons of influence were to be removed from their communities where there was reason to believe this precaution was necessary.[22]

David Mathews, whom Governor Tryon appointed mayor of New York on February 14, 1776, was on June 20 dragged from his bed at 1:00 A.M., as he states, by a party of fifty armed men and carried before the Provincial Congress. After questioning, he was committed to the provost jail ''amongst Criminals of all descriptions and under the influence of a desperate Mob who daily threatened to Murder him.'' The congress had apparently gotten wind of a plot by Mathews and two accomplices to abduct General Washington and deliver him on board Governor Tryon's ship.

Under the heading ''July 4, 1776,'' an entry in the diary of William Smith, the last crown-appointed chief justice of New York, gives this brief mention of William Wickham:

> A soldier of the General's Life Guard was hanged in Town, as an Accomplice on the 28 June Mr. Wickham Saml Gale the Assemblyman and others were taken as suspected Persons at Goshen an[d] on the 3 July 100 Men were imployed in scouring the Woods back of my Residence to disarm 70 Privates. . . .[23]

Parker Wickham was forty-nine years old in 1776. In a census prepared by the Provincial Congress, Parker's is the first family listed for Southold. It was a considerably large family. There were his three sons, Joseph, John Parker, and Tommy; his daughters, Parnel, Sarah, and Hellen; his wife, Mary; and his mother, Abigail, now seventy-three. Probably his sister Jerusha was living with them too. There were also his servants and black field hands, seven in all, including James, York, and Osbons Catury. Besides the census data, only two other bits of information can be said about Parker for the year 1776—one recorded, the other presumed. On August 7 of that year, an instruction was given to Wickham by Colonel Josiah Smith, a Brookhaven militiaman serving the patriotic cause. The instruction, found in the colonel's diary in an entry for that date, reads: "I Sot oute Eastward to South hold and gave Capt Reves orders & Ingaged Major Wickham to Secure the Stock on Robings Island from the Enemy."[24] The other item concerning the magistrate, this we presume about, happened a little earlier in the year, on the morning of July 12, 1776, when Parker picked up the *Connecticut Gazette; and the Universal Intelligencer,* a New London weekly that served the North Fork area. Scanning the second page of the newspaper, he fixed his attention on an article that began—

ſent a File of Soldiers to releaſe the Veſſel, confined the Lieutenant of the Seaford ſeveral Hours, and ordered the Forts to be immediately repaired.

In CONGRESS, July 4, 1776.

A DECLARATION

By the REPRESENTATIVES of the

UNITED STATES OF AMERICA,

In GENERAL CONGRESS aſſembled.

WHEN in the courſe of human events, it becomes neceſſary for one people to diſſolve the political bands which have connected them with another, and to aſſume among the powers of earth, the ſeparate and equal ſtation to which the laws of nature and of nature's God intitle them, a decent reſpect to the opinions of mankind requires that they ſhould declare the cauſes which impel them to a ſeparation.

We hold theſe truths to be ſelf-evident, that all men are created equal, that they are endowed by their Creator with certain unalienable rights, that among theſe are life, liberty, and the purſuit of happineſs—That to ſecure theſe rights, governments are

Part II:
The Nature of State's Title

A State must be an organization of people for political ends; it must permanently occupy a fixed territory; it must possess an organized government capable of making and enforcing law within the community; and, finally, to be a sovereign State it must not be subject to any external control.

Freeman Snow, *International Law,* 2d ed., p. 5.

CHAPTER 6

The Rupture of New York

APPREHENSIVE AS HE MAY have been upon reading the article on page two, Wickham could scarcely have foreseen the importance of the Declaration of Independence as a milestone in American history. How many readers of that article did? Presumably not even the editors of the newspaper, having decided to place the Congressional announcement on page two.

The Declaration of Independence declared independence, but independence declared as of 1776 was far from being, at least in every colony, an accomplished fact. And of the Thirteen Colonies, in none was separation from the mother country more uncertain at this time, the Congressional announcement notwithstanding, than in the province of New York.

In the first six months of 1776, the colony of New York was thrown into political turmoil. No actual break with the mother country had taken place, yet the functioning of the old government had broken down. George D. Ludlow, judge of the Supreme Court of New York, states that the last court he held was in January 1776. "At that time the People were very violent, and it was expected to be broke up." The judge retired into Queens County about February, as he says, and "was obliged to conceal himself to elude the search of parties sent in quest of him."[1] Judicial functions, now out of the hands of the court, had shifted to the revolutionary committees. The closest thing to a central authority in New York at this time was the governing body known as the Provincial Congress. It happened that on July 4 of that year this congress was not in session. Not until July 9 did it reconvene and, after deliberating, formally approve the Declaration of Independence of the Continental Congress. Thereupon New York's Provincial delegates referred to themselves no longer as representatives of a province, but of a state. It is important, however, not to think of this "state" in modern terms. In the first place, the actual physical contours of the state's jurisdiction were about to undergo constriction and change. And secondly, the powers of the now independent government were limited. Its enactments and decisions were not laws but "resolutions," as they were called, having uncertain legal and enforceable status. For example, a resolution of July 16, 1776, declared that "all persons abiding within the state of New York, and deriving protection from the laws of the same, owe allegiance to the said laws, and are members of the state." Being members, any who should side with Great Britain were "guilty of treason against the State," and upon conviction would suffer death. Forty-six years later, the Supreme Court of New York, in considering this resolution, opined as follows:

> Although the delegates of this state adopted that declaration [of independence] on the 9th of the same month, and although we had committees, and temporary bodies of men, who took charge of the public safety, we had no executive, legislative or judicial authority, nor any organized government, until the 20th of April, 1777. It would be a very grave question, which I shall avoid discussing whether, until the adoption of our constitution, treason could be committed against that imperfect and inchoate government. . . .[2]

A New Yorker himself, Alexander Hamilton estimated in 1782 that "near half" the people in the province of New York at the beginning of the Revolution were more attached to the king than to the American cause.[3] As this estimate came from the American side, a British account of Staten Island's submission to the British forces, occurring seven days before the Provincial Congress approved the independence of the state, takes on credence. On July 2 Governor Tryon writes to the British secretary of state:

> General Howe disembarked the troops under his command on Staten Island the 2d instant without opposition, on which occasion the inhabitants of the Island came down to welcome the arrival of their deliverers, & have since afforded the army every supply & accomodation [*sic*] in their power.[4]

That the county of Richmond was not particularly enthusiastic about the cause of independence can be fathomed from its earlier conduct in the spring of 1775 when it had refused to subscribe to the association in support of the Continental Congress.

When the Provincial Congress convened on July 9, 1776, it did not meet at its customary location, the Exchange or similar meeting hall in the city of New York. Fearing that an attack would soon be made upon the city, this congress had decided on June 30 to evacuate its headquarters. Now in session at the Court House at White Plains, from where a second evacuation would shortly be made, it was here the revolutionary body cast its approving vote for independence and statehood. The decision was momentous, as had been the Declaration of Independence seven days earlier. And yet, it was one thing to decide upon that issue; it was quite another to implement it.

The decision for statehood hardly meant that the province of New York now no longer existed or that the people within its borders had universally transformed their national identities. The actual configuration of the state's jurisdictional domain within the province vis-a-vis the British was very much in flux on July 9, 1776. True, the position of the old government hung in a precarious balance. Governor Tryon was at present living on ship in New York harbor. His appointed mayor, David Mathews, had been seized June 20 on orders of the Provincial Congress. The legislative assembly had dissolved the year previous, its delegates refusing to the end to recognize the Continental Congress. On the other hand, the position of the revolutionary government in New York subsequent to its vote on independence wasn't that firm either. British troops had landed on Staten Island. The Provincial body had withdrawn from the strategic capital, New York City. On August 10, a report was received by the delegates at White Plains that the inhabitants of Kings County had determined not to oppose the "enemy." Then came the crisis in Queens County. Like Richmond, Queens had refused in 1775 to subscribe to the patriotic associations. It had balked as well at sending delegates to the Provincial Congress. Now on the twenty-seventh of August 1776, there couldn't have been total surprise in congress when news arrived that the main contingent of the British army had chosen to land in Queens. Here, in what became memorialized as the Battle of Long Island, the American army under Washington engaged the enemy under General William Howe.

At this time the president of the Provincial Congress, General Nathaniel Woodhull, was stationed in Jamaica, Long Island. A native of Brookhaven, Woodhull was commander of Long Island's militia forces. On that fateful day, August 27, he was awaiting orders from the revolutionary body he presided over. He sends this message:

> The people are all moving east, and I cannot get any assistance from them. . . . Unless you can send me some other assistance, I fear I shall soon be obliged to quit this place.

A day passes. On August 28 he writes:

> I must again let you know my situation. I have about seventy men, and about twenty of the Troop, which is all the force I have or can expect, and I am daily growing less in number. The people are so alarmed in Suffolk, that they will not, any more of them, march; and as to Colonels Smith's and Remsen's Regiments, they cannot join me, for the communication is cut off between us. . . . If you cannot send me an immediate reinforcement, I am afraid I shall have no men with me by to-morrow night, for they consider themselves in an enemy's territory. . . . I beg you would immediately send at least two members, as a Committee, that I may have their advice, for unless you do, I must quit, for I hope the Convention does not expect me to make brick without straw.[5]

BATTLE OF WHITE PLAINS. Archibald Robertson Portfolio. *Manuscripts and Archives Division, New York Public Library; Astor, Lenox and Tilden Foundations*. Photograph by Harvey Weber.

Then on August 30 came the terse missive from General Washington:

> Circumstanced as this army was in respect to situation, strength, etc. it was the unanimous advice of a counsel of General officers to give up Long Island.[6]

Alarmed by this defeat, the Provincial Congress packed up and removed farther north. On September 5 it met at the Episcopal Church in Fishkill. However, that church "being very foul with the dung of doves and fowls, without any benches, seats or other conveniences whatever, which renders it unfit for the use of this Convention," the delegates reassembled at the Dutch church in the same village. From the south the news that reached them continued grim. By week's end, the capital, New York City, had fallen. This was followed a month later by Washington's defeat at Chatterton Hill, near White Plains, and the storming of Fort Washington. Pummeled by these setbacks, Washington's army now retreated to New Jersey and the theater of combat moved to that state, where before long the commander in chief would come up with significant victories. But in New York, insofar as the southern region was concerned, the situation as he left it would remain essentially unchanged for the next seven years.

As the British recouped in Queens and southern New York, how Suffolk County was aligning itself can be ascertained from official accounts on the American side.

I. *The Conqueror's First Law in Suffolk County and How It Was Received*

On August 29, 1776, Sir William Erskine, the British general, issued a proclamation to the people of Suffolk from his headquarters in Queens.

> His Excellency General Howe having appointed me commanding officer for the eastern part of this Island, I do hereby strictly order and enjoin all persons whatsoever in your County of Suffolk, upon their peril, to use their utmost efforts to preserve the peace of said County; that all Committeemen, and others acting under the authority of the Rebels, immediately to cease and remain at their respective homes; that every man in arms lay them down forthwith, and surrender themselves, on pain of being treated as Rebels.

The announcement turns to other matters: that cattle, wagons, and horses are needed for His Majesty's forces, the suppliers of which will be duly paid; that the army, he informs, has been sent to protect, not to oppress;

and that the inhabitants on their part are expected to show a dutiful submission. Days later, a deposition to New York State's Committee of Safety told of enemy strength on Long Island at over 30,000 men and 10,000 lately arrived on Staten Island. Another told of Suffolk County having given up, that General Howe had ordered 200 wagons to be supplied by the county, and that "near 300" had passed his, the deponent's, house.

On August 31, an urgent letter from the Suffolk County Committee to Governor Trumbull of Connecticut, who, unlike Governor Tryon of New York, had taken the American side. Justice Robert Hempstead, chairman of the Suffolk Committee, writes that enemy troops have "surrounded our lines at the west end, and stopped our communications to the Army and Provincial Congress." Hempstead estimates the British regulars at 15,000–20,000 men. "We must beg the favour of you to aid and assist us with men and ammunition."[7] But this flickering voice of resistance is short-lived. The north-south channels of communication remain open, but that does not prevent Suffolk County from slipping—like Queens, its neighboring county in the southern district—into the fold of British power. Now, in the space of a few days, communications of a different kind begin reaching the Connecticut governor, reports of "some surprising conduct" from the people of Long Island's East End. To the Connecticut Council of War, on September 7, the American Colonel Livingston conveys intelligence that the inhabitants of East Hampton have driven all their livestock from Montauk westward, "in order to furnish the Ministerial troops." And that same day East Hampton's town clerk writes to the governor:

> Sir: In consequence of a report prevailing in town that the people of Connecticut are coming to take away our live stock and effects, the Trustees who transact the business of the town have met early this morning and unanimously agreed to send an express humbly requesting your Honour's prohibition of such measures, as apprehensive if prosecuted we shall be involved in perplexities and sufferings far beyond those we are now the subjects of, in that it may be construed we are somehow accessory thereto, which we are not, being subjects of his Majesty King George, and therefore mean not to act a part exposing of us to his displeasure. We have therefore thought proper to request your Honour's interposition as we judge in our favour.
>
> We are your Honour's humble petitioners. Signed per order of the Trustees:
>
> Abraham Gardiner, Clerk[8]

The "surprising" conduct was not limited by any means to East Hampton. Communiques and reports indicate a growing, county-wide adherence to British authority, even before British troops made any significant movement into the county.

Twenty-six-year-old Henry B. Livingston, appointed by Washington to command the East End of Long Island, writes to Governor Trumbull on September 8, 1776:

> Since I wrote to your Honour, the people of East and Southampton have almost universally taken an oath of allegiance to George III, King of Great Britain. It was tendered to them by Colonel Gardiner. They are now driving their cattle into the woods in order to hide them from us. They had brought them from Montauk-Point to Easthampton, in order to drive them westward to the enemy, in compliance with a proclamation issued by General Erskine.[9]

He adds: "If speedy measures are not used, the whole County of Suffolk will shortly be in arms against us."

While Gardiner was on the South Fork administering the king's oath, Colonel Phineas Fanning was on the North Fork doing the same, having shifted loyalties after the British victory on Long Island.[10] Ironically, it was Fanning who had tendered the patriotic association pledge a year earlier to the very townsmen who were now being sworn to the king's oath.

General Washington had known for some time from intelligence reports that the sympathies of the Long Island population lay generally with the British. On September 9, 1776, he corresponds with Trumbull:

> I have the honour of your favour of the 5th instant, and am sorry to say that, from the best information we have been able to obtain, the people on Long-Island have, since our evacuation, gone generally over to the enemy, and made such concessions as have been required—some through compulsion I suppose, but more from inclination. As a diversion upon Long Island has been impracticable under these circumstances, I think you have done well in assisting the removal of the persons and effects of our friends from thence.[11]

And on September 11, Livingston reports to Washington:

> The Militia of Southold, about one hundred and fifty in number, deserted me at the River-Head, on my way to Huntington, having heard that Long-Island was given up to the enemy. I received, at the same time, letters from the town of Huntington, praying me, for God's sake, not to advance any farther, as they had already submitted to the enemy, and much feared that terms would not be granted them should I proceed any farther.[12]

New York State's Provincial Congressman John Sloss Hobart was a native of Suffolk County. His home was at Eatons Neck, near Huntington, where he lived until the occupation. Writing now to the Provincial Congress on October 7, 1776, from Fairfield, Connecticut, he explains the sentiments of his former constituency, why the people of Suffolk reacted the way they did.

> Upon the retreat of the army from the island they viewed themselves as abandoned by the Continent, and expecting the enemy hourly among them, a general removal appeared impracticable; besides, to quit their pleasant habitations and throw themselves with their tender connexions upon the charity of an unknown world, was a degree of apathy to which they had not yet arrived. In a fit of despair they laid down their arms and made an unconditional submission to what they supposed the conquering army.[13]

Not all of Suffolk's inhabitants remained on Long Island when the British recaptured the territory. A considerable number of refugees from the island, like Hobart, settled in Connecticut. Yet, as he himself pointed out, a "general removal" had not taken place. On the contrary, reports told of people *en masse* turning themselves over to the British, and not only in Suffolk but elsewhere in the southern district. People were laying down their arms, taking oaths of allegiance to the king, bringing their fat cattle to the enemy. Seen from the American side, their behavior could not even be classified as "equivocal neutrality." America was at war. Americans were fighting for independence. Yet here in the southern district were other Americans demonstrating their allegiance to His Majesty, the sovereign they were at war with. Undoubtedly there were cases of coercion and intimidation, but by Washington's own estimate the Long Islanders were acting more from inclination than compulsion. What could explain this? Why were they conducting themselves this way? Had counties full of people become traitors? Or was there, some congressmen might have pondered, was there perhaps another explanation? These people in the southern district, perhaps they were, as the British thought of them, subjects of His Majesty, King George III, to whom they indeed owed what they believed was their rightful allegiance. Borrowing the words of Hamilton:

> The surrender . . . carries in itself a decisive implication that the inhabitants of the country surrendered are the subjects of the power to which the surrender is made.[14]

As for the inhabitants voluntarily remaining on the island after the British had taken over, the state's Council of Revision itself defended the action in its objection to a later bill of the state legislature:

> Because, by the first enacting clause, the voluntarily remaining with the fleets and armies of the King of Great Britain is made an offense highly penal, whereas, by the known laws of all nations, persons who remain with their possessions when the country is overrun by a conquering army, are at least excused, if not justified.[15]

From New York on November 28, Governor Tryon writes to Lord George Germain in England:

THE DIVISION OF NEW YORK.

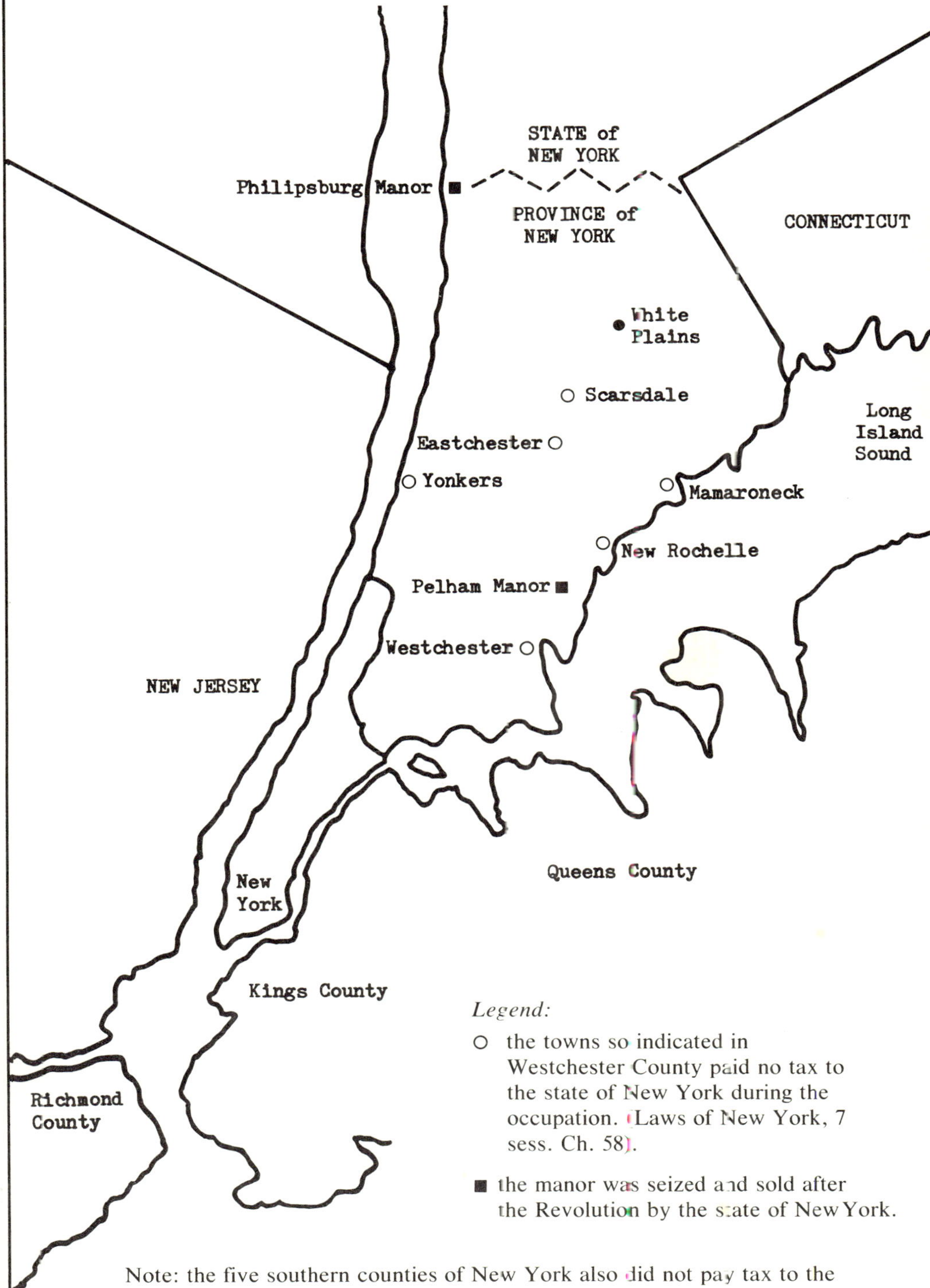

Legend:

○ the towns so indicated in Westchester County paid no tax to the state of New York during the occupation. (Laws of New York, 7 sess. Ch. 58).

■ the manor was seized and sold after the Revolution by the state of New York.

Note: the five southern counties of New York also did not pay tax to the state during the occupation. (See state law above).

My Lord,

It is with the most singular Satisfaction I have the honor herewith to transmit to Your Lordship Copies of the Addresses of the City and County of New York, and also of King's and Queen's County to the King's Commissioners, testifying their wishes to return under the King's peace and Government.

The Dissolution of the Committee of Suffolk County and the Committees of the several Townships in the same, with the Revocation of all their proceedings and orders under the Congress was effected at my particular recommendation to them for that purpose; Copies of all which are herewith transmitted.

Suffolk County's Committee announced its dissolution on October 24, and the declaration is signed by one person, Chairman John Brush. Brookhaven Committee's declaration is dated October 23, signed by seventeen. Islip's, undated, is signed by six. Huntington's was drawn up October 21, signed by fourteen; Smithtown's, October 19, signed by nine; East Hampton's, October 21, signed by four; Southampton's of the same date, also signed by four; and Southold's, October 25, signed by three, Barnabas Terrel, James Young, and Daniel Wells. The declarations of the committees were collected by Major Richard Floyd and Thomas Fanning, a newspaper informs us, and delivered to Governor Tryon. They were subsequently published in Gaine's *New York Gazette and Weekly Mercury* on November 11, 1776.[16]

By the spring Ambrose Serle, secretary of the British commander Lord Howe, could write to England:

Long Island (from the Tour of which I am just returned) is the only peaceful and happy Spot at present in this part of America. The Inhabitants are exceedingly benefited by supplying the Army, and are, excepting a few Presbyterians to the Eastward, eminent for their Loyalty, on which Account they suffered much while under the Terror of the Rebels.[17]

II. *The Jurisdictional Schism*

With the British conquest of Long Island and the southern New York counties, the jurisdiction of the state of New York was now reduced and constricted. Just how constricted is bluntly relayed on January 1, 1777, in a dispatch to Washington from the state's Committee of Safety, a military arm of the Provincial Congress.

On this occasion we beg leave to lay before your Excellency the true situation of this State. It formerly consisted of fourteen counties, of which five and a part of the sixth are in possession of the enemy, and a considerable part of the inhabitants of the counties of Gloucester, Cumberland and Charlotte appear determined to shake off their dependance upon us, so that above one half is lost; of the remainder, a considerable proportion is disaffected, and ready upon a favorable opportunity to join the enemy.[18]

The territory of what had been New York Province in pre-Revolutionary times was now in the throes of dismemberment. In the northeast, the counties of Gloucester, Cumberland, and Charlotte—claimed as sovereign territory by New York—banded together and revolted. Led by Ethan Allen and the Green Mountain Boys, the inhabitants of this region adopted their own constitution in the summer of 1777, which signified a declaration of independence from the state of New York. Out of that political rupture, Vermont was born. The other disjuncture took place in the south, involving five counties and a part of a sixth. New York, Richmond, Brooklyn, Queens, Suffolk, and a part of Westchester—comprising over a third of the counties of the old province of New York—had split off from the independent state and retained their alignment within the orbit of British rule.

In the southern region of New York, a provincial government functioned, performing military and civilian duties, dispensing justice as best it could, regulating commerce, etc., just as there was a state government to the north performing similar duties. With restoration of British law and order in the region, Tryon reestablished headquarters in New York City and continued as governor of the "province" of New York. However, his power was now curtailed by both geography and the decisions of the military commander. Escaping his imprisonment behind American lines, Mayor Mathews returned to the British capital in December 1776, and thereupon resumed his duties of office. Like Mathews, numerous other officials who lived in the southern district continued to perform their duties: the superintendents of police, the magistrates, town officials, and to a limited extent the New York Council, all acting under the authority of the British crown.

Among the old papers at the Manor of St. George, Suffolk County, is an October 15, 1776, loyalist handbill, on the back of which is found this scribbled message apparently intended for the American side:

Parker Wickham of Southold, Frederick Hudson of Wading River & Thos. Sanford of Sag are appointed Judges of the Interior [Inferior] Court of Suffolk County. Justices in Southold, Matthus Wills [Matthew Wells?]. John Gardner. Benj. Wills, Simon Moore. Joseph Mapes Jr. imployed by Muncy to buy up wheat & other provisions to carry to New York. James Muirson is Sheriff & very active. his family in Southold himself at Road Island. . . . Hudson is the most odious & has much distressed the Inhabitants by coming with parties of Tories carrying people to N. York in imprisoning, stealing Horses.[19]

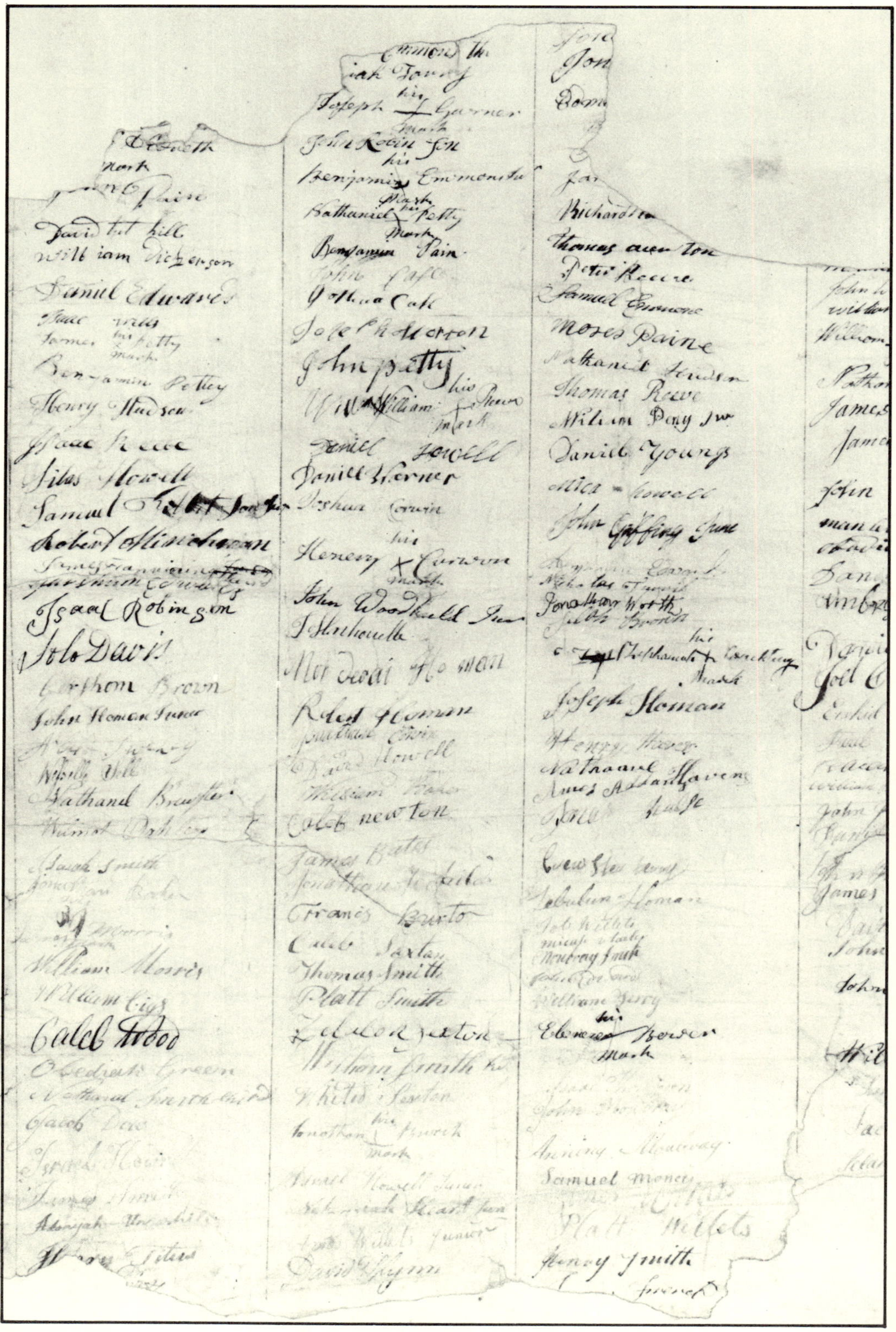
Paine
David tut hill
william Dickerson
Daniel Edwards
Isaac wells
James his petty mark
Benjamin Petty
Henry Hudson
Isaac Reeve
Silas Howell
Samuel [illegible]
Robert [illegible]
Isaac Robinson
Job Davis
Bethom Brown
John Homan Junr
Nathanel Brewster
Isaac Smith
Jonathan Baker
Morris
William Morris
Caleb Wood
Obediah Green
Nathanael Smith third
Jacob Dew
James Howell
Adonijah Underhill

Emmons
iah Terry
Joseph his mark Garner
John Robin son
Benjamin his Emmons mark
Nathaniel his Petty mark
Benjamin Pain
John petty
William his Reeve mark
Daniell Howell
Daniell Horner
Joshua Corwin
Henery his X Corwin mark
John Woodhull Jun
Mordecai Homan
Robert Homan
Jonathan Corwin
David Howell
William Baker
Caleb newton
Francis Burto
Caleb Saxton
Thomas Smith
Platt Smith
William Smith
Whitid Saxton
Jonathan his mark Smith
Daniel Howell Junr
Nehemiah Heart Jun
Willets Junior
David Glynn

Richardson
Thomas acen ton
Peter Reeve
Samuel Emmons
Moses Paine
Nathaniel Hudson
Thomas Reeve
William Terry Jun
Daniell Youngs
Mica howell
John Gaffing Junr
Jonathan Worth
his Stephen X Coaking mark
Joseph Homan
Henry Reeve
Joel Hulse
Zebulon Homan
Job Willets
Newbury Smith
William Terry
Ebenezer his Bower mark
Samuel Money
Platt Willets
Henry Smith

John
william
William
Nathan
James
James
John
Joel
John
James
John
John

THE DECLARATION OF DEPENDENCE:
the signatures on the appended fragments.
New-York Historical Society.

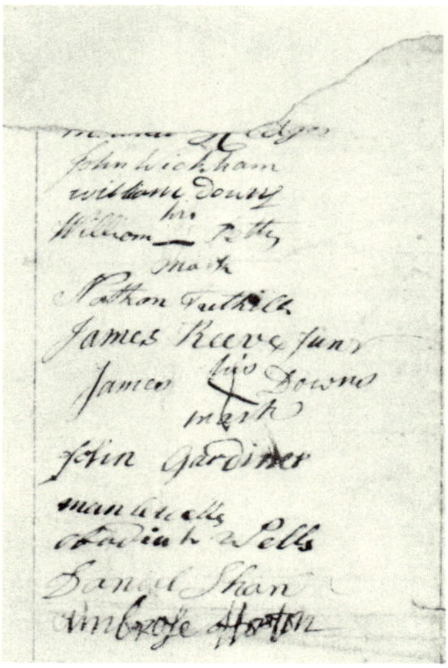

John Wickham
William Downs
William his mark Petty
Nathan Tuthill
James Reeve Junr
James his mark Downs
John Gardiner
Ambrose Horton

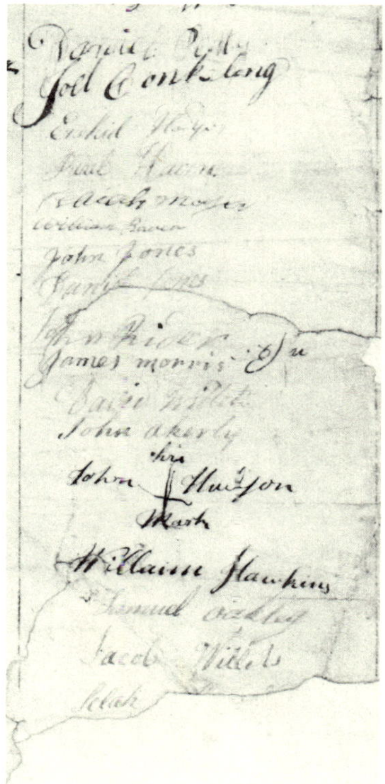

Joel Conkling
John Jones
James Morris
John Akerly
John his mark Hudson
William Hawkins
Samuel Oakley
Jacob Willets

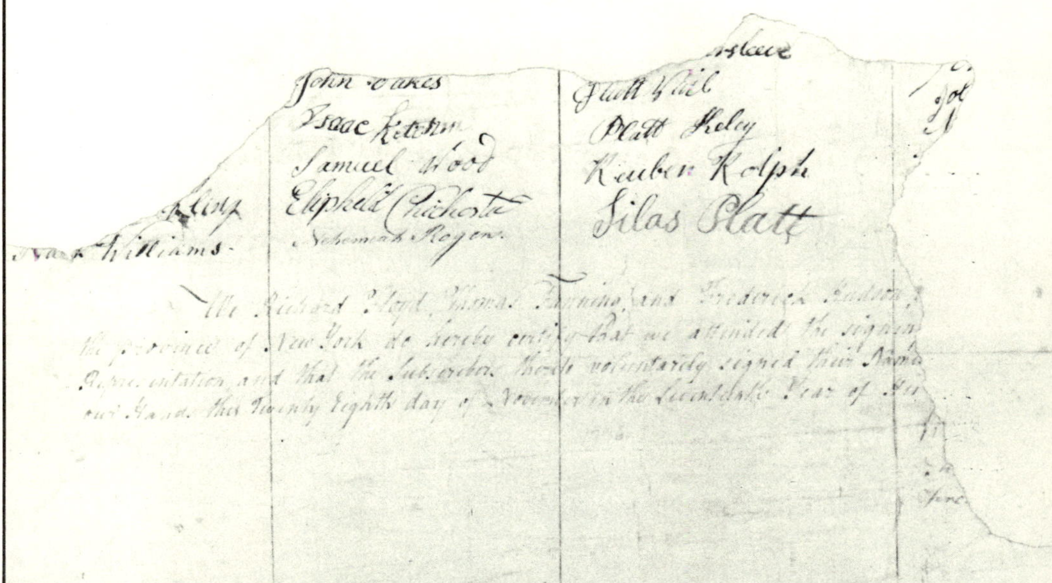

Williams
John Oakes
Isaac Ketcham
Samuel Wood
Eliphalet Chichester
Nehemiah Rogers
Platt Vail
Reuben Rolph
Silas Platt

We Richard Floyd, Thomas Fanning, and Frederick Hudson ... the province of New York do hereby certify that we attended the sign... Representation and that the Subscribers thereto voluntarily signed their Names ... our Hands this Twenty Eighth day of November in the Seventeenth Year of ...

Despite the suggestion in this anonymous message of mistreatment by the appointed justices, the men referred to had strong roots in their communities. Wickham was the elected supervisor of Southold and had held local office for many years—long before the Revolution. Whatever the opposition against him, there must also have been a base of support among his constituency. In addition, evidence suggests that the British authorities themselves enjoyed a degree of support not only in Suffolk County but in the occupied region as a whole. Contingents of loyalist American militia were successfully recruited, particularly in Queens. Suffolk had its loyalist militia. About New York County, Mayor Mathews testifies that he was able to form seven companies, amounting to "near 500 Men of the most wealthy & zealous Inhabitants in a few days."[20] As in the pre-occupation period, allegiance petitions were circulated, these supporting the occupation government. They contained declarations of allegiance to "our Rightful Sovereign George the Third" and were subscribed to by large numbers, especially in counties that had formerly been lax in associating. One petition to the British commander William Howe and his brother Admiral Richard Howe asserts that they, the subscribers, have maintained "inviolate our loyalty to our Sovereign" and "have ever with unshaken fidelity, borne true allegiance to His Majesty." The document speaks of the petitioners as inhabitants of the city and county of New York, but it is signed both by subscribers from the city (over 700) and, on two separate fragments, by signers from Suffolk (157). What the original number of Suffolk signers to this address was is not known. In any case, the fragments are dated November 28, 1776, and the original documents consisting of this address, the city subscriber list, and the fragments have survived.[21] The Suffolk subscribers are shown on pages 76–77.

The situation in the territory of New York was a demonstration of just how much the Declaration of July 4, 1776, had fallen short of securing and establishing independence throughout the Thirteen Colonies. It would take a Revolutionary War and the concluding of several treaties and agreements before this situation would change. In the meantime, there were still shifting loyalties, and much of the territory and population of New York remained out of the possession of the United States. From 1776 to November 25, 1783—the date of the British evacuation—there was in fact not one New York but two. The state to the north and the province to the south were each independent of the other, each sealed off from the other by military lines across Westchester County. Except for minor shifts in those lines from time to time, the American and British jurisdictions were as distinct and defined as New York's and Vermont's are today.

It was during this period of New York's history that the newly organized legislature of the state of New York enacted, on October 22, 1779, "An Act, for the forfeiture and sale of the estates of persons who have adhered to the enemies of this State, and for declaring the sovereignty of the people of this State in respect to all property within the same." Known as a bill of attainder, the act—in a stroke—accused and convicted fifty-nine alleged offenders, sentenced them to banishment, and declared their property forfeited. Declaring something to be so is one thing, however. The fact of its being so can be quite another. Failure to keep that distinction in mind reduces history to myth and fact to dictate. The Act of Attainder declared the state's sovereignty within its borders. It declared the estates of offenders forfeited. What it could not do, by the simple declaring, was change the configuration of those borders. It could not pretend the British were not there, in possession of five counties and a part of a sixth.

Estates declared forfeited under the Act were in some instances situated in the southern counties, then under British rule and law. One estate in particular, belonging to Parker Wickham, was located in Suffolk County, Long Island, a territory neither in the possession of the state nor of the United States at this time. Under such circumstances, how could the forfeiture of Wickham's estate take effect?

CHAPTER 7

A Skirmish

It was intended as a three-pronged American offensive. General Samuel Parsons's three divisions were to cross the Sound, heading to different locations on the north shore of Long Island. One division, under the command of Colonel Meigs, was to have left from Sawpits (Port Chester) and attack an enemy regiment encamped near Jamaica. But Meigs's unit never got off the mainland because of heavy seas. The middle division under Colonel Webb was to land near Huntington, support Meigs to the west or the eastern division as necessary, and destroy whatever had been collected in that part of Suffolk for use of the enemy. Colonel Webb's division sailed from Norwalk on the evening of December 9, 1777. The next morning, however, the colonel's armed sloop fell in with a British sloop of war, the *Falcon,* and was forced aground near Setauket. Webb and several of his officers, twenty privates, and forty militiamen were taken prisoner. That ended the prospects of the middle contingent. The eastern division, under the command of General Parsons, saw a different conclusion. Here there were some successes, yet it is unclear exactly how much of what happened in this excursion met with the military objectives that Parsons had in mind.

Sailing out of Norwalk also on the evening of the ninth, Parsons made a first stop on the Connecticut coast, at the town of Guilford, picking up Captains David Landon, Peter Griffing, and others in their group—the Guilford volunteers as they were called. Griffing had been given a commission by Connecticut's Governor Trumbull on September 2 to seize and make prize of all vessels and property on the high seas or below high water mark belonging to the subjects of the king of Great Britain. Captain Landon was the brother of Jared Landon, a surrogate of Southold. Their father, the judge whom Parker Wickham had once confronted in court, was now living in exile in Connecticut. Parsons and the Guilford volunteers agreed to terms. The latter knew the Long Island terrain intimately and would receive specified wages for their assistance. They would be under the same command as Parsons's own troops.[1]

On Wednesday, the tenth, the expedition landed at a place called Hockaback (Aquebogue?), about forty miles, as Parsons states in a deposition, from the east end of Long Island. Once landed, they went about their objective, which was to destroy the timber and boards then being loaded, or so they thought, on a fleet of transports in Southold Bay, material that would go into the construction of barracks in New York. A body of troops under Captain Hart, including Captains Landon and Griffing, was deployed east to the region of that bay. Arriving there, the men discovered that most of the fleet had left. However, one loaded sloop was captured, and a quantity of stored wood awaiting another fleet was destroyed. Adding some success to their mission, they came across Captain James Asycough, the commander of the *H.M.S. Swan*, a sloop of war in Southold Bay. At the time, Asycough and some of his crew were at a house in Southold and were ill-prepared for the raiding party. Hastening to their ship, the Britons, closely pursued, had scarcely enough time to board and weigh anchor, and were not out very far before receiving a fusillade of shots from Hart's company. The *Swan*'s log reports:

> Light Breezes & thick hazey W: the Rebbels Came Down and fird on our Boats Wounded Capt. Ayscough & the Surgeon and Ken McKenzie Wm Searl Geo Davis Seaman & Jos Pickford Marine and took Prisoners. . . .[2]

The subject of prisoners does not come up in a letter on the twenty-ninth, where Parsons discusses the results of his mission and what happened to the other divisions. However, in his deposition to the Continental Congress on January 5, he speaks of Captains Griffing and Hart returning to him on the sixteenth "with their Prisoners." Where exactly on the north shore Parsons had been at the time of the skirmish is unclear, presumably at the same place where he had landed—forty miles from the east end of Long Island. It could also be presumed that the prisoners spoken of were the sailors captured from Ayscough's crew, except for one thing: that other letter Parsons wrote to Governor Clinton on December 28, giving the names of several persons brought off from Long Island, among them Major Wickham, Major Hudson, Orange Webb, and Matthew Wells of Southold township. So there were not only British seamen taken prisoner on this expedition but local inhabitants as well, one of them the supervisor of the town of Southold.[3] The question is why were these townspeople—civilians all but one—taken prisoner? Parsons writes: "The well-affected inhabitants of Suffolk County are anxious to have Wickham, Hudson and Ireland kept upon the main; they much fear their

GENEALOGY OF THE GUILFORD VOLUNTEERS

Captains Peter Griffing and David Landon

Jasper Griffing

- John Griffing
  - John Griffing Jr. a refugee; died in exile at Lyme or Middletown.
    - John Griffing b. 1737; proprietor of the Griffing farm on west bounds of Wickham's "River Head"; remained on the island during the occupation.
- Robert Griffing
  - Samuel Griffing neighbor to Ezra L'Hommedieu in Southold; both he and State Assemblyman L'Hommedieu were Guilford refugees. = Elizabeth Landon m. 1732
    - **Capt. Peter Griffing** b. 1742; a Guilford refugee; died in prison ship *Jersey*, 1781 or '82.

Nathan Landon

- Elizabeth Landon m. 1732
- Judge Samuel Landon 1699-1782
  - **Capt. David Landon** b. 1743; a Guilford refugee.
  - Jared Landon 1740-1816; surrogate; purchased Wickham's Neck farm in 1784.

Sources:

1) Clara J. Stone, comp., *Genealogy of the Descendants of Jasper Griffing* (n.p., 1881), pp. 6, 10;
2) James O. Landon, comp., *Landon Genealogy* ("Part 2 Boardman Genealogy;" New York: Clark Boardman Co., 1928), pp. 21, 26;
3) Frederic G. Mather, *The Refugees of 1776 from Long Island to Connecticut* ([Rep. Ed.] Baltimore: Genealogical Publishing Co., 1972), pp. 439-440, also Landon mentioned on p. 410.

return." That may have been true. But there may have been something more behind it.

A newspaper in New York, the loyalist *New York Gazette and Weekly Mercury,* reported the landing of a troop from Parsons's second division that had then marched on to Wading River to the east. In this account, a straggler in the rear was asked what they wanted on the island. His answer, as quoted by the newspaper, was "that they intended to oblige the People of Suffolk County to swear Allegiance to the Congress, and those that refused to take the Oath were to be plundered, and carried off Prisoners to Connecticut." Whether there were instances of plundering by Parsons's troops cannot be verified. Thomas Jones, the loyalist writer, claims that Hudson was plundered, and in his testimony Wickham's son claims that his father's homestead was plundered three or four times but does not give the dates when this happened. Certainly Parsons would not have condoned such practices if he had known they were going on. He was also aware of Washington's strong sentiments against the plundering of Long Island's inhabitants.[4] But Parsons was not, it appears, in Southold at the time Wickham and the other residents of the town were taken. What he did know, and this was the reason for his deposition of January 5, was that Landon and Griffing had exceeded their authority under his command by claiming a captured vessel, the *Peggy,* that was also claimed as prize by one of his own men, Captain Hart.

Parsons's expedition returned to Saybrook on Wednesday, the seventeenth. Three days later in Southold, Jared Landon was arrested and sent to the British capital, New York City, where he was put in the provost, or jail.

Meanwhile, Wickham at this time was under the supervision of the Commissary of Prisoners at Hartford and on parole, like the other inhabitants taken from Long Island. On the twenty-eighth of December, Parsons sent a note to Thomas Mumford of Groton, proposing Mr. Wickham as an intermediary in effecting the exchange of Mumford's son, who was a prisoner of the British. Parsons's plan of an exchange was not approved in New York, as he soon learned, and so the idea was dropped. Thereafter, several months pass, during which time nothing is heard of the Southold magistrate. It is not known if he wrote any letters or received any, or under what conditions he was living. It is certain only that his status had not changed. He was a civilian prisoner like the others from Long Island, none of whom acted under military commissions except Hudson. All the rest, as Parsons explained, fell within Governor Clinton's jurisdiction, "being subjects of your State." Though described as a subject of New York State, Wickham doesn't appear to have ever been transferred to that state or to have benefited from any of the civil protections—trial by jury, the right to counsel, and so forth—under that state's first constitution of 1777.[5]

On April 27, 1778, the deputy commissary of prisoners at Wethersfield records Wickham's name in a "Return of Prisoners belonging to New York State." But Wickham at this time seems no longer to have been in Connecticut. In an undated personal memorandum, the magistrate records that on April 18, 1778, as he recalls, he took up lodging at Captain Stephen Hewlett's in Hempstead, Long Island. Violating his parole in Connecticut, which he appears to have done, may have been one of the reasons for the extraordinary legislative sentence which awaited him. Perhaps at this time he had a premonition of that impending decree, for in the middle of May he wrote out two deeds. In one he conveyed to son Joseph in fee simple (i.e., with full rights of ownership) all his Neck of land in Southold where he "now" lives, also all his island known as Robins Island. The other deed conveyed to his three daughters, Parnel, Hellen, and Sarah, other property and personal effects. Neither document speaks of the River Head property, but that still belonged to his mother Abigail, who was alive in 1778. Whether these deeds of Wickham were ever availed of is not known. They were probably considered useless by the family, as a clause in the Act of Attainder purported to invalidate all deeds since 1776 which had been made by those condemned under the Act.

Also in May, the same month as the date of the deeds, Wickham sold his horse to Captain Hewlett for twenty pounds. On June 2, as he writes, "My Negro York came to me and worked for Mr. Hewlett untill 14th October. I was absent from his house from the 27th December untill the 27 April 1779. . . ." Thereafter, the magistrate returns to Hewlett's at intervals until March 2, 1782, according to the memorandum spoken of earlier.[6]

Judging from his notations, Wickham was not in Suffolk County in the autumn of 1778, when Governor Tryon (now a British major-general) was in the region on two occasions. This would explain the absence of Wickham's name from the list of inhabitants taking the king's oath at this time. Under the directions of Tryon, the oath was administered to the male inhabitants of every town in Suffolk, and their names, ages, and occupations were recorded by town. Containing 2,677 names, the list serves as a virtual census of Suffolk County for the occupation period. One story about this oath suggests that the magistrate may indeed have been around while it was being taken, contrary to the other indications. According to an early historian of Long Island, a Major Isaac Reeve was purportedly informed against by Major Parker Wickham. The story goes that Reeve, eluding the light horse, was later caught, pinioned at his house, and carried before Tryon at Mattituck two miles away. There, it is said, he was threat-

"A PLAN OF MERRITUCK IN THE TOWNSHIP OF SOUTHOLD ON LONG ISLAND SURVEYED BY MAJOR HOLLAND" [1778]. Clinton Map 125. *William L. Clements Library, Ann Arbor, Michigan.*

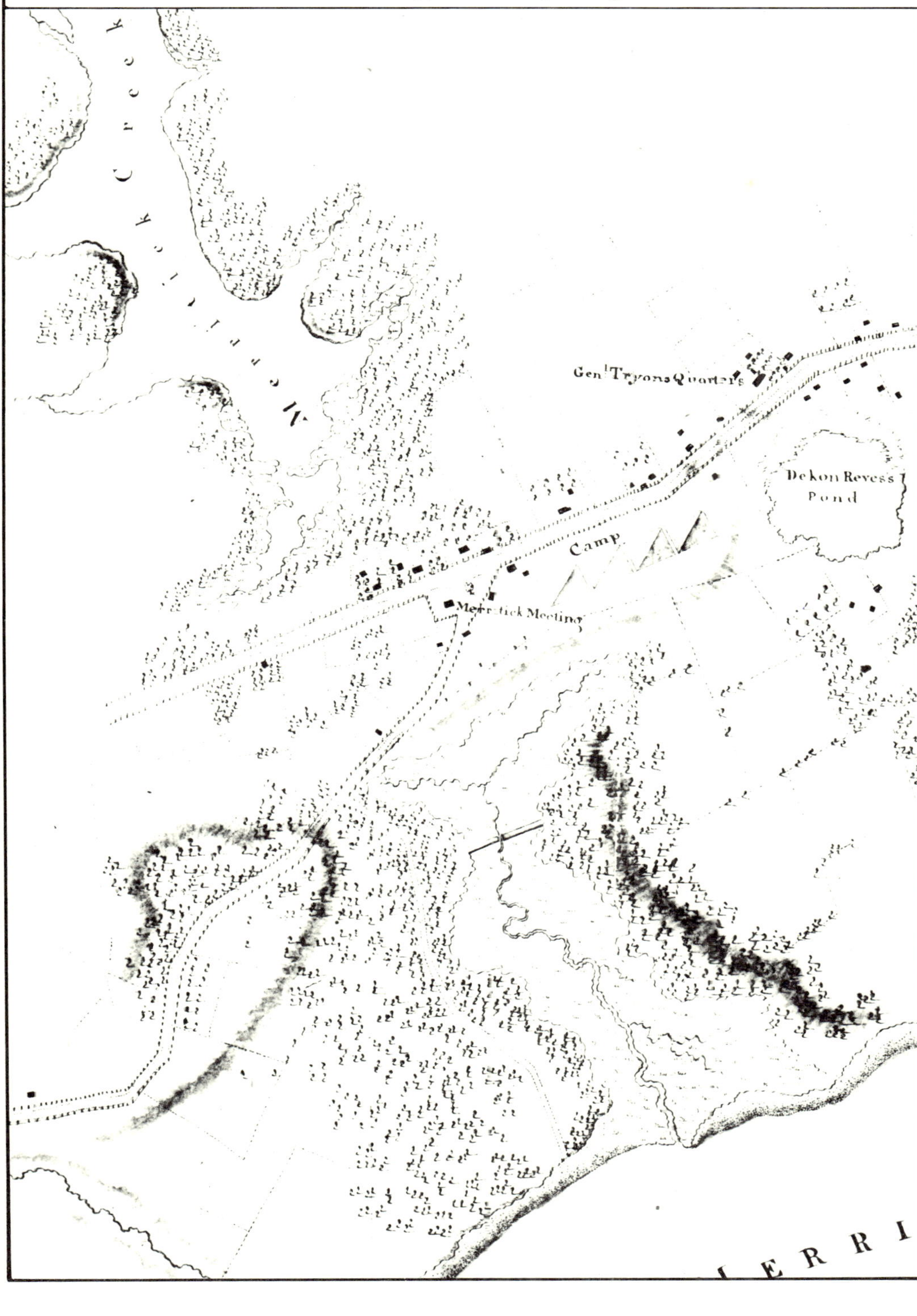

SUFFOLK COUNTY CHANGE OF POPULATION, 1776 - 1778

white adult males 17 and over*

Town		percent of decrease in 1778
SOUTHOLD (including Riverhead and Shelter Island)		
1776 pop.:	755	
1778 pop.:	506	33%
difference	249	
SMITHTOWN		
1776 pop.:	144	
1778 pop.:	102	29%
difference	42	
SOUTHAMPTON		
1776 pop.:	679	
1778 pop.:	518	24%
difference	161	
EAST HAMPTON		
1776 pop.:	318	
1778 pop.:	255	20%
difference	63	
BROOKHAVEN		
1776 pop.:	566	
1778 pop.:	505	11%
difference	61	
ISLIP		
1776 pop.:	83	
1778 pop.:	84	
difference	1	none
HUNTINGTON		
1776 pop.:	no figures recorded	
1778 pop.:	528	

*Sources: 1.) 1776 census under the Provincial Congress
2.) 1778 king's oath census (see n. 7)

ened with hanging, whereupon he took the oath "but spurned the Bible from his lips."[7] Unfortunately, no source is given for this curious anecdote, and the basis for the allegation against Wickham is not mentioned.

In the spring of 1779, Wickham's presence in Southold is suggested in two letters of Jared Landon, who had been released the previous year and returned from his detention in New York City. He writes to his father on May 22, 1779, and in the letter comments: "As to P. Wickham & T Fanning I think their influence no great with British generals." On June 23 he writes another letter, remarking: "As to P.W. he must not live hear. I do not think Southold will hold us both, if peace comes among us."[8] Landon's wishes were to be fulfilled. Four months later the legislature of the state of New York would pass the Attainder, and eventually Wickham, after the Revolution, would be banished.

CHAPTER 8

The Act of Attainder: What Did It Do?

The Name of the Claimants Father was inserted in the Act of Proscript: by a professed Enemy who meant to make his property his own.

> Dr. James Muirson, Sheriff of Suffolk County (1774–1776), testifying on the claim of Wickham's son.[1]

WITH THE ADOPTION OF New York State's constitution in April 1777, the state's first system of government by a congress and committees was replaced by a new government comprising a governor, a legislature, and a judicial branch. The constitution called for the election of the governor and members of the legislature, but of course no elections could take place in the southern district during the British occupation. Consequently, delegates who were said to represent this region were appointed to the legislature. Under the constitution a Council of Revision was also set up that was essentially a judicial body. Consisting of the governor, the chancellor, and the judges of the state supreme court, the Council had the power to veto bills of the legislature; however, its veto could itself be overridden by two-thirds of both houses of the legislature.

Among other things, the constitution of New York expunged from the statute books the treason laws of England. This was natural considering that under these laws the government of New York would itself have stood accused of treason. The abolishment of English treason law meant that such statutes as Henry VIII's "Act Whereby Divers Offences Be Made High Treason" were no longer on the books. It was that statute which was judged to have made estates tail, as well as unrestricted fee simple estates, liable to forfeiture in cases of high treason. At the same time, article 35 of the New York constitution reinstated all the other old body of English statute and common law. This included, of course, *De Donis,* the English statute which created estates tail.

The constitution also spoke of civil rights. One of its provisions on this subject was article 13. This article declares that "no member of this state shall be disenfranchised or deprived of any of the rights or privileges secured to the subjects of this state by the constitution, unless by the law of the land or the judgment of his peers." By "law of the land" is meant due process of law or—to quote Daniel Webster—"the general law—a law which hears before it condemns, which proceeds upon inquiry, and renders judgment only after trial."[2]

Another civil rights provision found in the New York constitution was article 41. While this article permitted acts of attainder to be passed by the legislature for crimes committed before the termination of the war with England, it also stipulated that such acts "shall not work a corruption of blood." The prohibition against corruption of blood safeguarded the rights of heirs in cases where there had been an attainder but not an absolute forfeiture. For example, if an actual forfeiture for some reason had not been carried out or if, after attainder and forfeiture, there remained an inheritance of property from an ancestor of the attainted parent, the rights of heirs would be respected.[3] Their blood would not be deemed corrupted just because of the alleged wrongdoing of their parent. Put another way, person B would not be punished because of the crimes of person A. The principle has been aptly expressed in a recent decision of the U.S. Supreme Court:

> Even if the State found it expedient to control the conduct of adults by acting against their children, legislation directing the onus of a parent's misconduct against his children does not comport with fundamental conceptions of justice.[4]

Two and a half years after the state adopted its constitution, the legislature of the state passed "An Act, for the forfeiture and sale of the estates of persons who have adhered to the enemies of this State, and for declaring the sovereignty of the people of this State in respect to all property within the same." Made law on October 22, 1779, the Act of Attainder was an extraordinary piece of legislation even for its time. A few months before its enactment the state's first chancellor, Robert R. Livingston, writes: "Never was there a greater compound of folly, avarice, and injustice than our confiscation bill." It drew this reaction from New York State's first chief justice, John Jay, writing to the governor of New York on May 6, 1780, from Spain, where he was then serving as foreign minister: "An English paper contains what they call, but I can hardly believe to be, your confiscation act. If truly printed, New-York is disgraced by injustice too palpable to admit even of palliation."[5] While dispensing with judicial procedure in its purpose of confiscating the estates of fifty-nine alleged offenders, it was not this which made New York's Attainder different either from legislation of this sort as it had been known in England or from the attainder enactments that were being passed in other states at this time. What made New York's Act different was, for one thing, the civil liberties articles in the state's constitution, which imposed restraints on the judicial prerogatives of the Act.[6] For example, attainder could not work a corruption of blood. Heirs of alleged offenders therefore had certain rights, those in particular who, like Parker Wickham's sons and heirs, had not been named in the Act.

There were other things in the contents of the enactment which made it different as well. One of these differences, noted by Alexander Hamilton, was that the named offenders are not described as subjects or citizens of the state. Yet neither are they termed aliens, but are described simply as persons. Another peculiarity, this one remarked on both by Hamilton and New York's Chief Justice Kent: the offense is described as adhering to the enemy. It was not, to quote Kent, "declared, or understood, to amount to treason, because many of the persons attainted had never owed any allegiance to this state."[7] That put this kind of attainder in a different ballpark altogether, distinguishing it from the attainder acts in other states such as New Jersey and Pennsylvania, where the offense was stated to be high treason. Why this mattered, how the defining of the offense changed the nature of New York's Act, is explained by reference to the long established rule in English jurisprudence, upon whose principles and precedents the laws of the young state were founded. This was the rule that only the offense of high treason could incur the forfeiture of property of the type which Wickham had title to—namely, entailed property.[8]

But even more important, New York's Attainder is not speaking about confiscating property in the sense of land. It is not worded like Henry VIII's Treason Act of 1535, which forfeited "all such landes tenemetes, and hereditametes, which any such offender or offenders shall have of any estate of inheritance." Indeed, the word used in New York's Attainder Act is "estates," as the title of the Act makes clear: "An Act, for the forfeiture and sale of the estates of persons who have adhered to the enemies. . . ." If we examine the end of section 1 of the Act, we learn more precisely what is being taken from the purported offenders:

> all and singular the estate both real and personal held or claimed by them the said persons severally and respectively, whether in possession, reversion or remainder, within this State, on the day of the passing of this act, shall be and hereby is declared to be forfeited to, and vested in the people of this State.

The words "estate real" are here being used to signify, as Kent explains, a "condition or circumstance in which the owner stands, with regard to his property. . . . It must be an interest in the land existing in possession, reversion or remainder.''[9] The interest or right to the property was something different from the property itself. It could be an interest in fee or a limited interest, such as was the case with estates tail. What New York's Act of Attainder confiscated, in other words, was the interest of the offender, whatever interest he held or claimed, which left the legal interests of others in the same property unimpaired.

That it was the intention of the legislature to take, under this Act, only the offender's interest in the property he claimed is shown by its later enactment on behalf of an heir. On March 14, 1788, David Richard Floyd received permission by act of the state legislature to change his name to David Richard Floyd-Jones. This Floyd was the son of Richard Floyd, who had been attainted and banished and was now living in New Brunswick, Canada. The petitioner seeking the name change had a special reason for doing so, and it is in the will of his grandfather, David Jones of Fort Neck, Queens, that we discover the reason. The will was signed in 1768, but it was revised in the testator's first codicil of 1771, which presented the final instructions regarding the disposition of his property. In that document David Jones leaves all his property in Queens to son Thomas for his lifetime, and then to Thomas's first son, and that son's son ''in Tail Male.'' The will thus set up an entail with successive remainders, or contingencies. One of these contingencies was that if son Thomas had no children the property being devised would go to the testator's daughter Arrabella for life, and then to her first son, and so on, in the same manner as described above. Arrabella was the wife of the attainted Richard Floyd, and their first son was David Richard Floyd. But now the grandfather leaves a final condition for his daughter's son in case he receives the property: Upon taking the estate, he must adopt the surname ''Jones'' in addition to his own.

Thomas Jones, the testator's son, was one of the former judges attainted under the Act of October 22, 1779. He had no children of his own but an adopted daughter, who would not qualify for an estate tail, not being an heir of the body. Under these circumstances the estate tail, after the term of Thomas's life, would normally go to the first remainderperson, Arrabella, and thereafter to her son David Richard Floyd-Jones. There was one snag, however. Thomas Jones had been attainted. And so the question was: Would that affect the course of the entail? Did the state confiscate all right, title, and interest in the property or just the offender's? The legislature provided the answer in an enactment on February 20, 1790, when again the petitioner was Arrabella's son, who had previously obtained a change of name.

GENEALOGY OF DAVID RICHARD FLOYD-JONES

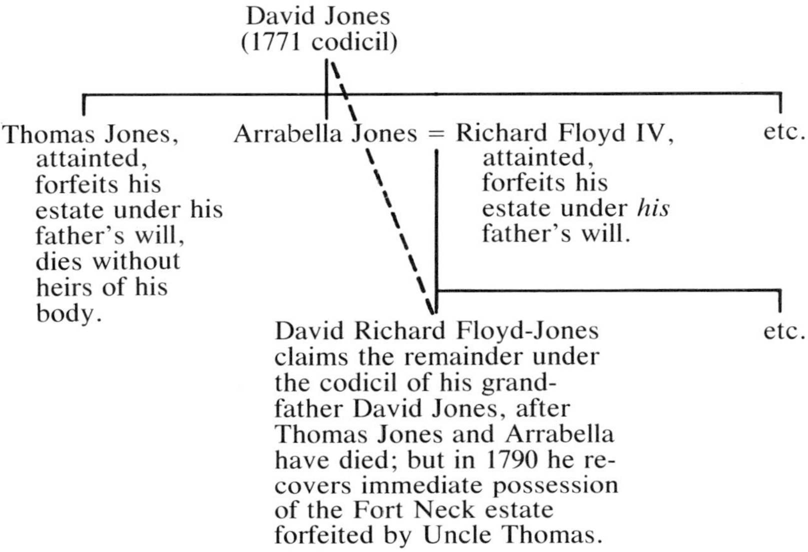

__________ = line of descent
– – – – – – = source of inheritance

Sources: Thomas Floyd-Jones, *Thomas Jones, Fort Neck, Queens County, Long Island, 1695, and his Descendents, the Floyd-Jones Family* (New York: the J. Grant Senia Press, 1906), pp. 45, 50, 53, 55.

Also Laws of New York, 13 sess., Chaps. 10, 11 (Feb. 20, 1790).

> Whereas David Jones late of Fort Neck in Queens . . . being at the time of his death seized of an estate of inheritance in the county aforesaid did by his last will and testament devise the same to the use of his son Thomas Jones for life with several contingent remainders over, And whereas the interest of the said Thomas Jones in the same estate by his attainder became forfeited to and vested in the people of this State And whereas David Richard Floyd Jones is the next remainder man to whom the estate is limited upon the death of the said Thomas Jones And whereas it is represented to the legislature that the premises aforesaid are much impaired to the great injury of those in remainder.
>
> Be it enacted . . . that all the right title and interest of the people of this State of in and to the estate aforesaid by virtue of the attainder aforesaid be and the same is hereby vested in the said David Richard Floyd Jones and his legal representatives for and during the natural life of the said Thomas Jones any law usage or custom to the contrary notwithstanding.

The lifetime interest of Thomas Jones, by the legislature's own admission, was the extent of what had been confiscated from the entailed estate, and that interest was now being turned over to the remainderman, David Richard Floyd-Jones.[10]

Besides the civil rights safeguards in New York's constitution and the restrictions in the Act of Attainder itself, there was yet another circumstance which stood in the way of this confiscatory decree of 1779, rendering it powerless, at least temporarily, in over one-third of New York's counties. That circumstance was British jurisdiction.

Enforcement of the Act of Attainder in British-occupied New York was of course impossible as long as enemy troops remained in the southern counties. Not surprisingly, the Act specified that no sales of confiscated property in the occupied zone were to be made until the enemy had left. And so such sales were held up until 1783. In November of that year 1783, the British evacuated the capital, New York City, and the surrounding territory. Taking possession of the formerly occupied counties, the state was now free to enforce the Confiscation Act within them. Or was it?

Before the British evacuation, two treaties had been made between the United States and England, both of which barred future confiscations of property. The only way, therefore, the state of New York (or any state) could initiate its confiscations after the war, without seeming to violate the treaties, was to justify them as having taken place before the treaties.

Future confiscations became a controversial issue after the war. In one case a person named in the Act of Attainder, Christopher Billop, owned lands in Richmond County. Before the British evacuated, he sold his lands to several purchasers. But subsequently, the state of New York sold the very same lands to someone else. The case went to court. The trial was moved from Richmond County because of the "strong prejudice" in that county. As explained in the pleadings, this prejudice was fostered by a general opinion held by the people there that no act of the state legislature could confiscate lands lying within the limits of the authority and power of the British government at the time such act was passed. Subsequently the court ruled against the purchasers of Billop, and the case was taken to the state legislature. There, a committee gave the following opinion, which was endorsed by the state assembly:

> Whether the peculiar situation of Richmond county, when it fell within the power of the British army, can entitle the petitioners to protection under the general treaty of peace, is a matter that cannot be taken into consideration by the committee. . . .

The report goes on to say that in other cases purchasers from persons attainted had to repurchase from the state. Consistent with that policy, therefore, the prayer of the petitioners could not be granted.[11]

After the Revolution, Alexander Hamilton practiced law in New York, and his services were solicited by various clients who had suffered property losses under the Act of Attainder. One of these was a purchaser of property from Robert Bayard, who had been attainted in 1779. Located in New York City, Bayard's property had been purchased in 1782 by John Middagh. Middagh had not been attainted, but in any case the state did not recognize the purchase and, with the gaining of territorial control over the southern counties in late 1783, the state's Commissioners of Forfeiture sold the property to someone else. Middagh wrote to Hamilton, asking for an opinion on his case. What if any reply the attorney gave is not known.

Another letter to Hamilton came from John Murray, a former governor of New York. Attainted by the state in 1779, Murray owned lands in Vermont, which had seceded from New York. The question he raises is whether the 1779 Confiscation Act could have reached his lands in Vermont if that state had broken off from the territory of New York before the Act was passed. Again, the attorney's reply, if any, is not known.[12]

In his political writings, Hamilton does address the issues raised in these letters, though there is an element of uncertainty about his position. On the one hand, he asserts that in the framing of the treaty between the United States and England, the latter agreed to give up New York City and its adjacent territories. "As she was in possession, by right of war, of all these objects, whatever may have been our original pretensions to them, they are, by the laws of nations, to be considered as so much given up on her part."[13] Here Hamilton seems to be suggesting that England had jurisdiction over the occupied territory by right of war, and that it was her law—and not the state's law—that prevailed there during the schismatic period. For otherwise it would make little sense to argue that one country had possession of a territory if another country's law prevailed in that territory. In his tract "Second Letter from Phocion," Hamilton further states that the inhabitants of the occupied region were "bound to pay a temporary and qualified obedience to the conqueror," but that "they could not transfer their eventual allegiance from the state to a foreign power." That comment suggests too that during the occupation it was enemy law which prevailed in the enemy zone, not state law. The inhabitants were bound to pay a temporary obedience to the conqueror. But the thrust of Hamilton's argument in his "Second Letter" is not this. His intent is not to show the political separation of the inhabitants of the occupied region, but the contrary: that even in their obedience to the British they did not lose their citizenship in New York State. The context of Hamilton's argument here is important. He was writing early in the year 1784. The state legislature was in a vindictive mood, preparing to enact a law that would declare large groups of inhabitants in the formerly occupied region aliens of the state. Hamilton saw the injustice of this, and his tract is a polemic against such a legislative move. Speaking in their defense, he reasons that these inhabitants, if they had become aliens during the war, would have ceased to be traitors, "and all the laws of the state passed during the revolution, by which they are considered and punished as subjects, would have been, by that construction, unintelligible and unjust."[14] Were these people, then, subjects of state law at the same time they were subjects of British law? Was state law operating in enemy-held territory? Actually, Hamilton is here not so much rendering an opinion about the extra-territorial power of state law as he is merely noting that state law had been framed during the war in the belief that it extended to the people in the occupied region.

Less than a year after Hamilton's "Second Letter from Phocion," state law jurisdiction became a controversial issue again, this time in the Mayor's Court of New York. The case before the court was *Rutgers* v. *Waddington,* with the attorney general of New York State arguing for the plaintiff and Alexander Hamilton retained by the defendant, James Waddington. At issue was the jurisdictional prerogative of the Trespass Act, passed by the state legislature in March 1783, while the British were still in possession of southern New York. The Act authorized legal actions against loyalists for wartime trespasses. In February 1784, Elizabeth Rutgers filed suit against Waddington, claiming the right to rents under the Trespass Act. The defendant had occupied her property in New York City and established a business there. Hamilton argued that the Trespass Act, being inconsistent with the treaty, which barred future confiscations and war-related prosecutions, was therefore void. He pointed out that the army of the king on September 10, 1776, "conquered subdued and took possession of the said City, and continued in firm and uninterrupted possession of the said City, from the time of the said conquest and reduction, until and after the seventeenth day of March, 1783." In its decision, the court echoed much of Hamilton's reasoning. It ruled that the law of nations [international law] and the Treaty of Paris gave protection to the defendant while acting under proper military authorization: "Restitution of the fruit—i.e. rents and issues of houses & lands, which have been collected under authority of the British Commander, while he held possession of the city, cannot, according to the law of nations, be required."[15] It was a bold decision for its time, considering the mood of American patriots toward loyalists after the Revolution. The court, in so many words, was repudiating the notion that state law was supreme. Because of the British occupation, New York's law was constrained, it recognized, by jurisdictional limitations insofar as that law retroacted and affected the occupied zone. The peculiar situation of New York being such as it was, law other than state law had to be taken into consideration, namely treaty law and international law.

Though *Rutgers* v. *Waddington* concerned rents, not real estate, and though it said nothing about New York's Act of Attainder, the decision in the case raises questions about just what jurisdictional scope the Act of Attainder had. Could it have affected property in the British zone during the occupation period? On the American side, the closest we come to a judicial resolution of this question is found in the deliberations of a Chief Justice of the U.S. Supreme Court, Joseph Story.[16]

Justice Story was first of all aware of how the rules of international law applied to the general question of sovereignty and territorial rights. "The laws of one country," he writes in his *Commentaries on the Conflict of Laws,* "can have no intrinsic force, *proprio vigore,* except within the territorial limits and jurisdiction of that country." He cites Vattel, an authority on international law: "Sovereignty, united with domain, establishes the exclusive jurisdiction of a nation within its own territories, as to controversies, to crimes, and to rights arising therein." In another place Story talks specifically about real estate: "All the authorities in both countries [England and the United States], so far as they go, recognize the principle in its fullest import, that real estate, or immovable property, is exclusively subject to the laws of the government, within whose territory it is situate."[17] There is no doubt then on the matter of general principle, as far as this Justice is concerned. When it came to property in land, a law's jurisdiction extended only as far as its territorial jurisdiction.

But now let us see how Story applied this principle to particular cases. In *Shanks* v. *Dupont* he speaks about the inhabitants of Charleston, South

Carolina, during the Revolution when the city was occupied by the British. "They owed allegiance indeed to the conquerors during their occupation; but it was a temporary allegiance, which did not destroy, but only suspend their former allegiance. It did not annihilate their allegiance to the state of South Carolina, and make them *de facto* aliens."[18] Owing allegiance to the conquerors, the inhabitants by implication must have been obliged to obey the conqueror's laws. But Story here does not speak of that concern, nor does he draw any conclusions about the status of state law in occupied territory. He does, however, say that allegiance to the state had been "suspended" in the occupied region, which would suggest that state law had been suspended there too. In another case, and here Story writes a concurring opinion, the subject of ligeance, or the territory where allegiance is due, is taken up, and this time the venue is New York City. Supposing that the plaintiff in the case was born in that city while in the possession of the British, the Justice reasons: "Now in no just sense can the demandant be deemed born within the ligeance of the state of New York, if, at the time of his birth, his parents were in a territory then occupied by her enemies and adhering to them as subjects, *de facto*, in virtue of their original allegiance."[19] Story then goes on to discuss the Act of Attainder of 1779, describing it as an act which not only "purports" to be an attainder of citizens but also of persons who never were citizens. The Act, he continues, "seems, indeed, a summary exercise of the ultimate power of sovereignty, in inflicting the penalty of confiscation upon the property of enemies, *jure belli.*" Unfortunately, the Justice's words suggest that, like Hamilton, he was giving more a description of what the Act was about rather than drawing conclusions about its extra-territorial efficacy under international law. There is, however, one aspect of the Attainder which Story is clearly suggesting had immediate enforceability regardless of territorial jurisdiction. Without delving into questions of property or inheritance rights consequent to attainder (especially under conditions where confiscation could not have occurred), the Justice nevertheless considers the Act to have absolved the named offenders from allegiance and the duties expected of citizens, having likewise deprived them of citizens' rights and protection of the government.[20] But there is no extra-territorial question here. The invalidating of allegiance, civil protection, rights, and duties can be done without resorting to pretensions that one has the power to take (whether it be property, taxes, duties, or the like) in a jurisdiction where one, in fact, doesn't have that power.

It is in a third case before Justice Story, *U.S.* v. *Rice,* that we find the extra-territorial question tackled head on, and here Justice Story delivers the unanimous opinion of the court. The circumstances of the case involve the British capture of Castine, Maine, in September 1814, a territory which remained in their possession until after ratification of the treaty of peace in February 1815. The question at issue was whether American law regarding customs duties could be imposed retroactively in that territory during the period of its occupation. The court's answer is unequivocal:

> The sovereignty of the United States over the territory was, of course, suspended, and the laws of the United States could no longer be rightfully enforced there, or be obligatory upon the inhabitants who remained and submitted to the conquerors. By the surrender the inhabitants passed under a *temporary allegiance* to the British government, and were bound by such laws, *and such only,* as *it* chose to recognize and impose. From the nature of the case, no other laws could be *obligatory* upon them, for where there is no protection or allegiance or sovereignty, there can be no claim to obedience. Castine was, therefore, *during this period,* so far as respected our revenue laws, to be deemed a *foreign* port.[21]
>
> [Italics theirs.]

The Castine case involved, of course, a different war with Britain and a law different from the Attainder Act of New York State. Still it is here, in a case decided previous to the two above, that the position of the Supreme Court is made clear on the question of extra-territorial legislation. It can be summed up this way: A law under one sovereign cannot reach into another sovereign's territory and lay claim to anything by force of the law when, in fact, that law within another sovereignty does not have any force. Sovereign authority is a prerequisite to the operation of a law.

What the Supreme Court has to say on extra-territoriality sheds light on the nature of Parker Wickham's situation in British-held Suffolk County and how he was affected by the state's Attainder in 1779. First of all, borrowing from the opinion of Justice Story, we can conclude that the Act of Attainder did succeed in revoking Wickham's civil and legal existence in New York State.[22] He was condemned to banishment, and, as with Jimmy Hoffa after his disappearance, became dead in the law, a nonperson under state law. Second, however—and what is most important—the state's Act was powerless to work a confiscation of Wickham's property. It could not claim rights to property in the occupied zone—a foreign zone—any more than state law could claim rights to property or territory in Mexico or Australia. Nor could it seize property outside its jurisdiction and bring it into its own. There could be no traffic of land across territorial lines, just as there could be no traffic of taxes or import duties.

Consequently, Wickham's property in Suffolk County remained undisturbed, at least for the time being.

Overview of the Treaties and the Claim

1778: Parker Wickham deeds property to son Joseph.

1779: By Act of Attainder, Parker Wickham is deemed civilly dead under New York State law.

1783: The Provisional Treaty of Peace goes into effect on Jan. 20.

Art. 5 protects from the obstacle of any law the prosecution by all persons with interests in confiscated lands. [See *Ware* v. *Hylton*, 3 Dall. (U.S.) 199 (1796) 240, 278, 284].

Art. 6 bars future confiscations.

1783: The Definitive Treaty of Peace is signed on Sept. 3.

1783: About the time of the British evacuation, Joseph P. Wickham leaves for the West Indies and the Carolinas.

1783: New York State takes possession of Long Island after the British leave.

1783: The British army evacuates from New York on Nov. 25.

1789: Joseph P. Wickham receives compensation from the British government. By 1791, he is back in Southold, Long Island.

1794: The Jay Treaty confirms the titles of British subjects to lands they now hold in America, whether they are in actual possession of them or not. (See p.149, n. 21).

Part III:
The Title Under The Treaties

A treaty cannot be the supreme law of the land, that is of all the United States, if any act of a State Legislature can stand in its way.

Justice Chase in *Ware* v. *Hylton*, 3 Dall. (U.S.) 199 (1796) 236.

CHAPTER 9

Independence

THOUGH DECLARED BANISHED BY the state of New York, Parker Wickham remained on Long Island in the province of New York. Indeed, where was he to go? Scattered records document his whereabouts in Southold, at least at intervals. In 1780 he ordered a yard of buckram, eight yards of shalloon—a woolen lining—and other sundries from a dealer in Orient, a hamlet in the eastern part of the township. In May of that year he was a witness to a Southold deed. A month earlier he would have been in town too, attending the funeral of his mother. It was she to whom John Parker had deeded his considerable estate tail, the River Head, in 1727, and this property now automatically passed under English law to Abigail's oldest son, Parker Wickham, donee in tail. On another occasion too we know the magistrate was in town. That was on July 12, 1782, when again he was serving as a witness, this time to the will of Barnabas Wines. Probated under the state government in 1784, the will bears Wickham's signature as witness, even though he was supposed to have become dead under state law by Act of 1779. Yet here he appears in 1782, alive in the law to serve as witness.[1] Less than a year later—April 4, 1783—his wife, Mary, died at the age of 49. He would have been present in Southold then as well to attend her funeral.

On November 1, 1783, Parker Wickham came to New York City and drew up a power of attorney witnessed jointly by William Smith, the crown-appointed chief justice of the province, and by a relative of Smith's named Robert Torrans. Torrans brought the document to the city magistrate William Waddell, in whose presence Torrans submitted a deposition on Wickham's power of attorney. Waddell signed as witness, and the documents then went before Thomas W.W. Birvan, the royal notary, who attested to the person and office of Waddell and to the authenticity of his signature. The notary's statement was signed and sealed on November 17, eight days before the evacuation of His Majesty's troops and the cessation of British law in the southern district of New York.

Meanwhile, another kind of law had come into play in New York. Treaties had been signed between the United States and England, and these were now part of the supreme law of the land, binding in all the land.

Aboard the frigate *Ceres* the new commander in chief of British forces in North America, Sir Guy Carleton, arrived in the port of New York on May 5, 1782. In the eighteen months that followed, it would be his responsibility to maintain the defenses around the city and in other parts of the occupied territory, and to proceed under the terms of the Provisional Treaty between the United States and England, ensuring an orderly evacuation from the city of both military personnel and civilians.

The Provisional Treaty was signed on November 30, 1782, but was scheduled not to go into effect until the French and British signed a peace treaty of their own, which they did at Versailles on January 20 of the following year. Then in April Carleton and the American Congress, receiving word from abroad, issued proclamations that hostilities between their respective countries had ended and that the treaty signed in November had gone into operation. The war was now over, and the two countries turned their attention to the terms of the treaty. Of primary concern to the state of New York was article 7, which provided that the king would, with all convenient speed, withdraw his armies from the independent states, while at the same time seeing to it that Negroes or other "property" of the American inhabitants was not carried off in the departing ships. On April 8, Attorney General Egbert Benson was deputed by New York State's Governor Clinton to arrange a meeting with General Carleton in the city of New York. The purpose was to set up a timetable for his withdrawal and "the speedy obtaining Possession of the Southern District of this State."[2] Granted safe passage, Benson proceeded to the city and there conferred with the British commander on two occasions. His minutes of April 17 inform us what transpired between the men. Families, he explained to the commander, wanted to return to their homes. The presence of Carleton's army in New York obstructed elections, and in the opinion of many persons a proper legislature could not be formed under these conditions, the legislative power of government being in a manner suspended. The visitor discussed the "general advantages which would arise to the state from an exercise of government and Jurisdiction throughout the whole territory." Pointing these things out, he wished to learn what plan of departure the general had in mind so that "the Jurisdiction of the state might be extended without the imputation of encroachment." Carleton reportedly declined to offer any specific agenda. Instead, he turned the subject of discussion to the legislature's Trespass Act of March 17, 1783, which permitted suits against persons who had "occupied, injured, or destroyed'' estates within the power of the enemy. The general considered such an act hostile to peace, and was no doubt thinking of article 6 in the treaty. It barred future prosecutions against persons by reason of the part they may have taken in the late war. The conference of the two men was prolonged and apparently relaxed, but came to an end without the tangible results Benson had been seeking.[3]

On May 5 the two generals Carleton and George Washington met at Tappan to discuss further the terms of the treaty; a number of state officials were also present. Two days later Governor Clinton wrote the British commander, seeking confirmation that he would, as he had pledged at the meeting, now withdraw his forces from Westchester ''so that the Jurisdiction of the State might take Place.'' Sir Guy answered on the thirteenth, stating that such had already been assented to, ''in firm Reliance that the Letter and Spirit of the Treaty will on the Part of Congress, with all possible Speed, be carried into the most liberal Execution, and that the State of New York will not for itself, take or suffer to be taken any measure contrary to the 5th and 6th Articles. . . .''[4]

The treaty's article 5 consisted of two sections, the first recommendatory, the second not. The first part stipulated that Congress shall ''earnestly recommend'' to the legislatures of the states the restitution of estates, rights, and properties of various categories of people. These included (1) ''real'' British subjects, and (2) those persons residing in districts in the possession of the British. Belonging to the second category were those, for the most part, who had been forced to flee with their families to the British lines because of their refusal to swear allegiance to the American cause. Public warnings such as Washington's proclamation of January 25, 1777, and New York's Act of June 30, 1778, both of which were directed at persons who refused to commit themselves to the American side, would have compelled this class of people to seek refuge in British-occupied territory. Their estates having subsequently been confiscated, they had no districts to be resident of except those in British possession. On the other hand, born in America like their fellow countrymen, they would not have qualified as ''real'' British subjects.

The magistrate Parker Wickham considered that a recommendation of Congress to the states was tantamount to a requirement. In his letter of March 30, 1784, he writes, ''I observe Congress has peremtorily ordered the states to give up all confiscated estates, agreeable to [the] treaty.'' But he adds, apparently mindful of an existing polarity between federal and state law: ''What effect that will take I know not, nor is it possible to know any faster than proceedings opperate. A child born with two heads is a monster.''[5]

The second section of article 5 of the treaty was not recommendatory.

It had to do with all persons having legal interests in confiscated lands.[6] This section reads:

> And it is agreed that all Persons who have any Interest in confiscated Lands, either by Debts, Marriage Settlements or otherwise, shall meet with no lawful Impediment in the prosecution of their just Rights.

Unlike article 5, which concerned property and estates that had been confiscated, article 6 of the treaty concerned future confiscations. It declared:

> That there shall be no future Confiscations made, nor any prosecutions commenced against any Person or Persons, for or by reason of the Part which he or they may have taken in the present War, and that no person shall on that account suffer any future Loss or Damage either in his Person, Liberty or Property.

What this article did was to make it impossible, under the treaty, for states now to confiscate property on account of a person's allegiance and conduct during the Revolution, in cases where, for one reason or another, the property had not already been seized and taken possession of by the state.[7] It also became unlawful under the treaty for states now to commence prosecution against wartime offenders.

Subsequent to Carleton's evacuation from Westchester County, complaints were filed with the British commander in chief. The properties of several residents who had lived in the British sector of that county were being seized by officials of the state of New York.

Andrew Fowler writes in his deposition that he and his family had been in possession of their farm in Eastchester during the war but that on June 6, 1783, he received warnings to quit his farm. He was subsequently evicted, accused of aiding and assisting the enemy. The jurors at an inquisition on June 16 determined that Israel Honeywell, Commissioner of Sequestration, and others had "long since" been lawfully and peacefully entitled to the property in question. Another deponent, Edward Ward, asserts that he was the proprietor of a 300 acre farm in Eastchester that had been in his family for 80 years. While declaring that he had not taken up arms in support of the British, he admitted expressing his "disapprobation of the popular measures" and had taken an oath of allegiance before David Mathews, the crown mayor of New York. An inquisition on June 30, 1783, ruled that a David Williams had "long since" been lawfully and peacefully entitled to the property in question. Ward and his family were evicted on July 2. A third deponent, Benjamin Hunt, lieutenant colonel of the militia, states that he had owned an estate in Westchester for many years before the war and that it had been continually in his or his tenants' possession.

He testifies that on July 8, 1783, he was forcibly dispossessed, some of his goods were thrown out of the door, and he himself beaten with clubs, the assailants declaring that he should not remain in the country. Hunt sought the help of Ebenezer Burling, the justice of the peace, but the latter "refused to give any redress, said the Informant was an outlaw & an open enemy of the Country, and not entitled to any protection, that any person might use him ill; and that he as a Magistrate could not know him." Hunt was "induced" to leave for New York City.

The depositions of Fowler, Ward, and Hunt, and the records of inquisition were forwarded by General Carleton to Elias Boudinot, the President of the Continental Congress.[8] In his letter to Boudinot, Carleton speaks of the hostile proceedings under Governor Clinton's sphere of authority, the incidents of violence by Americans against their countrymen—after the cessation of hostilities—and how the general's plans for evacuation were being delayed by the numbers of refugees "who look to me for escape from threatened destruction." Repeated proofs of a disregard of the articles of peace were found in the newspapers, he asserts, and was probably calling to mind such notices as the one that appears in the patriot *New York Packet* on August 7, 1783. The issue of that date lists thirty-three persons indicted for adhering to the enemies of the state, including several from parts of the southern district. By order of Lewis Duboys, sheriff of Dutchess County, they were summoned to appear in state supreme court by a certain time to traverse the charges or be adjudged guilty and suffer the confiscation of all their real and personal estate.

In Clermont, a few miles to the north of Dutchess County, New York State's chancellor, Robert R. Livingston, writes to Hamilton:

> I seriously lament with you the violent spirit of persecution which prevails here and dread its consequences upon the wealth commerce & future tranquility of the state. I am the more hurt at it because it appears to me almost unmixed with pure or patriotic motives. In some few it is a blind spirit of revenge & resentment but in more it is the most sordid interest. One wishes to possess the house of some wretched Tory, another fears him as a rival in his trade or commerce & a fourth wishes to get rid of his debts by shaking of[f] his creditor or to reduce the price of Living by depopulating the town.[9]

Two days after his letter to Congress, General Carleton received a message from Governor Clinton informing him that the cases of Fowler, Ward, and Hunt would be immediately looked into. The governor adds: "I am led to believe however as it would appear from Ward's own Information [i.e., records of the inquest] that the Farm he claims was long since confiscated, that the other two may be under similar circumstances."[10] It appears that what the governor was suggesting by "long since" was that these confiscations had somehow happened before the treaty which would have barred them, and therefore while the estates allegedly confiscated lay in territory still under British jurisdiction and law.

On September 3, 1783, the Definitive Treaty of Peace was concluded between the United States and England. The treaty was identical to the Provisional Treaty in virtually all respects except a final clause concerning Florida. A week after the signing of the Definitive Treaty, the American peace negotiators in France wrote to the president of Congress, urging that America, for her part, had a duty to faithfully carry out the stipulations in the treaty concerning the tories. They write: "The unseasonable and unnecessary resolves of various towns on this subject, the actual expulsion of tories from some places, and the avowed implacability of almost all who have published their sentiments about the matter are circumstances which are construed, not only to the prejudice of our national magnanimity and good faith, but also to the prejudice of our government."[11] The complaint was remarkably similar in tenor to the one from Sir Guy on August 17.

In mid-November the British commander in chief notified General Washington of the imminent evacuation of his forces from New York. He informed Washington that he proposed to relinquish his posts at Kingsbridge as far as McGowan's pass on the twenty-first, to resign the possession of Herricks and Hempstead, with all territory eastward on Long Island, on the same day, and if possible the city and Brooklyn on the day following. He reiterated these plans in messages to Washington and Clinton on the nineteenth, but modified one part of the schedule. His forces would not be able to depart the city until the twenty-fifth, and the evacuation from Staten Island and several outlying posts would need a few days more. Upon that final arrangement the evacuation was carried out. On the twenty-fifth Carleton's army proceeded to withdraw from the city and board the king's ships. Now as the withdrawal continued to completion, marking the end of a vestige of British rule that had survived seven years after the Declaration of Independence, the province of New York contracted its lines until it was no more. At the same time, the state of New York slowly extended its jurisdiction throughout the southern district.[12]

In Suffolk County, three alleged offenders named in the Act of Attainder of 1779 suffered the sale of their property in the late summer of 1784. One of the three, the former county sheriff George Muirson, writes to his wife on July 22 from New Haven, Connecticut:

> Be glad if you would use your best influence with Judge Strong to procure the money to Redeame the Estate . . . to Leave no Stone on Turnd untill It is Dun as there is no time to Luse.

The gavel fell on Muirson's hopes on August 3 and 5, when his property was sold in two installments to Brookhaven purchasers. However, a "pittance" of the property was not accounted for in the state treasury and was eventually, by state law, granted to his daughter Mary Heathcote Muirson.[13] Richard Floyd was more fortunate. Not only did he receive compensation from England, but most of his property was purchased from the state by his brother, Benjamin, the former supervisor of Brookhaven. There was also a portion of it that did not get sold by the commissioners, and it was allowed to go, again by state decree, to Floyd's son, David Richard Floyd-Jones. His son had another bit of good fortune. It all began with the efforts of David's mother, Arrabella, before the British occupation had ended. On May 26, 1783, a friend of the family, John Willett, writes to her:

> Dear Maddam,
> I assure you it was not in my power to answer yours of the 11th Instant by David as I really had not time to attend to it, am really greatly concerned at the disagreeable prospects of us all as I fear they will not soon take a favourable turn. . . . With respect to the claim you propose making I fear it will not avail any thing as a Law is passed in New York state breaking all intails, however you can make the experiment. . . .[14]

Arrabella's experiment was to lead seven years later to an act of the state legislature which would transfer the confiscated estate of Judge Thomas Jones to Arrabella's son, who would thereby gain immediate possession of this property as well as the rights to the property as remainderman after the death of Judge Jones. Today, a well-known portion of the Floyd-Jones estate, Jones Beach, still bears that family's name, a circumstance due in part to the estate's survival after the Revolution.

Shortly before the British evacuation from New York on November 25, 1783, the family of Parker Wickham brought their attainted father to New London, Connecticut. He had been too ill to make the journey by sea to England or Canada as others in the city were doing, the many who either had been condemned as loyalists like him, or if not condemned, were fearful for their lives if they remained in the state. The threat of the banishment decree, together with Wickham's precarious health, left his family with no choice but to take him to a neighboring state, and in Connecticut they believed he would be granted asylum. It was not to New London proper that they brought him but to Pine Neck, two miles above the Rope Ferry, near the Niantic River. Here they found lodging for him and people to take care of him. A few days after that, the magistrate's son Joseph took leave of his father, boarded a ship and sailed for Antigua and the Carolinas. Joseph would return to Long Island one day, but he was never to see his father again.

Meanwhile, Wickham, forced into exile, had abandoned home and property in Suffolk County. What was to become of that ancient legacy now, the estates tail that had belonged to him and his family for half a century?

One of his tracts, the River Head, Wickham inherited at the death of his mother, Abigail, in 1780. That had happened while Suffolk County was under British law. Now with the withdrawal of the British, however, political jurisdiction had changed. State law had gone into effect on Long Island, and it was state law that in 1779 had declared Wickham attainted. The magistrate's other property, Robins Island and Wickham's Neck, had been deeded by him to his oldest son, Joseph Parker Wickham, in 1778. But would state law recognize this deed? Or had it been voided by the Attainder Act, which purportedly invalidated all such property transactions made since 1776 by those the Act denounced as enemy sympathizers?

In fact the questions we are asking are the wrong ones. To know what really happened to Wickham's property in 1783 and subsequently, we must ask not what state law purported to do or not do at that time, but what state law could or could not do under the terms of the treaties. Despite the Attainder, Wickham's property remained unconfiscated, as we have seen, during the period the British were in possession of Long Island. State law was powerless to extend beyond its jurisdiction. It was powerless to cross enemy lines and be law where enemy law prevailed. But then in November 1783, political jurisdiction had changed in the occupied counties. State law replaced British law. By this time, however, treaties of peace had been concluded, barring all future confiscations. This made it lawfully impossible for the state now to carry out confiscations which had not already taken place. Any such actions against property owners would now be in violation of the treaties and void by law.[15] Wickham's property, therefore, could not be confiscated even after state law went into effect in Suffolk County. Not having been confiscated before the treaties, it could not now be confiscated after the treaties, except in violation of them.

It is true that by Act of 1779 Wickham had lost his civil rights and civil existence under the law in New York State. But the Attainder could do nothing about his property, which until 1783 lay on foreign soil. Nor could it deny his family and heirs their right of inheritance to property that the state could not lawfully confiscate. Wickham's oldest son, Joseph, who was the heir at law, had in fact been deeded part of the estate in 1778. That property could not later be forfeited in 1783, anymore than the other property, without constituting a "future confiscation." The only state law which, under the treaties, was competent to affect Wickham's property after the New York government acquired jurisdiction of Suffolk County was the Act to Abolish Entails, passed in 1782. By that law, those possessed of entailed estates became possessed of unrestricted estates in fee simple. Consequently, with the change to state jurisdiction, Joseph Parker Wickham, who had inherited the entailed legacy of the River Head, Robins Island, and Wickham's Neck, became "seised" of these lands (i.e., held title to them) in fee simple. His father couldn't hold title now to any of these lands, being without rights under New York State law.

Having seen what really happened after the Revolution—the fact that there could be no lawful confiscation of Wickham's property—we can now turn from reality to the presumptions that were put in place of reality. First, there was the presumption that state law was supreme. State officials presumed that their law determined the meaning of treaties, when in fact it was treaties that determined the power and interpretation of state law, where the two conflicted. State officials presumed that their law could take effect in occupied territory, and that therefore the Act of Attainder, upon enactment in 1779, had worked immediate confiscations not only in state-held territory but also in British territory.[16] They presumed, in other words, that state law could have jurisdiction in places where in fact it had not had jurisdiction. From these presumptions it was not difficult for state officials to make yet another: that the confiscation of Wickham's property, along with that of others in the occupied zone, had occurred not after the treaties but before, even while the British were in possession of the territory.

It is therefore not surprising that the state proceeded to confiscate Wickham's property, in violation of the treaties, after it had obtained jurisdiction of Suffolk County. The magistrate's tracts of land were located by prospective buyers in the spring of 1784, appraised, and sold by the state's Commissioners of Forfeiture in the late summer of that year. The abstract of these sales, prepared by the Commissioners, notes that the properties so sold became "forfeited to the people of this state by the attainder of Parker Wickham."[17]

Parker Wickham, meanwhile, passed the last year and a half of his life at his Connecticut refuge. "The time Draws nigh that Abraham must Die that is the Case with us all, and I look for my Departure Daily," he writes in his letter of April 2, 1785. On the twenty-second of the following month, he died at the age of fifty-eight.

Wickham's children had not been attainted. In fact one of them, his daughter Parnel, had been spoken of as a reputed "friend" by the governor and Council of Safety of Connecticut, which in 1778 had acted on her behalf following an incident involving a stolen horse. Even so, despite whatever favorable opinion there may have been in Connecticut, neither

By the Commissioners of Forfeitures, for the Southern District of the state of New-York.

PUBLIC NOTICE is hereby given, that pursuant to a law of this state, entitled, "An act for the speedy sale of the confiscated and forfeited estates within this state, and for other purposes therein mentioned," the estates formerly belonging to the persons herein-after named, have been located on, and an application made for the appraisment of each of the said estates, respectively, viz.

Frederick Philipse, Edmund Ward, Robert Bayard, John Rapalje, Daniel Kissam, John Pell, Johannis Polhemus, David Colden, John Gidney, Griffen Corey, Benjamin Hunt, Roger Morris, Richard Floyd, Miles Oakly, Jeremiah Travis, Peter Drake, James Leonard, Christopher Billop, Joseph Gidney, Henry Lloyd, Joshua T. De St. Croix, Waldron Blauw, Thomas Jones, Joseph Ford, David Husted, Frederick Devoe, Archelaus Carpenter, Isaac Titus, George Cornwall, Nathan Whitney, Isaac Williams, George Muirson, Lewis Palmer, Gabriel Ludlow, Shubal Sniffen, Thomas Merrit, Adam Seaman, James Jauncey. Hugh and Alexander Wallace, William Axtel, John Bates, Israel Seaman, Solomon Fowler, Parker Wickham, George Foliot. Beverly Robinson, William Reed, George D. Ludlow, Shubal Brush, Gilbert Miller, Philip Jones, John Harris Cruger, Robert M'Ginnis, Benjamin Seaman, Thomas Barker, Dow Van Dine.——Therefore, every person who has any claim or mortgage on any of the estates, formerly belonging to either of the persons herein before mentioned, are notified and desired to exhibit the same without delay to the subscribers, Commissioners aforesaid, dated May 18, 1784. 86 4

ISAAC STOUTENBURGH, } Com'rs.
PHILIP CORTLANDT,

PUBLIC NOTICE in the *New York Packet,* May 20, 1784. *American Antiquarian Society.*

to Parnel nor to any of her brothers or sisters was the state of New York about to restore their father's property now that he was dead. Their blood had become corrupted under the doctrine of corruption of blood, so that they were incapable of inheriting despite the enjoinder in the state constitution which prohibited acts of attainder from working a corruption of blood. In any case, the River Head, Robins Island, and Wickham's Neck had all been sold the previous year by the Commissioners of Forfeiture. The deeds the purchasers received conveyed "all estate right title and interest" which had "become forfeited" to the state. But what exactly was the right and title that had become forfeited to the state? And what right and title did it sell? No doubt there were some who wondered.

In the Caribbean, Joseph Parker Wickham endeavored to support himself as an itinerant merchant for several years, sailing the trade routes between the islands of Antigua, Montserrat, St. Christopher, and the Carolinas. Then in 1788, while in North Carolina, he learned of the death of his father. He also found out at this time that British commissioners were inquiring into the losses of American loyalists for the purpose of dispensing compensation to those who had served the British cause. In October of that year he was in London presenting his case before the British commissioners. He submitted testimony about himself and his father, and included supporting documents as evidence. One of these was an affidavit by New York's Commissioner of Forfeiture, Isaac Stoutenburgh, attesting to the fact that Robins Island, among other parcels, had been sold "in Fee Simple by Indenture" on August 5, 1784. The British claims board heard Joseph's case, and in December 1789, awarded him 2,800 pounds sterling for property loss, less a deduction for a temporary allowance he had been given of 36 pounds per annum. The compensation for property loss was short by a little over 400 pounds (in the currency of that time) of the estimated value of his father's real estate. Personal property losses could not be claimed for reimbursement.[18]

There was nothing in the treaties between the United States and England that made it the British government's responsibility to compensate loyalists and refugees for property losses suffered under the new American state governments. Thus, the relief that England did provide was gratuitous and not obligatory in any contractual sense. The United States, of course, remained obligated by the treaties. Where, on the American side, a treaty infraction did occur, as in instances where property was confiscated in violation of article 6, it was the duty of the federal courts to provide restitution. There is no evidence in any of the treaty cases this author has seen to suggest that the court saw a link between the issue of restitution and what, if any, compensation the British had awarded the party claiming a loss.[19]

On October 6, 1790, Joseph writes from Dublin, Ireland: "I have recovered near one half my property and am as hearty as ever you saw me." And in the same letter he comments, "I never more expect to see my Native Country. In Short the sufferings of our Family have been so Great in it that I don't want to see it. I am a Single Man and the World is before me."[20]

But Joseph was to return to his native country. In 1791, two years after the federal Constitution had been adopted, he appears in Southold, Long Island. It wasn't the old North Fork he remembered eight years back. The homestead of his father was now occupied by Jared Landon, the town justice. And Robins Island no longer belonged to his family either. Half, later all, of it was owned by the state senator and former member of the Continental Congress, Ezra L'Hommedieu. In Southold, Joseph bought a farm and married. It was a second marriage for Joseph, for his first wife, Mary, had died in 1780 at the age of twenty. This son of Parker Wickham would die in 1806 and in his will would leave the farm and personal effects to his nephew, brothers, and sisters. (He had no children of his own.) As for that other property, the legacy that had been seemingly forfeited by the attainder of Parker Wickham, Joseph makes no mention of it in his will but still it was not forgotten.

Now, under the treaties, the heirs of Parker Wickham would have a legal claim to it, a claim that would not die.[21]

CHAPTER 10

A Right Conferred by Treaty

For the first time in Indian land claim litigation a federal court is asked to invalidate land purchases made by a state from Indian tribes prior to the adoption of the United States Constitution, allegedly in violation of the Articles of Confederation.

> *Oneida Indian Nation of N.Y. v. State of N.Y.*, 691 F. 2d 1070 (1982) 1073.

SEEMINGLY FORFEITED BY THE attainder of Parker Wickham, the ancient legacy of John Parker and Joseph Wickham Sr.—the River Head, Robins Island, and Wickham's Neck—was actually protected by treaty restrictions against confiscation. But that was in 1783.

Now, over 200 years later, could the legacy be claimed by Parker Wickham's surviving heirs, his descendants living today? Would their case stand up in court, or would it be quashed by state laws, statutes of limitations and adverse possession laws which would ordinarily bar a claim this old?

At the time of New York's confiscation and sale of estates in its southern district, which covered the five southern counties, treaties entered into by Congress were binding on the states and paramount to any conflicting acts on the part of their legislatures, just as they are today.[1] The United States Constitution, which in 1789 replaced the Articles of Confederation as this country's federal constitution, affirmed the supremacy of all treaties which would be, and which had been, made by the federal government. Article 6, clause 2, of the Constitution reads:

> This Constitution, and the laws of the United States which shall be made in pursuance thereof; *and all treaties made,* or which shall be made, under the authority of the United States, shall be the supreme law of the land; and the judges in every State shall be bound thereby, anything in the Constitution or laws of any State to the contrary notwithstanding.
>
> [Emphasis added.]

As it applied retrospectively, Article 6 was "to be considered in the same light as if the Constitution had been established before the making of the treaty of 1783," writes Justice Chase in *Ware* v. *Hylton*.[2] Furthermore, where a treaty and state law conflicted, judges in every state were to be bound by the treaty. This meant, of course, that judges were not to use state law to interpret treaties, but were to interpret treaties according to their true tenor and "according to the rules and maxims established by the laws of nations for the interpretation of treaties."[3] Law of nations—i.e., international law—would lead to a consideration of such questions as jurisdiction, the rights of war, and the state of things at the instant the treaty was made.[4]

The supremacy of treaties means not only that they are above state law but also that state law cannot subsequently be thrown up in the way of treaties to block their implementation. One attempt to do this occurred in 1794 when the state of Vermont enacted legislation granting property to New Haven. However, this property, which belonged to British wardens, was protected against confiscation by the Treaty of Peace with England. Ruling on the case in 1823, the Supreme Court states: "The above act was utterly void, being passed in contravention of the treaty of peace, which, in this respect, is to be considered as the supreme law."[5] Another attempt to impose state law constraints on the same treaty occurred in 1797 when the legislature of New York passed an act for limiting the time period for bringing claims against confiscated estates. The act was challenged in a case before the federal circuit court of New York in 1812. In that case, *Fisher* v. *Harnden,* the court found the 1797 statute of limitations to be inapplicable to claims either of the attainted party himself or of his heirs and assigns. The Fisher case was then appealed to the U.S. Supreme Court, which ruled on another issue altogether, letting stand as law the time bar findings of the circuit court. In yet another case, this one involving the question of a creditor's rights under the 1783 treaty, Chief Justice John Marshall asserts, "Whenever a right grows out of, or is protected by, a treaty, it is sanctioned against all the laws and judicial decisions of the states; and whoever may have this right, it is to be protected."[6]

Treaties, especially treaties of peace, must have a permanent character when stipulating about permanent or vested rights and territorial arrangements. Otherwise, as the high court puts it in *Society for the Propagation of the Gospel in Foreign Parts* v. *Town of New-Haven,* "even the treaty of 1783, so far as it fixed our limits, and acknowledged our independence, would be gone, and we should have had again to struggle for both upon original revolutionary principles."[7] Moreover, for a court to freely impose a state statute of limitations upon a treaty, blunting its implementation, would be to weaken the treaty-making powers of the executive and legislative branches of our federal government. It would violate a fundamental

U.S. BICENTENNIAL STAMP, issued 1983, shows American peace commissioners Benjamin Franklin, John Adams, and John Jay observing while British commissioner David Hartley signs treaty document. *Public Affairs Office, Postal Headquarters.* Photograph by Harvey Weber.

principle of our Constitution: separation of powers. Were that to happen, would any foreign government feel secure in concluding a permanent treaty with the United States? Or would it believe that a firm compliance on our part could be had only by making separate treaties with each of the fifty states, and with the Supreme Court as well?

These considerations aside, it should be pointed out that even when a treaty does end—by agreement between sovereigns, for example—"the termination of a treaty cannot devest rights of property already vested under it."[8]

The principle of the supremacy of federal treaties and federal law over and above state law defenses has been taken up in recent times in American Indian cases. Regarding the claim of the Narragansett tribe, a federal court writes in 1976, "The broad principle dictated by the Supremacy Clause of the United States Constitution and the sovereign immunity of the United States that state statutes cannot supersede federally created rights has been applied with especial vigor to the question of Indian title."[9] In an Oneida Indian suit, the violation of a federal act—the Nonintercourse Act—occurred in 1795 when a purchase of Indian land was made. But here as in similar cases the court ruled that the 1795 purchase, in violation of the federal act, "had no validity then nor does it today. New York's statute of limitations and the doctrine of laches, adverse possession, and bona fide purchaser cannot validate this transaction." "If a transfer of

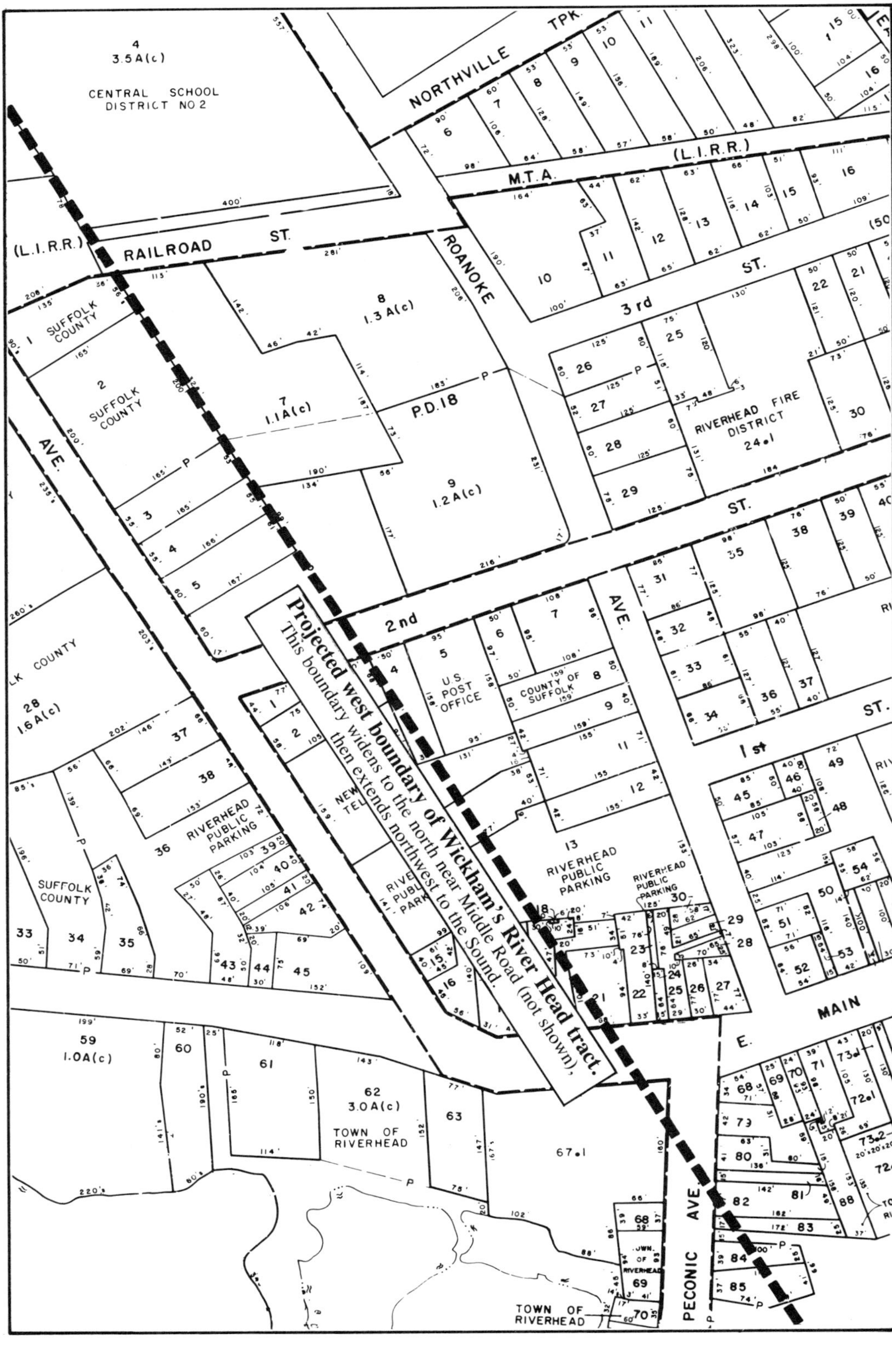

Projected west boundary of Wickham's River Head tract.
This boundary widens to the north near Middle Road (not shown), then extends northwest to the Sound.
CENTRAL SCHOOL DISTRICT NO 2
NORTHVILLE TPK.
M.T.A. (L.I.R.R.)
(L.I.R.R.) RAILROAD ST.
ROANOKE AVE.
3rd ST.
2nd ST.
1st ST.
E. MAIN
PECONIC AVE.
SUFFOLK COUNTY
P.D.18
RIVERHEAD FIRE DISTRICT
U.S. POST OFFICE
COUNTY OF SUFFOLK
RIVERHEAD PUBLIC PARKING
TOWN OF RIVERHEAD

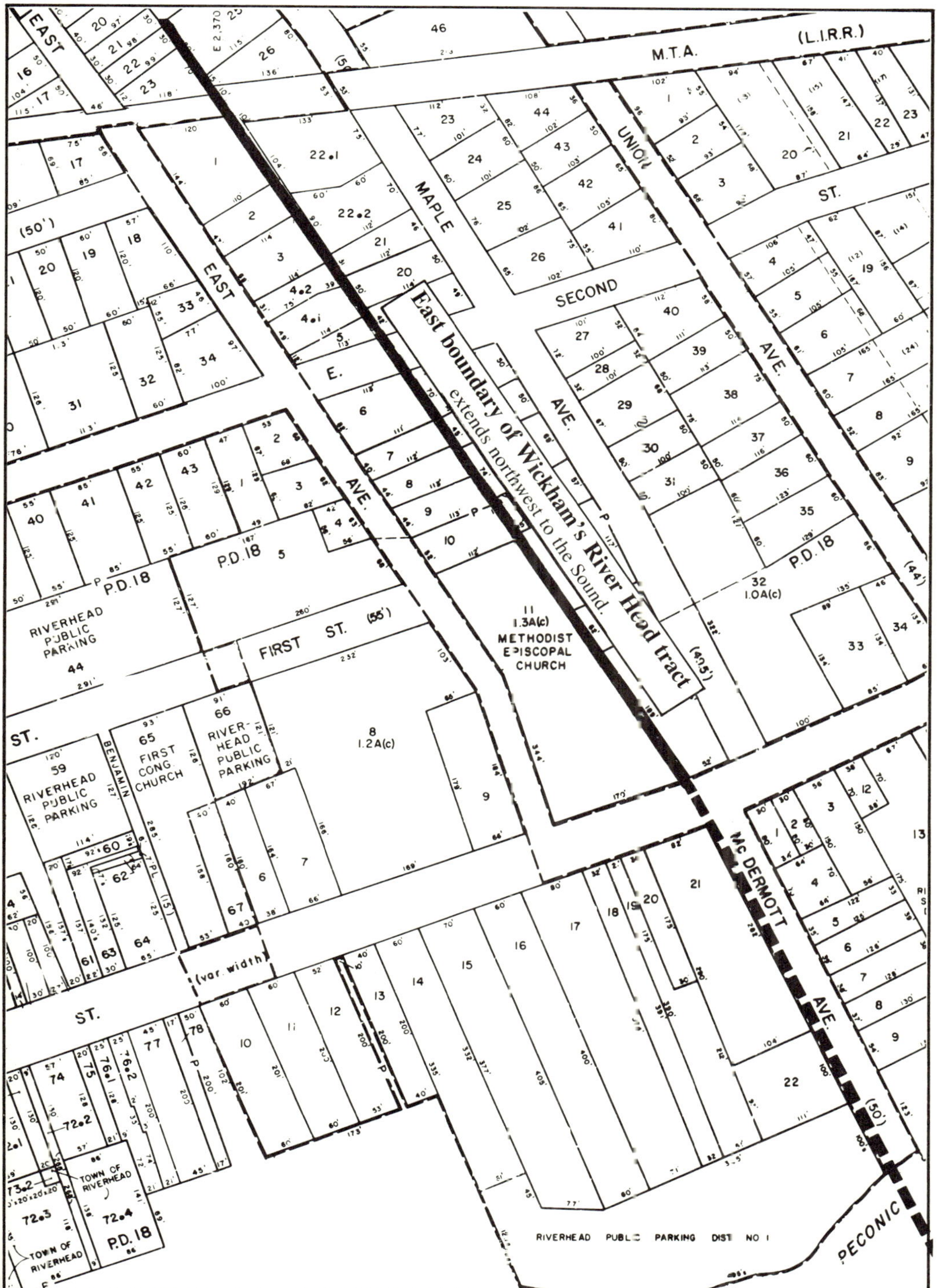

RIVERHEAD, L.I., PROPERTY MAP.
Sections 128-9, year 1981, with contours of the original Wickham property indicated by the author.
County of Suffolk, Real Property Tax Service Agency.

Indian land is void under federal law, see e.g., 25 U.S.C. Sec. 177, it cannot later be made valid by operation of state law." Citing cases which support its opinion, the court makes clear the principle they set forth: "These cases emphasize the supremacy of federal law, which forbade the transfers, over state statutes which would validate them after the fact."[10]

Federal treaties, like federal law and like the federal Constitution itself, are the supreme law of the land. No state law can override a treaty or violate its provisions, and any state law that attempted to do so would be unconstitutional. The convictions and confiscations under New York's Act of Attainder, insofar as they contravened the 1783 Treaty of Peace, were *coram non judice,* and absolutely void.[11] That and all subsequent state acts which come in the way of treaty-protected rights, including rights to property, must fall prostrate before them. The Wickham claim rests on such treaty-protected rights.

Today the house of John Parker, the man who in 1727 entailed the River Head and deeded it to the Wickham family, is still standing but it has changed. For one thing, it has been removed from the traffic circle on the Southampton side of Riverhead Village, and now lies east of the traffic circle on Route 27, behind the A.M.E. Church. The visitor has trouble seeing it at first until he walks around the church, stepping along an overgrown path into a vacant lot. Witnessing the house, the viewer is apt to think, "Obviously no one lives here," and then be left with a lingering incertitude. On either side of the ancient structure are signs of human habitation: an upended kitchen cabinet, a dog house, a discarded lounge chair, a picket fence buried in weeds. The house itself has indications of human occupancy, if not at present then in the not too distant past. An antenna perches on its roof. Telephone wires connect to the second floor. All but one of the windows have glass intact, the exception boarded up with a makeshift sign reading "FIX THIS NDOW." On the other hand, the general condition of the hovering edifice attests compellingly to utter abandonment. The porch lies half obliterated by an ungainly hedge growing, it seems, under, through, and in front of it. The roof eaves sag precariously. And under the eaves an improbable needle of light gleams through from the sky, evoking a sense of misgiving as one would feel looking at what one believed to be a person and then detecting a leak of light through some pore. Parker Wickham, were he here today, would probably not even recognize his grandfather's house.

To the right of the ancient structure, seen between overgrown brambles and leaves, flows the Peconic River, and on the opposite shore lies the village of Riverhead. What would the magistrate make of this tract of land he had known as the River Head? He would probably not even recognize it, anymore than his grandfather's house. The south end of his tract had become a village. He would gaze uncomprehendingly at the rear edifice of Sweezey's Department Store. The forest was gone. The gristmills were gone. The old court house, he would find, was gone too. The only thing left of that building was a placard on a wall where it once stood:

SITE OF
SUFFOLK COUNTY COURT HOUSE
1729–1855

Even the names had changed. The Country Road was now Main Street. Roan Oaks was now Roanoke Avenue. The River Head had become the village of Riverhead. Had everything changed?

Perhaps so. Perhaps everything has changed in the last 200 years, everything except one thing—the legal title to the River Head. That, given the evidence before us, remains as it was for centuries, one constant amid all the changes that on the surface would seem unrecognizable to Wickham. Astoundingly yet to this day, the ancient legacy of Parker and Wickham looms like the tomb of Tutankhamun, the claim of present or future generations, descendants of Parker Wickham.

[Note: In the winter of 1984–85, the house of John Parker was bought by Edmund Carpenter and removed to Further Lane, East Hampton.]

CHAPTER NOTES

CHAPTER 1

1. *Journals of the Continental Congress,* Vol. 1, pp. 82-3.
2. Letter of Parker Wickham to James Reeve Jr. [inside salutation: "Jemme and Parnal"], 30 March 1784. (J. Parker Wickham papers). The initials W^{m}‿F and E^{a}‿L stand for William Floyd and Ezra L'Hommedieu. The latter, a native of Southold, Long Island, was one of three state assemblymen of New York appointed to prepare the confiscation bill (*Assembly Journal,* October 15, 1778). Floyd was a Suffolk delegate to the Continental Congress and a signer of the Declaration of Independence. See L'Hommedieu's letter of February 9, 1779, to Floyd, *infra,* Chap. 8, n. 8.

   At the time of Wickham's letter in 1784, L'Hommedieu was Clerk of Suffolk County.
3. Suffolk County Clerk's Office, "Conveyances in Forfeiture, 1784". See also: New-York Historical Society, "Abstracts of Sales of Forfeited Lands in the Southern District upon Locations," p. 10.
4. By corruption of blood, they could not inherit from their attainted parent or through him to a more remote ancestor. Blackstone, Bk. 4, Chap. 29, p. 381; also Bk. 2 p. 252. Corruption of blood is discussed also by Joseph Story in his *Commentaries on the Constitution of the United States,* Vol. 2, Bk. 3, Chap. 28, sec. 1299, pp. 183–5. The prohibition against corruption of blood appears in the U.S. Constitution, Art. 3, Sec. 3. The concept is further discussed on p. 89 and *infra*, chapter 8, n. 3.
5. Laws of New York, 3 sess. Ch. 25. See Appendix II for full text of the Act. This kind of enactment was not unique to New York. During the Revolutionary period, almost all the states passed bills of attainder, as they are called. Bills of attainder are prohibited by the U.S. Constitution, Art. 1, Sec. 9.

   For discussion of bills of attainder, see *Calder* v. *Bull,* 3 Dall. (U.S.) (1798) at 389. Further discussed in: "The Constitutional Prohibition of Bills of Attainder: A Waning Guaranty of Judicial Trial," *Yale Law Journal* (63) 1954, p. 844. See also *supra,* Chap. 8.
6. J. Parker Wickham, Joan Silleck, and Margaret Tooker are the grandchildren of Charles W. Wickham, who in turn was the great-grandson of Parker Wickham. John Wickham and Henry Wickham are the grandsons of William Wickham, a former Suffolk County district attorney who was the great-grandson of Parker Wickham. The Case branch (including Nancy Marschean) derives from Hannah F. Case, the sister of William Wickham. Annie W. Beebe was the daughter of Hannah F. Case. Margaret Mullen is a descendant of Sarah Reeve, one of Parker Wickham's daughters.
7. *Oneida Indian Nation of N.Y.* v. *State of N.Y.,* 691 F. 2d 1070 (1982).

CHAPTER 2

1. Southold Town Records, Liber C, p. 37. The published abstract is in *Southold Town Records,* Vol. 2, p. 91, which mistakenly has "doctor" instead of "fuller". The deed was recorded on January 10, 1758, thirty-one years after it was signed.
2. Sources: 1) Paul Bailey, ed., *Long Island, A History of Two Great Counties: Nassau and Suffolk* (New York: Lewis Historical Publishing Co., Inc., 1949), Vol. 1, p. 195; 2) Virginia Wines, *West from Canoe Place* (Riverhead, N.Y.: Suffolk County Historical Society, 1979), p. 18. See also Riverhead title searcher J. Francis Maggee, "Fanning History on Tombstone," *Long Island Forum,* Vol. 9 (Dec., 1946), p. 241.

   The later title history of the River Head has been worked out in Holbrook's "Reconstructing the River Head". The early title history of this property is given in Muirson's testimony, Public Record Office, A.O. 13, Bundle 56/659 and in A.O. 12, 30/410-411. Transcripts of this record are found in the New York Public Library, MS Div., American Loyalists, Audit Office Transcripts, Vol. 46; and in Calendar of Original Memorials, Vol. 3. American loyalist papers in the Public Record Office are available on microfilm from Kraus-Thomson, Ltd.
3. John Parker did not use the term "River Head" or "River-head" to describe his property north of the Peconic River, but Parker Wickham (his grandson) did, according to "Corwin and Gardiner's Affidavit of the Value of Parker Wickham's Estate," April 19, 1786, Public Record Office, A.O. 13, 56/651-3. The name is used by the Commissioners of Forfeiture to describe, in one instance, the above property, and in another instance, the location of the above property. "Conveyances in Forfeiture," (leaf 2); "Abstracts of Sales of Forfeited Lands," p. 10.
4. New York County, Surrogate's Court, Record of Wills, 12/205.
5. The statute *De Donis* is found in Westm. 2, 13 Edw. 1, Chap. 1, sec. 2. In England, in the centuries that followed, there was some loosening of entailment restrictions. See further, Kent, *Commentaries on American Law,* Vol. 4, Lec. LIV, sec. 13, p. 12.
6. "Though it was in the power of the tenant in tail to bar them [i.e. the heirs] by a particular conveyance, that not being done, the court cannot take away a right, which they derive not from the tenant in tail, but from the original donor." Woodeson (1852 ed.), Vol. 3, p. 188. Hence, sheriff's grantee takes only an estate for life of the tenant in tail: *Hazzard* v. *Hazzard,* 29 Del. 94; 6 Boyce (1916). "The power of barring the entail was personal to the tenant in tail." *Borland* v. *Dean,* Fed. Cas. No. 1,660, at 908 [4 Mason, 174] (1826). See also *Hinchman, Denn* v. *Clark,* 1 N.J. Law (Coxe) 340 (1795) 360.

   New York State law abolished entails in 1782.

   The title of the tenant in tail is described as a "life estate" in *Hazzard* v. *Hazzard, supra,* at 94. But others describe it differently. "Something approaching an estate for life," according to T.F.T. Plucknett, *Legislation of Edward I,* p. 134. See also Aron, *Aron's Digest of New York Real Property Law,* p. 22.

   The distinction was drawn between a life estate and an estate tail in the case of William Pepperell, a Massachusetts loyalist whose property was confiscated under the "Act to confiscate the Estates of certain notorious

Conspirators. . . ." Massachusetts Acts and Laws, Chap. IX, April 30, 1779. Pepperell's son argued that his father had had only a life estate and that therefore the inheritance was protected from the state's confiscation act. The state court ruled otherwise, asserting that the father had held an estate tail, the whole of which had been comprised by the Massachusetts act. That act had declared forfeited all "Rights and Credits, Lands, Tenements and Hereditaments, of every Kind" belonging to the named conspirators, one of whom was William Pepperell. On Pepperell, see: New York Public Library, MS Div., American Loyalists, Audit Office Transcripts, Calendar of Original Memorials. . . , Vol. 2, p. 525 *et seq.*

7. Protection from forfeiture rested not on the principle, according to Foster, that the power to alienate and the power to forfeit went hand in hand, but on a "much stronger foundation, *viz.* upon the words of the act itself; 'The land shall *remain* to the issue. . . .' " Foster, *A Report of Some Proceedings on the Commission for the Trial of the Rebels in the Year 1746,* p. 99. Compare also Kent: "It is a rule of law, that the state, on taking lands by escheat, and even by forfeiture, takes the title which the party had, and none other. It is taken in the plight and extent by which he held it; and the estate of a remainderman is not destroyed or devested by the forfeiture of the particular estate." Kent, *Commentaries on American Law,* Vol. 4, Lec. LXVI, Sec. 427 (p. 474).

   In England, estates tail first became liable to forfeiture in the reign of Henry VIII. His enactment of 1535 declared what offenses would be classified as high treason. The act subjected perpetrators of such offenses to forfeiture of "all such landes, tenemetes, and hereditametes, which any such offender or offenders shall have of any estate of inheritance. . . ." 26 Hen. VIII Chap. 13. This act was adjudged to comprise, within its scope, both estates tail as well as estates in fee simple.

   During the American Revolution, the confiscatory enactments of the various states did not necessarily extend to the seizure of estates tail, as court decisions make clear. Compare, for example, the Pepperell ruling above (n. 6) with the decision in (1) *Hinchman, Denn* v. *Clark, supra,* 340, and (2) *Borland* v. *Dean, supra,* 908.

8. Robert Lowth, *The Life of William of Wykeham, Bishop of Winchester* (3d. ed.; Oxford, England: Clarendon Press, 1777), appendix no. II (p. ii).

9. Upon arriving in this country Wick took on a slightly new identity, possibly to escape detection by his creditors. The link between his old and new identities becomes apparent by taking two letters, both from the Wick papers, and comparing certain details of each.

   The first letter, actually a draft of a letter, is written by John Wickham of Southampton to his brother, whom we gather lives in Sodbury, England. In it we learn something of what the writer's ties are to the old world, matters there of concern to him.

Dr: Bror:

Yors: of Aprell 23d: 1703 & Desemr: 23d: 1708 Now Lyes before me & cannot but acknowled my thankes for Your love & truble in giving to my frindes & in p'tickuler ~~in giveing~~ me account of the tranceactions of Our family but am hartely glade to finde after all stormes in ye: family Is over ~~to finde~~ that a sunshine of peace appeare the wish I pray god Continiew amongs yee the Death of our ffather I rec from You ~~not~~ not withought Dew Effection also Brothr Thoms; but since wee grow fewer in Number lett us labour to grow more loveing. I am Verrey sorrey that You live so ought of the way of sea faireing men I woul now send three ore 4 times in a Yeare sum small adventuer If only to have oftenn acount of Your well fare I have had account that Cussn: Nickolas Hickes Is liveing & Driveing a trade in highstreat in Bristol I have writen to him but have no answer- If not give me adviz of sum othr man to Consine [consign] to in Bristow for the packett bote now Cumes onese Every Munth ore 2 & wee may heare from one & Other Very oftenn ~~I have good friends in New York~~ I left my place You know for Dept [debt]. pray give me account who of my Creditors. Is in Most want I will send ett according to Your Direction & in both of Your letters You give me account of sumthing wase given Unto Brother Thomas & his Male heires hee deying with Ought ~~Issew~~ sun I suppose ett to be mine but You never gave me account what ett wase only that ett wase given by Anthony Wickham pray searve me in giveing me a prtickuler account what ett Is & what ett may beworth P amn [per annum] I have now altred my mind in Cuming for England & have sent to London to have my Goods Returned to me that I had Remited in Order to my Vidge [voyage] for ~~I now live Much better with my Wife then I have & hope ett may Continew~~ am God bepraysed much better in health then I have bine for a Yeare or too past I suppose my sicknes did much arrise from a discontented sperett the wich I shall God inableing me indever to prevent in Not giveing way to Ett as I have dun but I am not withought strone hopes of seeing Sodbury againe I have God Know my harte a greate Desire to see Your face & the faces of those few of my Brothers & Sisters that Is now Left & the seade of those Desesed I rest and am as In Deuty bounde Your Effectionate Brother Whiles I am

John Wickham

John Wickham speaks of something left by Anthony Wickham, an inheritance which John is anxious to know more about. Note also the reference to Cousin Nickolas Hickes of Bristol. John has written to him but has not yet received a reply. Let us turn now to our second letter, the Hickes letter. It is addressed to John Wick and was written the same year as the first letter, 1711.

Hickes begins his letter by discussing whale-bone cargo that Wick has consigned to him. The Bristol merchant then takes up another subject:

I am a stranger at Sodbury have Enquired of Severall of the town about Anthony Wick ___' will but can not get information to my full Satisfaction. will employ Mr. [?] Bircomb in that affair as soon as have opportunity, am glad to hear from you & of your prosperity; the packet is this minute going to be seald Bloine [Blowing?] well [?]

ye affect Kin:
& Servt

Bristoll 5/Xen [eleven?] 1711 N. Hickes

verso: To Mr John Wick
Paid IN
To be left with Capt. Robt.
Walter at New York

The Anthony Wick___ is obviously Anthony Wickham, N. Hickes is Nicholas Hickes, and with these pieces of the puzzle fitting together, the final piece drops in place: John Wick is John Wickham. The identity of Wick with Wickham explains why various Wickham letters are found in the Wick papers. It also explains why genealogists have had trouble tracing back the family origins of John Wick. They've been searching after the wrong surname.

A little about Wick's family back in Sodbury can be sifted from records. The names of his brothers and sisters—Henry, James, Daniel, William, Edith, Margaret—nearly match those that Wick would give the rest of his own children after his first son Job. Wick gets a letter from his father, one that we know of, telling of those in the family that have died, and then his father dies in 1706. In his will John Wickham Sr. leaves a guinea of gold to Daniell and John, "my best drawing table" and two guineas of gold to William, assorted other items to grandchildren.

Sources: 1) "Letter of John Wickham of Southampton," *American Genealogist,* Vol. 33 (1957-8), pp. 190–1; 2) The New York Public Library, Wick-Blachly-Colles Papers (MSS), Box 1, F 2.

The will of John Wickham Sr. is in the Gloucestershire, England, Records Office ("Wills Proved in the Consistory Court of the Bishop of Gloucester"), 1706/146. The original of his letter has not been located. A typed transcript is at the Morristown, N.J., Public Library, folder "Wick (Wickes, Wickham, Weekes, Week)" H/VF/G. Date of letter (the year) is not shown.

10. The story is quoted in James T. Adams, *Memorials of Old Bridgehampton,* (Bridgehampton, L.I.: By the author, 1916), pp. 97-8.
11. New York County, Surrogate's Office, Record of Wills, 9/74 (old liber p. 64).

CHAPTER 3

1. "Memorandum," unsigned, undated; (Parker Wickham papers). The Williams and Morris patent is found in New York State Archives, Patents II, 1731-39, Series 450, No. 16, pp. 134–7. "Patent to Charles Williams and Frederick Morris," April 1, 1734. See also: Land Papers, Vol. II, pp. 53, 76, 82.

2. Joshua Hempstead, *Diary of Joshua Hempstead of New London, Connecticut, 1711-1758* ("Collections of the New London County Historical Society," Vol. 1; New London, Conn.: New London County Historical Society, 1901), pp. 397–8, 516.
3. New York Public Library, Wick-Blachly-Colles Papers (MSS), Box 1, f 2. The line after Wick's surname is in the original.

   References to the Antigua Wickhams are found in Vere L. Oliver, *The History of the Island of Antigua* (London: Mitchell and Hughes, 1896), Vol. 1, p. xciii; Vol. 3, pp. 228, 304. The gentleman-planter class is described in R.B. Sheridan, "The Rise of a Colonial Gentry: A Case Study of Antigua, 1730–1775," *Economic History Review,* Ser. 2, 13, no. 3 (1961), p. 347.
4. Great Britain, Public Record Office, *Calendar of State Papers, Colonial Series, America and the West Indies, 1708-9,* Vol. 24, p. 293, *487 ii. The details of the uprising are taken from George French, *The History of Col. Parke's Administration* (London: London and Westminster, 1717), p. 189. Presenting a partisan viewpoint, the book is nevertheless a surviving eyewitness account of events occurring on the island during this period.
5. *Letter Book of John Watts of New York, 1762-1765* ("Collections of the New-York Historical Society," LXI; New York: Printed for the Society by J.J. Little and Ives Co., 1928), pp. 166, 358–60, 362–3.
6. Document D70.1904, Sterling Historical Society, Orient, Long Island. Parker's commissioner assignment appears in Edmund B. O'Callaghan, *Calendar of New York Colonial Commissions, 1680-1770* ("John Divine Jones Fund Series of Histories and Memoirs," Vol. 7; New York: New-York Historical Society, 1929), p. 62.
7. Undated letter of Parker Wickham (J. Parker Wickham papers).
8. Suffolk County Clerk's Office, Common Pleas Minutes.
9. *Public Papers of George Clinton,* Vol. 2, p. 609. Wickham's record as supervisor is in *Southold Town Records,* Liber D (Part 3), pp. 246–260.

CHAPTER 4

1. William's lineage is confirmed by two pieces of evidence linking him to Joseph Wickham of Southold. First, the marriage of his father (William Sr.) to Ann Miller appears in the *Salmon Records,* which lists Southold marriages of that time. Second, there is a deed known as a "common recovery" at the Goshen library. It gives the name of the younger William Wickham and describes the lands on Robins Island Neck, Cutchogue, Long Island, which Joseph Sr. in his will had devised to the elder William.
2. William Wickham, "Supream Court Register," Vol. 2, p. 195; Vol. 3, p. 91 (Columbia University Law Library, N.Y.). *Fanning* v. *Landon* appears in Vol. 2, p. 57.
3. Moot Club Minutes, New-York Historical Society, N.Y., (MS), p. 1.

   William Wickham appears in the list of "Non-signers, or such as refuse to sign" the Association (patriotic loyalty oath) at Goshen, N.Y. Peter Force, *American Archives* (Washington, D.C.: By M. St. Clair Clarke and Peter Force, under an act of Congress, 1843), Series 4, Vol. 3, p. 591.
4. Worthington C. Ford, ed., *Wills of George Washington and His Immediate Ancestors* (Brooklyn, N.Y.: Historical Printing Club, 1891), pp. 54, 76. The quotation is from Moot Club Minutes, p. 6.

CHAPTER 5

1. Peter Force, ed., *American Archives* (Washington, D.C.: By M. St. Clair Clarke and Peter Force, under an act of Congress, 1837-1846), 4th Series, Vol. 1, pp. 297-8. A facsimile of Isaac Low's "Letter to Massachusetts Colony by the New York Colony" is in the New-York Historical Society.
2. Franklin Burdge, *A Second Memorial of Henry Wisner* (New York: Privately printed, 1898), p. 14. The source of Burdge's information on the number in attendance is not given. Perhaps he gathered it from the size of Stephen Slot's house, where the meeting was held. The house, located in the town of Sloatsburg, is still standing. The original letter of certification, reporting the fact that Wisner and Haring had been chosen delegates at "a general meeting of all the Committees of the County of Orange assembled at the House of Stephen Slot," is at the Goshen library.
3. Letter from Isaac Low, Sept. 6, 1774, Goshen Public Library, Goshen, N.Y. (02-00166) The second letter is also at the library.
4. Memorial of Isaac Low, New York Public Library, American Loyalists, Audit Office Transcripts, Vol. 43 (New York Claimants), p. 140.
5. *Journals of the Continental Congress*, Vol. 1, pp. 75–80.
6. New York State, Legislature, *Journals of the Provincial Congress . . . 1775-1777* (Albany: Printed by T. Weed, 1842), Vol. 1, p. 18 (May 29, 1775).

   Suffolk County, compared with other counties in the province, appears to have taken a lead in committee organization. We gather this in a letter of Cadwallader Colden, the lieutenant governor of New York, writing to the Earl of Dartmouth on August 2, 1774:

   > Great pains have been taken in the several Counties of this Province, to induce the People to enter into Resolves; and to send Committees to join the City Committee; but they have only prevailed in Suffolk County, in the East End of Long Island, which was settled from Connecticut, and the inhabitants still retain a great similarity of manners and sentiments.
   >
   > E.B. O'Callaghan, ed., *Documents Relative to the Colonial History of the State of New York* (Albany: Weed, Parsons and Co., 1857), Vol. 8, p. 486.

7. The Westchester declaration of loyalty to the king appears in Kenneth Scott, comp., *Rivington's New-York Newspaper, Excerpts from a Loyalist Press, 1773-1783* (New York: New-York Historical Society, 1973), pp. 110-112.

   Colonel Herd's incursion into Richmond County is discussed in the *Journals of the Provincial Congress*, Vol. 1, p. 310 (Feb. 17, 1776). The incursion into Queens and the compulsory oaths that followed are described in a letter, *American Archives*, Series 4, Vol. 4, p. 858. The names of the oath-takers are given on that page. There was, besides this, a small Queens Association of seventeen names. But like the other, it is dated 1776, not 1775. In: New York State, Secretary of State, *Calendar of Historical Manuscripts Relating to the War of the Revolution, in the Office of the Secretary of State*, Albany, N.Y. (Albany: Weed, Parsons & Co., printers, 1868), Vol. 1, p. 209.

The 1775 associations from throughout the province appear in the above source and in *American Archives,* Series 4, Vol. 3, pp. 581–620. In neither source is found a patriotic association for that time period from Queens, Richmond, Kings, or Westchester.

8. The Southold (militia) Association is found in *Calendar of Historical Manuscripts,* Vol. 1, p. 61. A scattering of additional Southold names appears in a "County Hall" list on p. 59 and elsewhere. The Southold Association described above also appears, in slightly varied format, in *American Archives,* Series 4, Vol. 3, pp. 616, 618.

   One of the few—perhaps only—loyalist subscriptions from Suffolk County at this time was initiated by Benjamin Floyd, said to have obtained the signatures of 100 men in the first company of that township. Mentioned in Hugh Gaine's *New York Weekly Mercury,* February 6, 1775, [p. 3]. No signatures are shown. Also in *American Archives,* Series 4, Vol. 2, pp. 117–118. Floyd spoke out strongly on behalf of Brookhaven opposition to having that town represented in the County Committee of Observation. See his letter to Rivington, *American Archives,* Series 4, Vol. 2, pp. 36–7.
9. Taken from Hamilton: "The idea indeed of citizens transforming themselves into aliens, by taking part against the state, to which they belong, is altogether of new invention, unknown and inadmissible in law, and contrary to the nature of the social compact. (His "Second Letter from Phocion," April 1784, *The Papers of Alexander Hamilton,* Vol. 3, p. 534).

   However, the context in Hamilton is completely different. He is arguing that the people in New York's southern district were not aliens during the Revolution but citizens of the state of New York.
10. Editorial entitled "To the Printers of the Massachusetts Gazette," *American Archives,* Series 4, Vol. 2, p. 106.
11. "To the Inhabitants of the Province of Quebec," October 26, 1774. In *Journals of the Continental Congress,* Vol. 1, pp. 105–110.
12. "To the Americans," Suffolk County, February 4, 1775. In *American Archives,* Series 4, Vol. 1, p. 1212. Political editorials at this time were customarily left unsigned or given a pseudonym.
13. "A Fragment (8 pp.) of the Proceedings of the Old Committee of Safety of the Town of Brookhaven, Manor of St. George and Patentship of Moriches . . . 1775," Manuscript Division, New York Public Library. Typed transcript of the missing portion, which was published in Holt's newspaper, is also in the library, along with a photostat of the 1776 "Brookhaven, L.I., Committee of Safety, etc., Minutes." A copy of the latter is also in the Pennypacker Collection, East Hampton Library, Long Island, N.Y. The location of the original is uncertain.
14. The Brookhaven letter is in *Journals of the Provincial Congress,* ("Correspondence of the Provincial Congress"), Vol. 2, p. 75. The congress's consequent resolutions are in the *Journals,* Vol. 1, p. 131.

   Thomas Fanning, whose confrontation with the Committee of Safety shows him to have been an adamant opponent of their cause, nevertheless appears to have changed his position from an earlier sympathy to the patriotic cause. Described further in Chester G. Osborne, "Thomas Fanning of Bellport," *Long Island Forum,* May 1966, p. 50.

15. The Floyd-Fanning sources are: 1) Thomas Floyd-Jones, *Thomas Jones and His Descendants* (New York: [the J. Grant Senia Press], 1906), pp. 53, 55. 2) on Floyd: William S. Pelletreau and John H. Brown, eds., *American Families of Historic Lineage* ("Long Island Edition;" New York: National Americana Society, n.d.), Vol. 1, pp. 105–6. 3) wills of various members of the Floyd family. 4) Walter F. Brooks, *History of the Fanning Family* (Worcester, Mass.: Privately printed, 1905), Vol. 1, pp. 103, 105, 135–9, 144–5; Vol. 2, pp. 651–2. Another Fanning son, William (b. 1728) was ordained in England into the Anglican ministry in 1754.
16. Ewald Gustav Schaukirk, *Occupation of New York City by the British* (New York: New York Times and Arno Press, c. 1969), p. 2.

    [Rev. John Vardill] to [William Eden]; letter contains reference to Edmund Fanning. In Benjamin F. Stevens, comp., *B.F. Stevens's Facsimiles of Manuscripts in European Archives Relating to America, 1773-1783* (Reprint ed.; Wilmington, Del.: Mellifont Press, [1970]), Vol. 4, #438.
17. *Documents Relative to the Colonial History of the State of New York,* Vol. 8, p. 589.
18. *Journals of the Continental Congress,* Vol. 3, p. 280. In the debates on this resolution the previous day, the motion had been made to apprehend Governor Tryon (p. 483).

    Delancey's departure is recounted in his memorial, New York Public Library, American Loyalists, Audit Office Transcripts, Vol. 41, p. 269.
19. Letter dated Dec. 24, 1775, in *John Jay, the Making of a Revolutionary, Unpublished Papers 1745-1780,* ed. Richard B. Morris (New York: Harper & Row, c. 1975), Vol. 1, p. 214.

    On December 21 the Provincial Congress had resolved that the inhabitants of Richmond County were guilty of a breach of the General Association, although in fact there is no report of the inhabitants having subscribed to any such association until February. Persons in Queens County who had prevented the election of delegates to the Provincial Congress were likewise said to be guilty of a breach of the General Association, although again an attempt at an association in Queens is not recorded until the next year. That same day, December 21, the congress sent a letter to New York's delegates in the Continental Congress advising that the latter body was free to deal further with the "delinquents" in Queens and Richmond, adopting any of its own action deemed necessary. *Journals of the Provincial Congress,* Vol. 1, p. 230.
20. *Documents Relative to the Colonial History of the State of New York,* Vol. 8, p. 663. According to the *Journals of the Provincial Congress* (Vol. 1, p. 289), Col. Herd's request to be discharged of the prisoners in his charge was received on February 10, at which time the Provincial Congress decided that the prisoners were to be each confined to a house of their choice in New York City, and kept under guard at their own expense
21. *Journals of the Provincial Congress,* Vol. 1, p. 277 (entered Feb. 1, 1776).
22. *American Archives,* Series 4, Vol. 6, pp. 1368–1370. Lists of particular persons wanted for questioning at that time are entered in the *Journals.* The names are grouped by county and every county from the southern district is represented except Suffolk County. Apparently at that time no one from Suffolk County was considered by the congress sufficiently dan-

gerous or threatening to the American cause to require being put on the summons list.

23. William Smith, *Historical Memoirs from 16 March 1763 to 25 July 1778 of William Smith,* ed. William H.W. Sabine (New York: New York Times and Arno Press, 1956), Vol. 1, p. 282.

    The information on David Mathews is taken from his memorial, New York Public Library, American Loyalists, Audit Office Transcripts, Vol. 41, p. 472 (transcript of original in Public Record Office). Mathew's attempt to seize Washington was of course matched by plentiful exertions of this kind on the other side. The Continental Congress had ordered committees of safety to seize "dangerous" persons. On January 30, 1776, Washington's instructions to General Lee had been to disarm the Tories and seize those most active in opposition. "And happy should I be if the Governour could be one of them." *American Archives,* Series 4, Vol. 4, p. 895.

24. "Diary of Colonel Josiah Smith, from July 23 to September 7, 1776," (typescript) Long Island Historical Society, Brooklyn, N.Y. (unpaged). ("Copied from the original in possession of Mr. Conlin Havens, East Moriches, Long Island, and contributed to the MAGAZINE by Mr. W.T. Avery.")

CHAPTER 6

1. Ludlow's memorial, New York Public Library, American Loyalists, Audit Office Transcripts, Vol. 41, p. 505. (Transcript of original in Public Record Office).

    In Suffolk County, minutes of the Court of Common Pleas continued until March of 1775, and so with the Court of General Sessions. Another court at Middle Island shows by its records that it remained in session until March of 1776. "Middle Island, Court Records" (MS), Long Island Historical Society.

2. *Jackson* v. *White,* 20 Johns. Rep. 313 (N.Y.) (1822), at 323. Implicitly, the court was recognizing that the state's sovereignty (or power of law) depended not on the Declaration of Independence but on the state's ability to function under an organized government, make laws and execute them. See also: *Respublica* v. *Chapman,* 1 Dall. (U.S.) 53 (1781) 57.

    The allegiance resolution of New York State is found in *Journals of the Provincial Congress,* Vol. 1, p. 527. This resolution and the restricted nature of New York State's jurisdiction are further discussed in *Inglis* v. *Trustees of the Sailor's Snug Harbour,* 3 Peters (28 U.S.) 99 (1830) 125, 167.

3. Harold C. Syrett, ed., *The Papers of Alexander Hamilton* (New York: Columbia University Press, 1962), Vol. 3, pp. 132, 141.

4. E.B. O'Callaghan, ed., *Documents Relative to the Colonial History of the State of New York* (Albany: Weed, Parsons and Co., 1857), Vol. 8, p. 681.

5. Peter Force, ed., *American Archives* (Washington, D.C.: By M. St. Clair Clarke and Peter Force, under an act of Congress, 1837-1846), Series 5, Vol. 1, pp. 1544, 1549. The August 28 letter is cut off in the published *Journals of the Provincial Congress* (Vol. 2, "Correspondence," p. 274). For a study of Nathaniel Woodhull's actions at this critical point in the

Revolution, see William H.W. Sabine, *Murder, 1776 and Washington's Policy of Silence* (New York: Theo Gaus' Sons, Inc., 1973), p. 162 *et al.*

6. *Journals of the Provincial Congress,* Vol. 1, p. 603.
7. Erskine's proclamation is in *American Archives,* Series 5, Vol 1, p. 1211; the report and Ogden communication are in *Journals of the Provincial Congress,* Vol. 1, p. 617 (Sept. 9, 1776); the Suffolk County Committee letter is in *American Archives,* p. 1261. Trumbull speaks of the "surprising conduct" in his letter to Livingston, responding to the intelligence Livingston has given him, in *American Archives,* Series 5, Vol. 2, p. 266.
8. Gardiner's letter is in *American Archives,* Series 5, Vol. 2, p. 225. Following Gardiner's letter is a short note by Samuel Buell, East Hampton's Presbyterian minister, indicating his acquiescence to the trustees' request and subscribing his name as one of the petitioners.

   The intelligence conveyed by Col. Livingston is on the same page.
9. *American Archives,* Series 5, Vol. 2, p. 252.
10. *Ibid.,* p. 252, 1042
11. *Ibid.,* p. 257.
12. *Ibid.,* p. 295.
13. *Ibid.,* p. 935.
14. Syrett, Vol. 3, p. 547.
15. Alfred B. Street, *The Council of Revision of the State of New York* (Albany: William Gould, 1859), p. 254.
16. The letter from Tryon to Germain is in *American Archives,* Series 5, Vol. 3, pp. 892–3. The committee declarations appear in Series 5, Vol. 2, p. 1219, and in the *New-York Gazette and Weekly Mercury,* Nov. 11, 1776, p. 1. The published Southold declaration is similar to the others and virtually identical to the model provided in Tryon's instructions. However, the transcript of Southold's declaration found in the Public Record Office, London, has certain variations from the text published in the gazette.

Published Text	Transcript (C.O.5/1107.f414 verso)
We, the Committee of Southold, in the County of Suffolk, being thoroughly convinced of the injurious and criminal tendency of our former meetings and resolutions, and willing to manifest our hearty disapprobation of all such illegal measures, do hereby dissolve this Committee, and [as far as in us lies] renounce and disavow [revoke and disannul all former orders and] resolutions of all Committees and congresses [whatsoever] as being undutiful to our lawful Sovereign, repugnant to the principles of the British Constitution, and ruinous in the extreme to the	We the Subscribers, being part of the Committee of the Township of Southhold in the County of Suffolk, being thoroughly convinced of the Injurious Tendency of our former meetings and Resolutions, and willing to manifest our hearty disapprobation of all such Illegal Measures, do hereby Dissolve ourselves from this Committee, and as far as in us lies, Revoke all former Orders and Resolutions of this Committee, and Renounce the Orders and Resolutions of all other Committees and Congresses whatsoever, as being undutifull to our Lawful Sovereign,

happiness and prosperity of this country.

Barnabas Terrel
James Young
Daniel Wells

[] = *American Archives* version

repugnant to the Principles of the British Constitution and Ruinous to the Happiness and prosperity of this Country.

We beg the favor of Major Richard Floyd and Mr. Thos. Fanning to communicate this our Declaration, to His Excellency Governor Tryon.

Southhold 25th October 1776

Barnabas Terrel
James Young
Daniel Wells

Appearing in the same newspaper on December 16 was a published declaration from Kings County, "the Members of the Provincial Congress of New-York, the County Committees, and the respective Committees of the different Townships, elected for and by the Inhabitants of Kings County." The signers, whose names were listed, asserted the dissolution of their organizations, rejecting and disclaiming all power of congresses and committees, etc. It was Kings County to which, on August 10, 1776, a committee of the Provincial Congress had been instructed to proceed in order to determine if a report were true that the inhabitants of the county had determined not to oppose the enemy. The congress resolved that if the report were well founded, the committee was empowered to disarm and secure the disaffected inhabitants, remove or destroy the stock of grain, and if necessary "lay the whole county waste." Military assistance would be provided if needed. (*Journals of the Provincial Congress,* Vol. 1, pp. 567-8).

17. The quotation from Serle is in Benjamin F. Stevens, comp., *B.F. Stevens's Facsimiles of Manuscripts in European Archives Relating to America, 1773-1783* ("Reprinted from the edition of 1898, London;" Wilmington, Del.: Mellifont Press, [1970]), Vol. 24, *2057.
18. *Journals of the Provincial Congress,* Vol. 1, p. 754.
19. Chester Osborne, "Thomas Fanning of Bellport," *Long Island Forum,* May 1966, p. 89.
20. American Loyalists, Audit Office Transcripts (12), "Examinations in London," Vol. 41, Bk. i, pp. 471–2 (New York Public Library); and for Suffolk County, *Ibid.,* "Examinations/Nova Scotia/New York," Vol. 17, p. 497 (Richard Floyd's memorial).

    See also Tryon's letter to Lord George Germain, in E.B. O'Callaghan, ed., *Documents Relative to the Colonial History of the State of New York,* Vol. 8, p. 693.
21. This petition is catalogued as the "Loyalist Declaration of Dependence" (MS) in the New-York Historical Society, and is described by R.W.G. Vail in the *New-York Historical Society Quarterly,* Vol. 31, no. 2 (April 1947), p. 68.

    The fragments are dated the "Twenty Eighth day of November in the Seventeenth Year of His [Majesty George III]", i.e. 1776.

A transcription of the Suffolk County names follows, with additional information supplied by the New York Revolutionary government's census of 1776 and the British census of 1778.

Explanation Key

Sthd. = Southold
Bkhn. = Brookhaven
Htgn. = Huntington
Sthpn. = Southampton

( ) = data supplied by 1778 British census and oath. (Public Record Office, C.O. 5/1109 [old America & West Indies 188]). Note that the ages given are as of 1778.

[ ] = data from the June 1776 census of the Revolutionary government.

Sthd., Bkhn. = the name on the petition could belong to someone by that name in one of these two towns.

Sthd. (2) = there are two people by that name in this town.

Transcription of the Names
with Information Supplied by Censuses

Name	Town	Age	Occupation
John Pain	Sthd. (2)		
David Tuthill	(Sthd.	16	farmer)
William Dickerson			
(William Dickinson	Sthd.	61	farmer)
Daniel Edwards	(Sthd.	35	farmer)
Isaac Wells	(Sthd.	32	carpenter)
James Petty	Sthd., Bkhn.		
Benjamin Pettey			
(Benjamin Petty	Bkhn.	22	carpenter)
Henry Hudson	Sthd., Sthpn.		
Isaac Reeve	(Sthd.	42	carpenter)
Silas Howell	(Sthd.	27	carpenter)
Samuel . . .			
Robert Hinchman	(Sthd.	42	innkeeper)
James Fanning	Sthpn. (2)		
Gurshum Edwards			
(Gershom Edwards	Sthd.	33	farmer)
Israel Robinson	(Bkhn.	56	farmer)
Job Davis			

(Continued on next page)

Name	Town	Age	Occupation
Gershom Brown	(Bkhn.	31	farmer)
John Homan Jr.			
(John Homan	Bkhn.	44	farmer)
Abel Swezey?			
(Abel Sweasey	Bkhn.	35	farmer)
Wesell Sells			
(Westle Sell	Bkhn.	32	farmer)
Nathaniel Brewster	(Bkhn.	33	farmer)
Wilmot Oakley			
(Wm. Oakley	Htgn.	33	merchant)
Isaiah Smith			
Jonathan Baker	[Bkhn.]		
James Morris	Bkhn., Islip		
William Morris	Smtn., Islip		
William Bigs?			
(William Biggs	Bkhn.	30	farmer)
Caleb Wood	Islip, Htgn.		
Obedreih Green			
(Obadiah Green	Islip	61	weaver)
Nathanal Smith	Smtn., Islip		
Jacob Dow	(Islip	39	farmer)
Israel Howell	Sthd., Islip		
James Smith	(Bkhn.	28	farmer)
Adonijah Underhill	[Islip]		
Henry Titus			
. . . Emmons			
Josiah Terry?			
Joseph Gavner?			
John Robinson	(Bkhn.	67	farmer)
Benjamin Emmons Jr.			
(Benjamin Emmons	Sthd.	43	farmer)
Nathaniel Petty	(Sthd.	27	farmer)
Benjamin Pain	Sthd. (2)		
John Case?	(Sthd.	27	joiner)
Joshua Case	(Sthd.	67	cordwainer)
Joseph Morrell			
John Petty			
William Reeve			
[William Reves	Bkhn.]		
Daniel Howell	(Sthd.	52	farmer)
Daniel Warner	(Sthd.	48	farmer)
Joshua Corwin			
(Jos. Corwin	Sthd.	19	farmer)
Henery Curwin			
(Henry Corwin	Sthd.	26	cooper)
John Woodhull Jur.	(Bkhn.	31	farmer)
T H . . .			

Name	Town	Age	Occupation
Mordecai Homan			
(Mordicah Homan	Bkhn.	20	farmer)
Robert Homan	(Bkhn.	34	farmer)
Jonathan Corwin?	(Sthd.	57	farmer)
David Howell	Bkhn., Sthpn.		
William Baker	(Bkhn.	32	farmer)
Caleb Newton	(Bkhn.	49	farmer)
James Bates	(Bkhn.	43	farmer)
Jonathan . . .			
Francs Brinto?			
(Francis Barto	Bkhn.	68	farmer)
Caleb Saxton	(Islip	28	blacksmith)
Thomas Smith	(Islip	28	farmer)
Platt Smith	(Islip	32	farmer)
Zebulon Sexton			
[Zebulon Saxton	Islip]		
William Smith	Smtn., Islip, Htgn., Bkhn.		
Whited Sexton			
(Whitehead Saxton	Htgn.	23	carpenter)
Jonathan Burch	[Islip]		
Israel Howell Jr.	(see Israel Howell)		
Nehemiah Heart Jr.?			
(Nathanial Hart	Sthd.	19	farmer)
Amos Willets Jr.			
(Amos Willis Jr.	Islip	21	tailor)
David Flynn?			
Richard H . . .			
(Richard Hudson?	Sthd.	53	joiner)
Thomas Overton	(Sthd.	38	farmer)
Peter Reeve	(Sthd.	37	farmer)
Samuel Edward?			
Moses Paine	(Sthd.	18	farmer)
Nathaniel Hudson	(Sthd.	17	farmer)
Thomas Reeve	(Sthd.	52	farmer)
William Peny Jr.			
(William Penny	Sthd.	40	farmer)
Daniel Youngs	Sthd., Sthpn.		
Mica Howell			
(Micah Howell	Sthd. (2)		
John Griffing Jr.			
(John Griffing	Sthd.	40	farmer)
Benjamin Edwards?	(Sthd.	39	mariner)
Nicholas Turril?			
(Nicholas Terrel	Bkhn.	30	farmer)
Jonathan Worth	(Bkhn.	32	farmer)
Selah Brown	(Bkhn.	44	farmer)
Zephanicah Conkling			

(Continued on next page)

Name	Town	Age	Occupation
(Zepheniah Conkling	Bkhn.	29	farmer)
Joseph Homan	(Bkhn.	20	farmer)
Henry Havens?	(Sthd.	20	farmer)
Nathaniel Havens			
Amos Addams?			
(Amos Adams	Bkhn.	36	farmer)
Jonah Hulse			
Brewster Terry?	(Bkhn.	42	farmer)
Ebenezer Bowen?			
(Ebenezer Bower	Islip	33	farmer)
Isaac Thompson?	[Islip]		
John Moubray			
(John Mowbray	Islip	58	farmer)
Anning Moubray			
(Anning Mowbray	Islip	27	farmer)
Samuel Moncy			
(Samuel Muncy	Htgn.	62	cordwainer)
Amos Willets			
Platt Willets	(Htgn.	20	farmer)
Henry Smith	(Bkhn.	18	farmer)
. . . French			
[James? French	Bkhn.]		
. . . Hedges			
John Wickham	(Sthd.	43	hatter)
William Downs			
(Wm. Downes	Sthd.	37	farmer)
William Petty	(Sthd.	23	farmer)
Nathon Tuthill			
(Nathaniel Tuthill	Sthd.	19	cordwainer)
James Reeve Jr.	(Sthd.	44	farmer)
James Downs			
(James Downes	Sthd.	38	farmer)
John Gardiner	(Sthd.	50	farmer)
Manle Wells			
(Manly Wells	Sthd.	32	farmer)
Obadiah Wells			
Daniel Shaw	(Sthd.	36	cordwainer)
Ambrose Horton			
Daniel Petty			
Joel Conkling	(Bkhn.	23	farmer)
Ezekiel Hedges	(Bkhn.	60	farmer)
Darel Havens?			
Isaiah Moger?	(Bkhn.	31	farmer)
William Bowen			
John Jones	(Htgn.	24	farmer)
Daniel Jones	Bkhn. (2)		
John Rider Jr.			
James Morris	[Islip]		
David Willets	(Islip	62	farmer)

Name	Town	Age	Occupation
John Akerly			
(John Akerley	Bkhn.	25	farmer)
John Hudson	(Islip	56	farmer)
William Hawkins	(Bkhn.	23	farmer)
Samuel Oakley	(Htgn.	44	farmer)
Jacob Willets	(Islip	34	farmer)
Selah . . .			
N . . . Williams			
John Oakes			
(John Oaks	Bkhn.	22	farmer)
Isaac Ketchm			
(Isaac Ketcham	Islip	43	farmer)
Samuel Wood			
Elipheld Chickatu?			
(Eliphilet Chichester	Htgn.	40	carpenter)
Nehemiah Roger			
. . . Gildersleeve?			
Platt Vail	(Htgn.	47	farmer)
Platt Keley			
(Platt Kelly	Htgn.	22	farmer)
Reuben Rolph			
Silas Platt			
(Selah Platt	Htgn.	34	cordwainer)
Richard Floyd	(Sthpn.	47	farmer)
Thomas Fanning	(Bkhn.	56	farmer)
Frederick Hudson	[Sthd.]		

CHAPTER 7

1. The particulars on the expeditions, Parson's and Webb's, are taken from 1) Parsons's letter to Washington, Dec. 29, 1777, in George Washington, Pres. U.S., *Goerge Washington Papers* ("Presidential Papers Microfilm"; Washington: Library of Congress, 1961), Ser. 4; 2) Parsons's deposition, Jan. 5, 1778, in U.S., Continental Congress, *Papers of the Continental Congress, 1774-1789* ("National Archives Microfilm Publications;" Washington: National Archives, 1958-9), M247, r54, i42, V.3, p. 367; 3) Webb's letter to Washington, Dec. 29, 1777, quoted in J. Watson Webb, *Reminiscences of Gen'l Samuel B. Webb* (New York: Globe Stationery & Printing Co., 1882), p. 6; and 4) various newspaper accounts.

   Upon learning of Webb's capture, Washington advised General Putnam that he has "ever been averse to these small excursions, especially when they divert our attention from more material Objects." *George Washington Papers,* Ser. 4, reel 46, (Dec. 27, 1777).
2. Journal of H.M. Sloop *Swan,* Captain James Ayscough; in London, Public Record Office, Admiralty 51/960, (1921).
3. See p. 38. It is not clear from Parsons's deposition what he was doing during the time Hart and the others were in Southold. His letter to Wash-

ington suggests that he was also at Southold Bay, but the deposition shows that he was not.

4. Washington's letter to Parsons on March 20, 1777, warns against plunderers descending upon the island, under the pretense of distressing the enemy, when their purpose was in fact to plunder the inhabitants without respect to Whig or Tory. John C. Fitzpatrick, ed., *The Writings of George Washington, 1745-1799* (Washington, D.C.: U.S.G.P.O., [1932]), Vol. 7, p. 306.

   The newspaper account is in the newspaper cited, Dec. 15, 1777. A later issue, this time of a Whig newspaper (*New London Gazette,* Jan. 9, 1778) contains a January news release stating that 150 Tories under the command of Col. Hewlett were in Southold, robbing "the honest inhabitants to a large amount."

   The practice of plundering the Long Island inhabitants is described by Parsons as "in a very flourishing state" in a letter to the Continental Congress on May 20, 1779. At that time the general sought a definitive answer on whether the practice was to be condoned among his officers. *Papers of the Continental Congress,* M247, r179, p. 335.

5. During Wickham's confinement in Connecticut there is no evidence of his having been charged with a crime. The New York State constitution is further discussed in the next chapter.

6. Parker Wickham's undated memorandum; (J. Parker Wickham papers).

   The British farm censuses, taken in Southold on January 16 and August 21, 1778, show Wickham's name on Cutchogue lists of both dates. But Wickham didn't have to be present for either in order for his name to appear. There was no oath tendered. The farm censuses are titled, "Suffolk County. Census: heads of families, stock, crops. 1778." New York State Archives, Andrew Elliot Papers, Box 4, Folder 12. Also in published form, though abridged, in Kenneth Scott, "Suffolk County, Long Island, New York, 1778 Census," *National Genealogical Society Quarterly,* Dec. 1975, pp. 276–282.

7. The anecdote is found in Henry Onderdonk, Jr., *Revolutionary Incidents of Suffolk and Kings Counties* (New York: Leavitt & Co., 1849), p. 76 (*666).

   The 1778 king's oath is cited as "A List of Persons in Suffolk County, on Long Island who took the following Oath of Allegiance and Peaceable behaviour before Governor Tryon 1778," London, Public Record Office, C.O. 5/1109, fos. 1-49d. A copy of this list is in the East Hampton Library, Long Island Collection.

8. Landon's letter of May 22, 1779, negative of the original at the historian's office, Town of Southold. The original has not been located. His letter of June 23, 1779, is given in Wayland Jefferson, *Cutchogue, Southold's First Colony* (New York: 1940), p. 95. The original of this letter has not been located.

CHAPTER 8

1. "The Memorial of Joseph Parker Wickham," London, Public Record Office, A.O. 12/30, p. 414. Transcript of the record is at the New York Public Library, MS Div., (American Loyalists, Audit Office Transcripts, Vol. 46).
2. Quoted from Daniel Webster in *Dartmouth College* v. *Woodward,* 4 Wheat. (U.S.) 581 (1819). See also *Black's Law Dictionary.*

Explaining the phrase as it appeared in the state constitution, Hamilton writes in 1784, "If we inquire what is meant by the law of the land, the best commentators will tell us, that it means due process of law; that is, by indictment or presentment of good and lawful men, and trial and conviction in consequence." Syrett, ed., *The Papers of Alexander Hamilton*, Vol. 3, p. 485.

The phrase has a long history. Magna Charta (Chap. 29): "No freeman shall be taken, or imprisoned, or disseized, or outlawed . . . unless by the judgment of his peers or the law of the land." See also Coke's interpretation in Zechariah Chafee, *Documents in Fundamental Human Rights* ("Preliminary ed.; [Cambridge]: Harvard University Press, 1951-2), Vol. 1, p. 247. Discussed further in Thomas M. Cooley, *The General Principles of Constitutional Law in the United States of America* (Boston: Little, Brown, & Co., 1880), pp. 222–4.

Further reference to article 13 of the state constitution is made by New York's Council of Revision, in its criticism of the pending attainder bill. See Street, *The Council of Revision of the State of New York*, p. 222.

3. See *Inglis* v. *Trustees of the Sailor's Snug Harbour* 3 Peters (28 U.S.) 99 (1830) 136.

   Corruption of blood is also discussed in (1) Blackstone, Bk. 4, Chap. 29, p. 381; Bk. 2, p. 252; (2) Wooddeson, Vol. 2 Lec. 36, p. 507; (3) Story, Commentaries on the Constitution of the United States. Vol. 2, Bk. 3, Chap. 28, Sec. 1299, pp. 183–5; (4) Kent, *Commentaries on American Law*, Vol. 4, "Of Title by Forfeiture," Lec. 66, Sec. 426.
4. Justice Brennan in *Plyler* v. *Doe*, 102 S. Ct. 2382 (1982) at 2396. See also *Wallach et al.* v. *Van Riswick*, 92 U.S. 210 (1875), where the high court discusses the prohibition against corruption of blood as stated in the federal Constitution.
5. Livingston's remark is contained in his letter to John Jay, dated April 21, 1779. Richard B. Morris, ed., *John Jay, the Making of a Revolutionary* (New York: Harper & Row, c. 1975), Vol. 1, p. 583.

   Jay's letter, with his quoted comment, is given in William Jay, *The Life of John Jay* (New York: J. & J. Harper, 1833), Vol. 1, p. 112. As William, Jay's son, noted, the Confiscation Act was unfortunately authentic. "Mr. Jay, in after-life, often spoke of it with strong indignation. He regarded the dispute with Britain as one in which men might conscientiously take opposite sides. . . ." (William Jay, p. 112).
6. This point was made by the state's Council of Revision in its opposition to an earlier version of the proposed bill. Street, *The Council of Revision of the State of New York*, p. 222.
7. Section XI of the Attainder Act distinguishes conviction under this Act from conviction for high treason according to the ordinary course of the law.

   Kent's comments are given in *Jackson* v. *Catlin*, 2 Johns. (N.Y.), 248 (1807) 260. Hamilton's notes on the Attainder Act are given in Goebel, ed., *The Law Practice of Alexander Hamilton*, Vol. 1, pp. 233–235. See also *Inglis* v. *Trustees of the Sailor's Snug Harbour*, 3 Peters (28 U.S.) 99 (1830) 167–8.
8. Blackstone, *Commentaries on the Laws of England*, Bk. 4, Chap. 29, p. 378.

The preliminary draft of New York's attainder bill was apparently intended as a high treason enactment. Assemblyman L'Hommedieu writes to William Floyd, Feb. 9, 1779:

> The Bill for confiscating the Estates of Persons inimical to these States, is now on the carpet, and I believe will at present, end in an Act of Attainder wherein a Number of Persons by Name being the Principal Tories in our Country, will be declared guilty of High Treason & their Estates confiscated. This is thought by Mr. Scot & others at present to be the most prudent & politick. They think the persons named will take in those that are objects, the others are open to the General Law of Treasons.
>
> MS letter, William Floyd Estate, Mastic Beach.

See also the objections of the senate dissentients to the Attainder bill. New York State, *Senate Journal*, March 9, 1779.

9. *Jackson* v. *Catlin*, 2 Johns. (N.Y.) 248 (1807) 260. The text of the Attainder Act is given in Appendix II. Though in a different context, "Estates, real" is similarly interpreted in *Inglis* v. *Trustees of the Sailor's Snug Harbour*, *supra*, 130.

   By way of contrast in phraseology, New York's Treasons and Felonies Act of 1788 speaks of forfeiting lands, not estates, and its wording is very close to Henry VIII's Treason Act of 1535.

10. The will of David Jones, which entailed his estate, also set up trustees to hold the residuary interests. I am indebted to Professor David Yale for pointing out that such a provision in a will is called a strict settlement.

    In another case involving entailment, Frederick Philips Jr. came to believe that his whole estate tail, not just his lifetime interest in it, had been entirely forfeited under New York State law. This may have been because *both* his father and he had been attainted by name under the Attainder Act. Furthermore, he points to a later state law as having confiscated the entirety of the estate, namely, the Act To Abolish Entails, passed on July 12, 1782. This law gave the grantee of a fee tail estate an enlarged fee simple interest, if the grantee had been in uninterrupted possession of the estate. As the Philips estate lay in the jurisdiction of New York State during the Revolution, it was probable that the state considered itself the grantee in possession of this property as a result of its Attainder Act and its territorial jurisdiction. Consequently, the Act To Abolish Entails would have given the state absolute ownership in fee simple, at least as Philips saw it. By contrast, Floyd-Jones's (and Wickham's) properties did not lie in the state's jurisdiction or possession during the Revolution. On Philips, see the transcript of his memorial, New York Public Library, MS Div., American Loyalist, Audit Office Transcripts, Vol. 41, pp. 604–613, 626–631, 639, 641–645.

    Cp. the Civil War confiscation case of *Day* v. *Micou*, 18 Wall. (U.S.) 156 (1873) at 158.

11. New York State, *Assembly Journal*, 13 Sess. (Feb. 5, 1790), p. 28. The pleadings of the case before the state supreme court are found in the New York County Clerk's Office, Hall of Records, *McFarren* v. *Ward*, Parchment Rolls 147 K8 (1786).

12. Goebel, ed., *The Law Practice of Alexander Hamilton,* Vol. 1, pp. 264–5, 263.
13. Syrett, ed., *The Papers of Alexander Hamilton,* Vol. 3, p. 490.

    Hamilton's view here is echoed by British complaints of American treaty violations. (1), *Journals of the Continental Congress,* Vol. 30, pp. 848–9, 851; (2), *American State Papers,* Vol. 1, Class 1, p. 195 (2d. 2.); p. 198 (the Act of New York, Oct. 22, 1779); p. 205, sec. 23; and p. 486, where Jay acknowledges the "forcefulness" of the British viewpoint.
14. Syrett, Vol. 3, p. 534. "An Act Declaratory of the Alienism of Persons Therein Described" was vetoed by the state's Council of Revision. The legislature did not override the veto. (Syrett, Vol. 3, p. 542 n.).
15. Goebel, Vol. 1, p. 411; also pp. 308, 324. And with regards to Suffolk County, p. 477.
16. In 1792 Secretary of State Thomas Jefferson presented the American government's position on confiscations, in answer to charges by England that American states had committed treaty violations. Although he cites Vattel and other then respected authorities on international law, his arguments totally avoid the question of territorial jurisdiction and whether British law prevailed over American law in territories the former was in possession of. His presumption was that all confiscations declared under a state attainder, and which predated the treaties, were able to take effect and be enforced before the time of the treaties. By contrast, Jay acknowledged the "forcefulness" of the British position on the jurisdictional question, raised in connection with freed slaves in the occupied city of New York. See above, n. 13 (2).

    There are actually two distinct issues here. One is what the Declaration of Independence did, by American law, in making the colonies sovereign and independent states. A sample of views on this point is found in: (1), Joseph Story, *Commentaries on the Constitution of the United States,* Vol. 1, Bk. 2, Chap. 1, *211,*215; (2), *M'Ilvane* v. *Coxe's Lessee,* 4 Cranch (8 U.S.) 209 (1808) 212; (3), *Johnson* v. *M'Intosh,* 8 Wheat. (21 U.S.) 543 (1823) 584; (4), *Respublica* v. *Chapman,* 1 Dall. (U.S.) 53 (1781) 57; (5), *Jackson* v. *White,* 20 Johns Rep. 313 (N.Y.) (1822) 323.

    The other issue is a very separate question of law concerning subsequent occupation of an enemy on American soil. *U.S.* v. *Rice,* 17 Wheat. (U.S.) 253 (1819) 254; *Inglis* v. *The Trustees of the Sailor's Snug Harbour,* 3 Peters (28 U.S.) 99 (1830) 125; and further sources below, n. 17. Jefferson failed to make the distinction between these two issues.
17. The quotations are from his *Commentaries on the Conflict of Laws,* *7, *8, *428; see also Chap. 2, *20; Chap. 14, (*539–540,*543. Story's jurisdictional tenet is echoed in Wheaton, Part 2, Chap. 2, *78; and in *Pennoyer* v. *Neff,* 95 U.S. 714 (1877) 722, among other places.

    The underlying principle, which is one of international law, is that exercise of sovereignty over a territory or property requires "the union of possession and the right to the territory which must concur to give *plenum dominium et utile.*" *Davis* v. *Police Jury of Concordia,* 9 How. (50 U.S.) 280 (1850) 289. See also (1), *The Fama,* Great Brit., High Court of Admiralty, 1804 (5 C. Rob. 106); (2), *U.S.* v. *Percheman,* 7 Pet. (32 U.S.) 51 (1833) 86. See further U.S. Secretary of War, Elihu Root, describing the circumstances of our country's limited sovereignty in Cuba in 1898.

U.S. War Department, *Reports on the Law of Civil Government in Territory Subject to Military Occupation by the Military Forces of the United States,* by Charles E. Magoon (Washington, D.C.: G.P.O., 1902), p. 602.

In its constitution of 1777, New York State adopted the common law of England. James Duane writes in his decision in *Rutgers* v. *Waddington:* "By our excellent constitution, the common law is declared to be part of the law of the land; and the *jus gentium* is a branch of the common law. *In republica maxime conservandi sut jura belli*, is an ancient adage." Goebel, Vol. 1, p. 402.

18. *Shanks* v. *Dupont,* 3 Pet. (28 U.S.) 242 (1830) 246.
19. *Inglis* v. *Trustees of the Sailor's Snug Harbour,* 3 Pet. (28 U.S.) 99 (1830) 167–8. He explains that the Act does not purport "to be an attainder of citizens of the state only, on account of their treason in adhering to the public enemies; for it embraces persons who never were, nor were pretended to be citizens."
20. By usual practice, the sentence of attainder was civil death—i.e., the offender no longer existed under the law nor had legal rights. The law considered him dead. Blackstone, Bk. 4, Chap. 29, p. 374; *Jackson* v. *Catlin,* 2 Johns. Rep. (N.Y.) 248 (1807) 262; *Platner* v. *Sherwood,* 6 Johns. Ch. (N.Y.) (1822) at 128. Cp. Hamilton: "When persons are to be considered as dead in law either by attainder or banishment, the sixth article [of the treaty] shall not operate restoratively to them, or remit any of the penalties of a sentence actually passed against them." Goebel, Vol. 1, p. 251.

However, the sentence of civil death under New York's Act of Attainder must be understood in the context in which it appeared. For one thing, civil death by New York's Attainder was severed from the collateral punishment of confiscation. This was so for two reasons. One, because of jurisdictional limitations, the state's Act was powerless to impose confiscation in the occupied zone during the period the British were there. Second, as the property of accused offenders in the occupied zone remained unconfiscated, the state could not withhold it from the offenders' heirs without committing corruption of blood, a practice which was barred by the state's constitution. See *Inglis v. Trustees of the Sailor's Snug Harbour, supra,* 136. Note also *Avery* v. *Everett,* 110 N.Y. 326 (1888):

> If civil death worked of itself a divestiture of his estate, either no entry would be necessary to complete the title of the crown by forfeiture, or the alternative result would follow, that the title would be in abeyance from the time of the attainder until entry by the king or lord, *for the heir could not take by reason of corruption of blood,* and the felon's title would be gone by his civil death. But we have not been able to find any case showing that, as a general rule, civil death modified in any respect the law of forfeiture, or deprived the attainted person of his lands before the forfeiture was enforced by entry.
>
> [Italics added].

Even without taking into consideration the jurisdictional question, civil death by attainder during the Revolution did not necessarily result in the confiscation of the offender's property. Examples are as follows. N.Y.:

The petition of Floyd-Jones, Laws of N.Y., 13 sess. Chs. 10, 11 (Feb. 20, 1790); N.J.: *Hinchman, Denn* v. *Clark,* 1 N.J. Law (Coxe) 360 (1795); Pa.: *Republica* v. *Gordan,* 1 Dall. (1 U.S.) 233 (1788); see also Mass.: *Borland* v. *Dean,* Fed. Cas. No. 1,660, p.908 [4 Mason, 174] (1826), where the offender had been deemed an alien.

21. *U.S.* v. *Rice,* 17 Wheat. (U.S.) 253 (1819) 254.

    A parallel situation occurred with respect to property in rebel-held territory during the Civil War, and on that subject a Massachusetts district court commented as follows in 1862: "Belligerent confiscations take effect only upon property of which possession is taken during the war. As against property which continues under the control of the enemy, they are wholly inoperative." *The Amy Warwick,* 1 Fed. Cas. No. 342 [2 Spr. 143; 24 Law Rep. 494] 808 (1862) 811.

22. See above, n. 20.

CHAPTER 9

1. Wines's will is in the Surrogate's Office, New York County, Record of Wills, L37/pp. 281–2. Suffolk wills of that time were generally probated under the occupation authorities if probated before the evacuation. One of the last to be done so was the will of Abraham Gardiner, signed August 18, 1782, and given the crown seal of the province of New York on March 5, 1783.

   Parker Wickham's power of attorney, Nov. 1, 1783, is in the Public Record Office, A.O. 13/Bundle 56, pp. 644–5.

   Abigail Wickham's date of death is given on her tombstone. Transcribed in Edward D. Harris, "Long Island Manuscripts," (bound manuscript), Vol. 3, p. 231, New York Genealogical and Biographical Society. However, the *Salmon Records* lists the date of her death as April 4, 1779.

2. Instructions from George Clinton to Egbert Benson, April 8, 1783, in U.S., Continental Congress, *Papers of the Continental Congress, 1774-89,* M247, r66, item 52, p. 173.

3. *Ibid.,* pp. 175–177. On Jan. 18, 1784, Benson and two others who were serving as American Commissioners of Embarkation wrote to Washington as follows:

   > Sir Guy Carleton, during the whole of the time from our arrival in this city until his departure on the 25th of November, exercised the same kind of jurisdiction in this city, and on Long Island, and Staten Island, and as fully as his predecessors in command had, at any period of the war.
   >
   > *Papers of the Continental Congress,* M40, r4, il20, V4, p. 336.

4. *Ibid.,* M247, r66, item 52, p. 179 (Clinton to Carleton); *Ibid.,* p. 181 (Carleton to Clinton).

5. Parker Wickham papers.

   Speaking of Congress, Hamilton writes to George Washington in 1783: "They have no right by the Confederation to *demand* funds, they can *only recommend.*" Syrett, Vol. 3, p. 307.

In 1782 Ezra L'Hommedieu, now a delegate to the Continental Congress, writes to John Taylor in Albany:

> I am now more induced to believe than ever I have been, that no restitution will ever be made of Tory property confiscated or sold. The Ministers from these States, as also the Court of France, have been so well informed of the insuperable obstacles and of the want of power in Congress, of the impractibility of their inforcing in the several States any such measures, that I have no expectation that such an Article will ever be agreed to, and if it should be, it never will be complied with by the different States.
>
> L'Hommedieu to Taylor, Oct. 9, 1782. MS letter #9584, New York State Archives, Albany, N.Y.

Subsequently the legislature of New York and of most other states decided not to abide by the recommendatory paragraph of article 5 of the treaty.

The persons residing in districts in the possession of the British, as described in article 5, included persons residing in these districts between November 1782 and January 14, 1784, according to the British view. *American State Papers,* Vol. 1, Class 1, p. 193.

6. U.S. Foreign Secretary John Jay explains this paragraph of article 5 as follows:

> The obvious meaning of which is, that all fair lawful contracts touching land, to which the parties were at the time competent, shall continue in full force and be executed in favour of innocent persons claiming the benefit thereof, notwithstanding the said lands may have been confiscated. The article clearly relates to grants or contracts which at the time they were made were valid, and not to grants or contracts which at the time they were made conveyed no rights to the grantees or contractees. The article expressly removes impediments to the prosecution of just or legal rights, and that idea excludes the supposition of its meaning to confer validity to claims not warranted by law, or to create rights which at no prior period had even existence.
>
> *Journals of the Continental Congress,* Vol. 31, p. 850.

The original deed of gift of John Parker and the will of Joseph Wickham Sr., both of which created in the Wickham family an estate of inheritance, were valid grants.

See also article 5's interpretation in *Ware* v. *Hylton,* 3 Dall. (U.S.) 199 (1796) 284; and with respect to debts: *Higginson* v. *Mein,* 4 Cranch (U.S.) 416 (1808) 419; *Owings* v. *Norwood's Lessee,* 5 Cranch (9 U.S.) 344 (1809) 345–8.

7. Importantly, article 6 does not say, "There shall be no future judgments or attainders," but rather, "There shall be no future confiscations." The question, then, is whether a confiscation—not whether an attainder—has or has not occurred at the time of the treaty.

Two pre-treaty Maryland laws which *declared* British real property in Maryland to be seized and in the possession of the state without office found (or entry), were deemed by the Supreme Court to have effected a confiscation before the treaty. *Smith* v. *Maryland*, 6 Cranch (U.S.) 286 (1810) 306. This case, however, did not involve a jurisdictional boundary issue. Furthermore, New York's Act of Attainder was not worded in the same way as these Maryland statutes. New York's Act is talking about the *rights* to property, which it deemed vested in the state, not the property itself, which by Maryland law was declared to be "in the full and actual seisin and possession" of its commissioners without the necessity of any office found, entry, or other act to be done.

Among the cases where property was deemed protected from confiscation by article 6 of the treaty are the following: (1) *Fairfax* v. *Hunter,* 7 Cranch (11 U.S.) 604 (1812)—The confiscation in this case had not been consummated by office found or entry; (2), *Orr* v. *Hodgson,* 4 Wheat. (17 U.S.) 453 (1819)—Here the property in question belonged to an alien; and (3), *Society for the Propagation of the Gospel* v. *Town of New-Haven,* 8 Wheat. (21 U.S.) 464 (1823) 493—Here a subsequent legislative act selling the property to someone else was deemed "utterly void, being passed in contravention of the treaty of peace."

Concerning when article 6 of the Treaty of Peace was to take effect, see: (1), *Papers of the Continental Congress,* M247, r114, p. 310, "Letter from the American Commissioners to Robert R. Livingston, July 18, 1783;" (2), *Public Papers of George Clinton,* Vol. 8, p. 259; (3), *American State Papers,* Vol. 1, Class 1, pp. 201, 486. See also case law: *Gordon* v. *Holiday,* 10 Fed Cas. No. 5,610 [1 Wash. C.C. 285] 798 (1805) 799, 801; *Fisher* v. *Harnden,* 9 Fed. Cas. No. 4,819 [1 Paine, 55] 129 (1812) 130; *Hylton* v. *Brown,* 12 Fed. Cas. No. 6,982 [1 Wash. C.C. 343] 1129 (1806) 1133.

8. *Papers of the Continental Congress,* M247, r66, item 52, pp. 217, 241–264.
9. Harold C. Syrett, ed., *The Papers of Alexander Hamilton* (New York: Columbia University Press, 1962), Vol. 3, pp. 434–5.
10. *Papers of the Continental Congress,* M247, r66, item 52, p. 272.
11. U.S., House of Representatives, *The Revolutionary Diplomatic Correspondence of the United States,* ed. Francis Wharton (Washington: G.P.O., 1889), Vol. 6, p. 689.
12. Carleton's communique is in George Washington, Pres. U.S., *George Washington Papers* ("Presidential Papers Microfilm;" Washington: Library of Congress, 1961), Ser. 4, reel 93.
13. Laws of New York, 15 sess. Ch. 74 (April 12, 1792); Muirson's letter is quoted in Kate W. Strong, "Times Do Change." *Long Island Forum,* June 1966, pp. 122–4. Muirson's son received from England a compensation of 660 pounds.
14. Letter Jn. Willett to Mrs. Arrabella Floyd, May 26, 1783, Papers of Richard Floyd, Box 2, file 3, Society for the Preservation of Long Island Antiquities, Setauket, L.I.

    The law referred to was New York State's first inheritance law, An Act

To Abolish Entails, passed on July 12, 1782 (Laws of New York, 6 sess. Ch. 2). The effect of this law, as far as tenants in tail were concerned, was to change the nature of the estates they held from fee tail to fee simple. It also meant that the instant a person inherited an entailed estate, at that moment the estate under this law was changed into a fee simple. See *Van Rensselaer* v. *Kearney,* 11 How. (52 U.S.) 297 (1846), 314–320, where the court ruled on virtually the same clause in the 1786 Act to Abolish Entails (Laws of New York, 9 sess. Ch. 12), which repealed the earlier act.

15. *Fisher* v. *Harnden,* 9 Fed. Cas. No. 4,819 [1 Paine, 55] 129 (1812) 131 [reversed on other grounds by the Supreme Court]; *Gordon* v. *Holiday,* 10 Fed.Cas. No. 5,610 [1 Wash. C.C. 285] 798 (1805) 801; *Society for the Propagation of the Gospel* v. *Town of New-Haven, supra,* 493.
16. This point of view is implicitly shared by Secretary of State Thomas Jefferson in his response in 1792 to British charges of treaty violations by the states. See *American State Papers,* Vol. 1, Class 1, pp. 201, 205

    That New York State had passed laws in violation of article 6 of the treaties of peace was acknowledged both by Foreign Secretary John Jay in his recommendations to Congress and by this state's own Council of Revision. *Journals of the Continental Congress,* Vol. 31, pp. 857, 862; Street, *The Council of Revision of the State of New York,* p. 255. See also Madison's admission, cited in Crandall, p. 37, n. 64.
17. The first sale recorded in the abstract does not have the words "the attainder of", probably because of oversight. All the other sales in the book do.
18. American Loyalists, Transcripts of Loyalist Claims, Liquidations, Vol. 11, pp. 314–5. And see above, chapter 8, n. 1.
19. The following are examples of claimants who were compensated by England. They (or their heirs) also sued in American courts and won lands back that had been confiscated: Lord Fairfax (Virginia); John L. Borland (Mass.); John Hinchman (New Jersey). Donald Fisher (N.Y.) lost in the Supreme Court, but the decision made no reference to his compensation from England. Floyd-Jones's attainted father and uncle were both compensated by England, yet the boy was able to recover a confiscated estate by act of the New York legislature.

    In 1784, the banished Parker Wickham writes from Connecticut: "As application is already made for redress of grievances to another quater, I think it scandalous and hypocritical to apply for redress of grievances to two opposite parties for the same thing." That may have been a consideration for Parker Wickham, or his children, but what of the rights of subsequent heirs—including the present living heirs—to the ancient legacy that was barred from them? Certainly there is no obligation for them to refuse any legal rights they may have.

    The total loss that Wickham's heirs sustained might well include not only the original real property loss, but also personal property loss, and the deprivation of their ancestral land for over 200 years, including loss of rental value and interest on the fair rental value for that length of time.

    The question of subrogation does not enter here because Joseph Parker Wickham's compensation from England was volunteered. Furthermore, it was less than the full value of the total loss. In any case, the English government was not in the position of an insurer suing the state of New York as the party bearing the primary liability. England's partial compensation did not relieve the state of New York, or other parties, from potential liability resulting from Wickham's losses. See George E. Palmer, *The Law of Restitution* (Boston: Little, Brown & Co., c. 1978), Vol. 1, p. 23; Vol. 4, pp. 410–412.

20. Letter of Joseph Parker Wickham, Dublin. (J. Parker Wickham papers).
21. In addition to the 1782, 1783 Provisional and Definitive Treaty provisions which pertained to the rights of people who held land in America, there was article 9 of the Jay Treaty of 1794, which spoke of the rights of British subjects to land held in America.

> It is agreed, that British subjects who now hold Lands in the Territories of the United States, and American Citizens who now hold Lands in the Dominions of His Majesty, shall continue to hold them according to the nature and Tenure of their respective Estates and Titles therein, and may grant, Sell or Devise the same to whom they please, in like manner as if they were Natives; and that neither they nor their Heirs or assigns shall, so far as may respect the said Lands and the legal remedies incident thereto, be regarded as Aliens.

Describing this provision of the Jay Treaty, the Supreme Court states in 1928, "Article 9 aims at perpetuity and deals with existing rights, vested and permanent in character, in respect of which, by express provision, neither the owners nor their heirs or assigns are to be regarded as aliens. These are rights which, by their very nature, are fixed and continuing, regardless of war or peace." *Karnuth* v. *U.S.*, 279 U.S. 229 (1928) 239; *accord, Akins* v. *U.S.*, 551 F. 2d 1222 (1977) 1227.

Furthermore a claimant, under article 9, does not need to show that he—or his ancestor—was in possession of claimed property as of 1794, but only that title to it was in him, or his ancestor: "To avail themselves of this treaty, the lessors of the plaintiff must show that their ancestor held the lands for which this suit was instituted, at the time when it was made. The court does not mean they must show a seisin in fact, or an actual possession of the land, but that the title was in him at the time." *Har[n]den* v. *Fisher,* 1 Wheat. (U.S.) 301 (1816) 304; *accord, Orr* v. *Hodgson,* 4 Wheat. (17 U.S.) 453 (1819) 464; *Hughes* v. *Edwards,* 9 Wheat. (22 U.S.) 490 (1824) 496.

Whether Joseph Parker Wickham, the son of the attainted Parker Wickham, could be adjudged a British subject in 1794—the date of the Jay Treaty—and so qualify under article 9 of that treaty, depends on his state of allegiance at the end of the Revolution. *Inglis* v. *Trustees of the Sailor's Snug Harbour,* 3 Pet. (28 U.S.) 99 (1830) 162, 169. The fact that he returned to Southold in 1791 and was undoubtedly treated as an American citizen (he bought property and devised it in his will) does not preclude his having been a British subject in 1794, from the point of view of the British government. *Shanks* v. *Dupont,* 3 Pet. (28 U.S.) 242 (1830) 249. See also Kettner, "Subjects or Citizens. . .", pp. 961, 966.

The question of whether a claimant's property had been confiscated by state law or whether it was protected from confiscation by the treaties of peace (1782, 1783) is an issue that falls within federal court jurisdiction.

Smith v. *Maryland,* 6 Cranch (U.S.) 286 (1810) 305; *accord, Martin* v. *Hunter's Lessee,* 1 Wheat. (14 U.S.) 304 (1816) 356–7, 359.

A constructive trust argument may also be available to Wickham's heirs. See Austin W. Scott, *The Law of Trusts* (3d ed.; Boston: Little, Brown, & Co., 1967), Vol. 5, Chap. 13. Secs. 462.2, 462.4, 465, 468, 481.1.

CHAPTER 10

1. *Oneida Indian Nation of N.Y.* v. *State of N.Y.,* 691 F. 2d 1070 (1982), at 1088.
2. *Ware* v. *Hylton,* 3 U.S. (Dall.) 199 (1796), at 236–7.
3. On Feb. 22, 1788, New York passed "an Act in the form of the act recommended by the resolution of the United States in Congress assembled. . . ." It was a public declaration of compliance with the instructions of Congress that infractions of the Treaty of Peace not be condoned and that the courts in the state interpret the treaty according to its true tenor.

   Reference to the rules and maxims of the law of nations for the interpretation of treaties is found in the resolution of Congress referred to above. See *Journals of the Continental Congress,* Vol. 32, p. 179; also Vol. 31, p. 799. See further, Brinton Coxe, *An Essay on Judicial Power and Unconstitutional Legislation* (Philadelphia, Pa.: Kay and Brother, 1893), pp. 281–2; and Chief Justice Jay's remarks in *Henfield's Case,* 11 Fed. Cas. No. 6,360 [Whart. St. Tr. 49] 1099 (1793) 1101.
4. As every power at war pretends to have right on its side, and this pretension is not liable to be judged by others, the state of things at the instant of the treaty is to be held legitimate, and any change to be made in it requires an express specification in the treaty; consequently all things not mentioned in the treaty are to remain as they were at the conclusion of it. This is also a consequence of the promised amnesty.

   Vattel, *The Law of Nations,* Bk. IV, Chap. 2, sec. 21.

   The point is also made by Hamilton. Syrett, ed., *The Papers of Alexander Hamilton,* Vol. 3, p. 490. See further: *Strother* v. *Lucas,* 12 Pet. (37 U.S.) 410 (1838) 438.
5. *Society for the Propagation of the Gospel in Foreign Parts* v. *Town of New-Haven,* 8 Wheat. (21 U.S.) 464 (1823) 493.

   Cp. with the following: (1), *Rutgers* v. *Waddington* (1784)—"No state in this union can alter or abridge, in a single point, the federal articles or the treaty." Goebel, ed., *The Law Practice of Alexander Hamilton,* Vol. 1, p. 413. (2), *Clark* v. *Allen,* 331 U.S. 503 (1946) 508—"If, therefore, the provisions of the treaty have not been superseded or abrogated, they prevail over any requirements of California law which conflict with them." See also *Hauenstein* v. *Lynham,* 100 U.S. 483 (1879) 488, 490; *De Tenorio* v. *McGowan,* 510 F. 2d 92 (1975) 95.

   See also *Journals of the Continental Congress,* Vol. 32, pp. 180–1; and the interpretation of articles 4 and 5 of the Treaty of Peace, in *Ware* v. *Hylton, supra,* 240, 284.
6. *Owings* v. *Norwood's Lessee,* 5 Cranch (9 U.S.) 344 (1809) 348.

The previous case is cited as *Fisher* v. *Harnden,* 9 Fed. Cas. No. 4,819 [1 Paine, 55] 129 (1812). The circuit court decision on that case was reversed in *Har[n]den* v. *Fisher,* 1 Wheat. (U.S.) 301 (1816). The Supreme Court ruled against the British claimants in the case, whose father—Donald Fisher—had been attainted by the state of New York. The problem with their claim, as the high court saw it, was Fisher's title to his property and whether there was sufficient evidence of this title in 1794, the year of the Jay Treaty which protected the rights of British subjects to lands held in America at that time (see further, Chap. 9, n. 21). The high court writes:

> The verdict does not find that Donald Fisher held his title until the treaty of 1794 was made, and although nothing is found to show that he has parted with it, yet the court cannot presume that he did not part with it.

Har[n]den v. *Fisher,* at 303.

7. *Society for the Propagation of the Gospel in Foreign Parts* v. *Town of New-Haven, supra,* 494. See also *Karnuth* v. *U.S.,* 279 U.S. 229 (1928) 237, 239.

   Bevans describes articles 4–7 of the Definitive Treaty of Peace as "terminated upon fulfillment of terms." Apparently this is his own opinion, as he cites no statute or authority that categorizes them as such. Charles I. Bevans, *Treaties and Other International Agreements of the United States of America, 1776-1949* (Washington, D.C.: G.P.O., 1974), (Dept. of State Pub. 8761).
8. *Society for the Propagation of the Gospel in Foreign Parts* v. *Town of New-Haven, supra,* 493. See also *Chirac* v. *Chirac,* 2 Wheat. (5 U.S.) 259 (1817) 277.

   The doctrine of separation of powers is mentioned in the dissenting opinion, n. 12, of *Oneida County, N.Y.* v. *Oneida Indian etc.,* 105 S. Ct. 1245 (1985) at 1266. See also *INS* v. *Chadka,* 462 U.S. 919 (1983) 951.
9. *Narragansett Tribe, Etc.* v. *So. R.I. Land Devel.,* 418 F. Supp. 798 (1976), at 804.
10. *Oneida Indian Nation of N.Y.* v. *Cty. of Oneida,* 434 F. Supp. 527 (1977), at 542–3.
11. *Fisher* v. *Harnden,* 9 Fed. Cas. No. 4,819 [1 Paine, 55] 129 (1812) 131. See also *Hamilton et al.* v. *Eaton,* 11 Fed. Cas. No. 5980 [1 Hughes 249; 2 Mart. (N.C.) 1] 339 (1792) 340; *Ware* v. *Hylton,* 3 Dall. (U.S.) 199 (1796) 236–7. See further, Chap. 9, n. 15.

Part IV: Appendixes

APPENDIX I

The Present-Day Heirs to the Ancient Legacy[1]

Explanatory key:	C? = Children, if any, are unidentified
	H? = Presumed heir

I. Line A

i. Parker Wickham; ii. Parnel W. Reeve; iii. Anna Reeve; iv. William Wickham (husband); v. William Wickham (son); vi. James Wickham

1. John S. Wickham of Cutchogue, N.Y.

children (H?): 2. Thomas Wickham of Kandy, Sri Lanka [his son: Jonathan Wickham]; 3. John L. Wickham of Baltimore, Md. [his children: Joseph, Benjamin, Barnabas, Prudence Wickham]; 4. Parnel Wickham-Searl of Cutchogue, N.Y. [her children: Julia, Stephen Wickham]

II. Line A

i. Parker Wickham; ii. Parnel W. Reeve; . . . James Wickham

5. Henry P. Wickham of Cutchogue, N.Y.

children (H?): 6. Peter Wickham [his children: Mark, Nancy Elizabeth Wickham]; 7. Virginia Uhl [her children: Thomas, Christian]; 8. Sarah Elizabeth [her son: Nicholas]; 9. Christopher (C?)

III. Line A

i. Parker Wickham; ii. Parnel W. Reeve; iii. Anna Reeve; iv. William Wickham (husband); v. William Wickham (son); vi. James Wickham; vii. James Parker Wickham

10. James Parker Wickham of Cutchogue, N.Y.

IV. Line A

i. Parker Wickham; ii. Parnel W. Reeve; iii. Anna Reeve; iv. William Wickham (husband); v. William Wickham (son); vi. William H. Wickham

11. William H. Wickham of Mattituck, N.Y.

children (H?): 12. Nancy E. Wickham of Cutchogue, N.Y.; 13. Abigail Wickham Bressler of Mattituck, N.Y.

V. Line A

i. Parker Wickham; ii. Parnel W. Reeve; iii. Anna Reeve; iv. William Wickham (husband); v. Hannah F. [i.e. Nancy] Case; vi. Wickham Case; vii. Oliver W. Case; viii. Corinne B. Case (wife)

14. Stanley Graham Case of Cutchogue, N.Y.

children: 15. Ernest Wickham Case of Cutchogue, N.Y. (C?); Stanley Oliver Case, deceased (C?); 16. Margery Boisseau Case of Cutchogue, N.Y. (C?); 17. Barbara Jean Case of Cutchogue, N.Y. (C?); 18. Nancy B.C. Marschean of Southold, N.Y. [her son: 19. Scott]

[Note: The will of Corinne B. Case (above) contains two residuary clauses and two codicils, raising a possibility of other qualifying heirs.]

VI. Line A

i. Parker Wickham; ii. Parnel W. Reeve; iii. Anna Reeve; iv. William Wickham (husband); v. Hannah F. Case; vi. Wickham Case; vii. Clifford T. Case

children (H?): 20. Clifford; 21. David; 22. a daughter

VII. Line A

i. Parker Wickham; ii. Parnel W. Reeve; iii. Anna Reeve; iv. William Wickham (husband); v. Hannah F. Case; vi. Wickham Case; vii. Ruth B. Case

VIII. Line A.

i. Parker Wickham; ii. Parnel W. Reeve; iii. Anna Reeve; iv. William Wickham (husband); v. Hannah F. Case; vi. George H. Case; vii. Frank H. Case

children: 23. Harrison Case [his son (H?): 24. Bruce]; 25. Henry Case (C?); 26. Russell Case of Cutchogue, N.Y.; 27. Ralph Case (C?); 28. Norman Case (C?)

IX. Line A

i. Parker Wickham; ii. Parnel W. Reeve; . . . vi. George H. Case; vii. Lizzie Horton

X. Line A.

i. Parker Wickham; ii. Parnel W. Reeve; . . . vi. George H. Case; vii. Lucetta Waite

child (H?): Harry Waite (C?)

XI. Line A

i. Parker Wickham; ii. Parnel W. Reeve; iii. Anna Reeve; iv. William Wickham (husband); v. Hannah F. Case; vi. Annie W. Beebe

children (H?): Theodore O. Beebe [his children: 29. William; 30. Theodore; 31. Marjorie; Sherwood C. Beebe, deceased]; 32. Gerald Beebe [his daughter: 33. Anna M. Robinson (C?)]

XII. Line A

i. Parker Wickham; ii. Parnel W. Reeve; iii. Anna Reeve; iv. William Wickham (husband); v. Henry D. Wickham; vi. Frances P. Wickham

residuary heirs: 34. Isabel C. Underhill of Mineola, N.Y. (C?); 35. Kenneth K. Underhill (C?); 36. Henry W. Skinner of Glen Cove, N.Y. (C?)

XIII. Line A

i. Parker Wickham; ii. Parnel W. Reeve; iii. Anna Reeve; iv. William Wickham (husband); v. Col. John Wickham; vi. William Wickham (and other C?)

XIV. Line A

i. Parker Wickham; ii. Parnel W. Reeve; iii. James Reeve (her husband); iv. Irad Reeve; v. Henry G. Reeve; vi. Henry W. Reeve (of Brooklyn, living in 1902) (C?)

[Note: the residuary clause in the will of Irad Reeve, above, uses the word "property" (real and personal), not "property and estate".]

XV. Line A

i. Parker Wickham; ii. Parnel W. Reeve; iii. James Reeve (her husband); iv. James W. Reeve; v. James Reeve (died 1891, in Southold Township) (C?)

XVI. Line B

i. Parker Wickham; ii. Hellen Hudson, iii. Helen W. Aldrich; iv. Herman D. Aldrich (H?); v. Elizabeth W. Aldrich (his wife)

children named in her will's residuary clause: James H. Aldrich (C?); Spencer Aldrich (C?); Helen Hudson Steele (C?); Mary Elizabeth Dudley of Louisville, Kentucky (C?); and the children of William W. Aldrich: namely, 37. Herman D. Aldrich (H?), 38. Elizabeth A. Underhill (H?), and 39. Arthur L. Aldrich (H?)

XVII. Line B

i. Parker Wickham; ii. Hellen Hudson; iii. Helen W. Aldrich; iv. James Aldrich (H?); v. Elizabeth Aldrich Ely

her children: Helen Steele Burleson (C?); Mary T. Ely (C?)

XVIII. Line C

i. Parker Wickham; ii. Sarah Reeve; iii. Samuel Reeve (her husband); iv. Sally Frazee of Auburn, N.Y.; v. Mary Mullen; vi. Andrew Mullen

children (H?): 40. Eloise; 41.Carrie Beavers; 42. James; 43. Enid Pultz [her children: 44. Saundra Dring; 45. Bruce Pultz]

XIX. Line C

i. Parker Wickham; ii. Sarah Reeve; . . . v. Mary Mullen; vi. Elizabeth Hovey of Long Island (C?)

XX. Line C

i. Parker Wickham; ii. Sarah Reeve; . . . v. Mary Mullen; vi. John Mills Mullen

children (H?): Clarence Albert Mullen of Hudson, Wis. (deceased, unmarried); 46. Marion J. Kane [her children: 47. Lucille E. Nelson; 48. Joseph Henry Kane; 49. Fred Kane of Minneapolis, Minn.]; Geraldine B. Pominville [her children: 50. Richard W. Pominville; 51. John Mills Pominville; 52. David H. Pominville]; 53. Hazel P. Briggs [her children: Mary Lou Ilers (deceased, left children); 54. Daniel H. Briggs; 55. Timothy J. Briggs]; 56. Jack Mills Mullen [his child: 57. Jane A. Peterson]; 58. George S. Mullen [his children: 59. Georgia A. Hatch; 60. Michael P. Mullen]

XXI. Line C

i. Parker Wickham; ii. Sarah Reeve; iii. Samuel Reeve (her husband); iv. Sally Frazee

her other children (H?): James Frazee of Throop, N.Y. (C?); Emina Frazee of Auburn, N.Y. (C?); Armenia Frazee of Throop, N.Y. (C?); William Frazee of Cayuga Co., N.Y. (C?)

XXII. Line C
i. Parker Wickham; ii. Sarah Reeve; iii. Samuel Reeve (her husband); iv. [J.] Parker Reeve
children: James Reeve [his children: Horace A. Reeve; Ida M. Reeve]; Warren W. Reeve [his children: Julia Reeve; Arthur Reeve]; Mary Comstock [her children: Paris Comstock; Willie Comstock; Earl Comstock (C?)]

XXIII. Line C
i. Parker Wickham; ii. Sarah Reeve; iii. Samuel Reeve (her husband); iv. Samuel Reeve Jr. (no children)

XXIV. Line C
i. Parker Wickham; ii. Sarah Reeve; iii. Samuel Reeve (her husband); iv. William Reeve
his children (H?): Caroline O. Reeve of Webster, Mich.; Mary A. Mills of Cayuga Co., N.Y. (C?)

XXV. Line C
i. Parker Wickham; ii. Sarah Reeve; iii. Samuel Reeve; (her husband); iv. Philip H. Reeve of Webster, Mich. (C?)

XXVI. Line D
i. Parker Wickham; ii. Thomas Wickham; iii. Joseph P. Wickham; iv. Charles W. Wickham; v. Cedric H. Wickham
children: 61. J. Parker Wickham of Mattituck, L.I. [his son: 62. Jay P. Wickham]; 63. Hull M. Wickham of Middletown, N.J. [his sons: 64. Spencer H. Wickham; 65. Wessel C. Wickham]

XXVII. Line D
i. Parker Wickham; ii. Thomas Wickham; iii. Joseph P. Wickham; iv. Charles W. Wickham; v. W. Raynor Wickham
children: 66. Joan Wickham Silleck of Mattituck, L.I. [her children: 67. Charles W. Silleck of Johnson City, N.Y.; 68. Cindy (Mrs. Douglas) Schuch of Birmingham, Alabama; 69. Betsy (Mrs. Richard) Thiel of Highland, Indiana]; 70. Margaret Anne Wickham Tooker of Riverhead, L.I. [her children: 71. Pamela Anne Brunell; 72. Mark Wickham Tooker; 73. David Scott Tooker; 74. Colin William Tooker; 75. Robin Elisabeth Tooker]

XXVIII. Line D
i. Parker Wickham; ii. Thomas Wickham; iii. Joseph P. Wickham; iv. Charles W. Wickham; v. Marie C.W. Griffin; vi. Howard T. Griffin (no children)

XXIX. Line D
i. Parker Wickham; ii. Thomas Wickham; . . . v. Marie C.W. Griffin; vi. Frank W. Griffin (no children)

XXX. Line D
i. Parker Wickham; ii. Thomas Wickham; iii. Joseph P. Wickham; iv. Charles W. Wickham; v. Helen M.W. Goldsmith
children (H?): 76. Sheila Wirsing of Mattituck, L.I. [her children: 77. Donald; 78. Virginia]; Phoebe Ross [her children: 79. Pamela M. Gay of San Francisco; 80. David A. Ross of San Francisco; 81. Nancy Carmean of New York City]

XXXI. Line D
i. Parker Wickham; ii. Thomas Wickham; iii. Joseph P. Wickham; iv.

Charles W. Wickham; v. Spencer Summers Wickham; vi. Marjorie S. Wickham (his wife) (no children)

XXXII. Line D

i. Parker Wickham; ii. Thomas Wickham; iii. Joseph P. Wickham; iv. William Hull Wickham; v. F. Ethel Wickham; Margaret v. Dunham (residuary heir)

children (H?): Margaret V.V. Corscaden; Lawrence B. Dunham; William P. Dunham (C?)

XXXIII. Line D

i. Parker Wickham; ii. Thomas Wickham; iii. Joseph P. Wickham; iv. Julia H.W. Evans

children (H?): Beryl E. Gray; Perry B. Coxe; Belton W. Evans; Brenda T. Evans (C?)

XXXIV. Line D

i. Parker Wickham; ii. Thomas Wickham; iii. Joseph P. Wickham; Sarah E. Wickham of Elberon, N.J. (C?)

---

[1] The list includes identified heirs only, based on substantial, but by no means exhaustive research.

The inheritance claim presupposes that there neither is, nor has been, a lawful impediment to the recovery of the legacy despite the passage of time. An enjoinder against lawful impediments is found in the treaties of peace, article 5, para. 2.

We have discussed one such impediment, the passage of time (see Chap. 10). Two others should be mentioned, even if a court of law were to find them to have no applicability to the Wickham claim.

The first of these is the old common law doctrine of England, *seisina facit stipitem*. Under this doctrine, which was abolished in New York in 1829, property could not pass by descent unless from a person who had been in actual possession of it or who had received it by will or deed—i.e. by "purchase." [This doctrine did not apply to estates tail, under which heirs claimed *per formam doni*, not by descent. Henry Chitty, *A Treatise of the Law of Descents* (London: Joseph Butterworth & Co., 1825), p. 155.] Were the *seisina facit stipitem* impediment sanctioned in the Wickham claim, inheritance lines A and B would be barred from the claim because they stem from an heir of Joseph Parker Wickham who died intestate before 1829. On *seisina facit stipitem*, see Kent, Vol. 4, Part 6, Lec. LXV, pp. 426–7. See also *The Revised Statutes of the State of New-York* (Albany: Packard and Van Benthuysen, 1829), Vol. 1, pp. 751, 754; and *Inglis* v. *The Trustees of the Sailor's Snug Harbour*, 3 Peters (28 U.S.) 99 (1830) 128–9.

A second impediment is found in what is known as an occupying claimant statute. New York's Act of May 12, 1784 (7 sess. Ch. 64) provided, among other things, that a winning claimant to confiscated property must pay the ousted occupant for all improvements (buildings and the like) made on the property. Were this requirement to prevail in the Wickham claim, the suit would probably only be feasible if limited to Robins Island, which except for two or three old buildings is virtually in its natural state.

In tracing the inheritance lines, the author has treated residuary clauses as directing the course of descent, where they appear in wills.

APPENDIX II

Text of New York's Attainder Act

CHAP. XXV.

An ACT *for the Forfeiture & Sale of the Estates of Persons who have adhered to the Enemies of this State, and for declaring the Sovereignty of the People of this State, in Respect to all Property within the same.*

Passed 22d October, 1779.

Preamble.

WHEREAS during the present unjust and cruel War, waged by the King of *Great-Britain*, against this State, and the other United States of *America*, divers Persons holding or claiming Property within this State, have voluntarily been adherent to the said King, his Fleets and Armies, Enemies to this State, and the said other United States, with Intent to subvert the Government and Liberties of this State, and the said other United States, and to bring the same in Subjection to the Crown of *Great-Britain;* by Reason whereof, the said Persons have severally justly forfeited all Right to the Protection of this State, and to the Benefit of the Laws under which such Property is held or claimed: *And whereas* the public Justice and Safety of this State absolutely require, that the most notorious Offenders should be immediately hereby convicted and attainted of the Offence aforesaid, in order to work a Forfeiture of their respective Estates, and vest the same in the People of this State: *And whereas* the Constitution of this State, hath authorised the Legislature to pass Acts of Attainder for Crimes committed before the Termination of the present War:

Persons by Name, *Ipso Facto*, attainted of the Offence of adhering to the Enemies of the State.

I. *Be it therefore Enacted by the People of the State of* New-York, *represented in Senate and Assembly, and it is hereby Enacted by the Authority of the same,* That John Murray, Earl of *Dunmore,* formerly Governor of the Colony of *New-York;* William Tryon, Esq; late Governor of the said Colony; John Watts, Oliver De Lancey, Hugh Wallace, Henry White, John Harris Cruger, William Axtell and Roger Morris, Esquires, late Members of the Council of the said Colony; George Duncan Ludlow, and Thomas

Jones, late Justices of the Supreme Court of the said Colony; John Tabor Kempe, late Attorney-General of the said Colony; William Bayard, Robert Bayard, and James DeLancey, now or late of the City of *New-York,* Esquires; David Matthews, late Mayor of the said City; James Jauncey, George Folliot, Thomas White, William McAdam, Isaac Low, Miles Sherbrook, Alexander Wallace and John Wetherhead, now or late of the said City, Merchants; Charles Inglis, of the said City, Clerk, and Margaret his Wife; Sir John Johnson, late of the County of *Tryon,* Knight and Baronet; Guy Johnson, Daniel Claus, and John Butler, now or late of the said County, Esquires; and John Joost Herkemer, now or late of the said County, Yeoman; Frederick Philipse, and James De Lancey, now or late of the County of *Westchester,* Esquires; Frederick Philipse, (Son of Frederick) now or late of the said County, Gentleman; David Colden, Daniel Kissam, the Elder, and Gabriel Ludlow, now or late of *Queen's* County, Esquires; Philip Skeene, now or late of the County of *Charlotte,* Esq; & Andrew P. Skeene, Son of the said Philip Skeene, late of *Charlotte* County; Benjamin Seaman, and Christopher Billop, now or late of the County of *Richmond,* Esquires; Beverly Robinson, Beverly Robinson, the Younger, and Malcom Morrison, now or late of the County of *Dutchess,* Esquires; John Kane, now or late of the said County, Gentleman; Abraham C. Cuyler, now or late of the County of *Albany,* Esq; Robert Leake, Edward Jessup, and Ebenezer Jessup, now or late of the said County, Gentlemen; and Peter DuBois, and Thomas H. Barclay, now or late of the County of *Ulster,* Esquires; Susannah Robinson, Wife to the said Beverly Robinson, and Mary Morris, Wife to the said Roger Morris; John Rapalje, of *King's* County, Esq; George Muirson, Richard Floyd, and Parker Wickham, of *Suffolk* County, Esquires; Henry Lloyd, the Elder, late of the State of *Massachusetts-Bay,* Merchant; and Sir Henry Clinton, Knight, be, and each of them are hereby severally declared to be, *Ipso Facto,* convicted and attainted of the Offence aforesaid; and that all and singular the Estate, both real and personal, held or claimed by them the said Persons severally and respectively, whether in Possession, Reversion or Remainder, within this State, on the Day of the passing of this Act, shall be, and hereby is declared to be forfeited to, and vested in the People of this State.

Their Estates forfeited.

The said Persons banished from this State.

II. *And be it further Enacted by the Authority aforesaid,* That the said several Persons herein before particularly named, shall be, and hereby are declared to be forever banished from this State; and each and every of them, who shall at any Time hereafter be found in any Part of this

State, shall be, and are hereby adjudged and declared guilty of Felony, and shall suffer Death as in Cases of Felony, without Benefit of Clergy.

For the Purpose of attainting other Offenders.

Courts to take Indictments.

Defects in the Proceedings remedied 5th Sess. Ch. 4.

Convictions confirmed 7th Sess. Ch. 64. Sec. 23.

III. *And to the End,* That for the Purpose aforesaid, Convictions and Attainders for the Offence aforesaid, may, in Pursuance of this Act, be had against other Offenders than those herein before particularly named; *Be it further Enacted by the Authority aforesaid,* That it shall and may be lawful for the Grand Jurors at any Supreme Court of Judicature to be held for this State, or at any Court of Oyer and Terminer and General Gaol Delivery, or General or Quarter Sessions of the Peace, to be held in and for any County within this State, whenever it shall appear to such Grand Jurors, by the Oath of one or more credible Witness or Witnesses, that any Person or Persons, whether in full Life or deceased, generally reputed, if in full Life, to hold or claim, or if deceased, to have held or claimed, at the Time of their Death respectively, real or personal Estate within this State, hath or have been guilty of the Offence aforesaid, to prefer Bills of Indictment against such Persons as shall then be in full life, for such Offence, and in Relation to the Offence committed by such Persons in their Lives Time, as shall then be deceased, severally and respectively, notwithstanding that such Offence may have been committed elsewhere than in the County for which such Grand Jurors shall be summoned: That in every Indictment to be taken in Pursuance of this Act, the Offence or Offences shall be charged to have been committed in the County where the Indictment shall be taken, notwithstanding such Offence or Offences may have been committed elsewhere; and it shall not be necessary to set forth specially, whether the several Persons charged in such Indictment, were respectively deceased or in full Life, or were reputed to hold or claim real or personal Estate within this State. And on every such Indictment shall be indorsed, that the same was taken in Pursuance of this Act, and the Day when the same was preferred into Court.

When Indictments are taken, Sheriff to publish Notices thereof.

IV. *And be it futher Enacted by the Authority aforesaid,* That whenever and as often as any such Indictment shall be taken, against any Person or Persons, the Sheriffs of the respective Counties, where such Indictments shall be taken, shall forthwith cause Notices therof, agreeable to such Form as is herein after mentioned, to be published in one or more of the public News-Papers within this State, for at least four Weeks.

On Neglect to appear and traverse, the Persons charged in the Indictment, to be adjudged guilty.

V. *And be it further Enacted by the Authority aforesaid,* That in every Case of a Neglect to appear and traverse agreeable to the Sheriff's Notice, the several Persons charged in such indictment, whether in full Life or deceased, shall respectively be, and hereby are declared to be, and shall be adjudged guilty of the Offences charged against them respectively. And the several Persons who shall in Pursuance of this Act, either by Reason of such Default, in not appearing and traversing as aforesaid, or upon Trial, be convicted of the Offence aforesaid, shall forfeit all and singular the Estate, both real and personal, whether in Possession, Reversion or Remainder, held or claimed by them respectively, within this State, to the People of this State; and Judgment shall accordingly be awarded in the Supreme Court of this State, against the said Persons respectively. And such Forfeitures, as well of the Estates which were at the Time of their Death, respectively, of Persons deceased, as of Persons in full Life, at the Time of Conviction, shall be deemed to have accrued; and the Estates accordingly attached to and vested in the People of this State, as and from the Day charged in each respective Indictment, most distant from the Day of the taking thereof. *Provided nevertheless,* That where a Trial shall be had upon any such Indictment, the Forfeiture shall in such Case be deemed to have accrued from the Day to be found by the Verdict of the Jury, by which such Persons shall be respectively convicted, most distant from the Day of the taking of the Indictment; any other Day to be charged in the Indictment notwithstanding. *And provided further,* That the several Persons who shall have been pardoned in Pursuance of a Declaration or Ordinance of the Convention of this State, passed the Tenth Day of *May*, in the Year of our Lord One Thousand Seven Hundred and Seventy-seven, offering free Pardon to such of the Subjects of the said State, as having committed treasonable Acts against the same, should return to their Allegiance; or in Consequence of any Proclamation or Proclamations, heretofore issued by the Commander in Chief of the Army of the United States of *America,* may respectively plead their Pardons to Indictments, taken in Pursuance of this Act, in like Manner as they might or could do to Indictments for High Treason, taken in the ordinary Course of Law. *And provided further,* That each and every Person, who shall at any Time before the Fourth Day of *April,* in the Year of our Lord One Thousand Seven Hundred and Seventy-eight, have taken the Oath of Allegiance to this State, before the Convention or Councils of Safety of this State; or before the Committee of the said Convention, appointed for enquiring into, detecting and defeating all Conspiracies, which may be formed in this State, against the Liberties of *America;* or the Commissioners appointed for the like Purpose, or a County,

Forfeiture on Conviction.

Judgment accordingly in the Supreme Court, and when Forfeitures shall be deemed to have accrued.

Proviso, in Favor of Persons pardoned.

Proviso, in Favor of those who shall have taken the Oath of Allegiance, before 4th of *April,* 1778.

District or Precinct Committee; shall and may plead such taking the Oath of Allegiance in Bar to any Indictment, to be taken in Pursuance of this Act, for Offences committed before the Day on which they respectively took such Oath.

All Indictments on this Law, taken in the other Courts, to be returned into the Supreme Court, and there tried.

VI. *And be it further Enacted by the Authority aforesaid,* That all Indictments to be from Time to Time taken in Pursuance of this Act, at any Court of Oyer and Terminer, or General Gaol Delivery, or General or Quarter Sessions of the Peace, shall, by the Clerks of the said Courts, respectively be returned, under their respective Hands and Seals, into the Supreme Court of this State, and shall be tried at the Bar of the said Court; and upon the Trial of any such Indictment, no greater Number of Witnesses shall be required than are required by Law in Cases of Felony, without Benefit of Clergy.

Sheriffs to return the News-Papers in which their Notices shall have been published.

VII. *And be it further Enacted by the Authority aforesaid,* That the several Sheriffs shall, from Time to Time, respectively return, under their Hands and Seals, into the Supreme Court of this State, the several Numbers of the News-Papers containing the Notices published by them respectively, there to remain as Records of such Notices, until Judgments shall be had against the several Persons named in such Notices respectively.

To prevent Advantages for Defects of Form,

It shall be sufficient to charge generally in the Indictment an Adherence to the Enemy.

VIII. *And to the End,* That in Prosecutions for the Offence aforesaid, in Pursuance of this Act, no Advantage may be taken of mere Matters of Form; and that the Defendants may notwithstanding be fully apprized of the several Matters charged against them; in order to their Defence, *Be it futher Enacted by the Authority aforesaid,* That it shall be sufficient in all Indictments to be taken for the Offence aforesaid, in Pursuance of this Act, to charge generally, that the several Persons therein charged, did, on the several Days, and at the several Places therein mentioned, adhere to the Enemies of this State, and the Grand Jurors shall, at the Time they deliver any such Indictment into Court, deliver into Court the Examinations or Depositions of the Witness or Witnesses, upon whose Testimony such Indictment was found, to be filed in Court, together with the Indictment; and the Defendants shall respectively upon Application, be entitled to Copies of the Indictments against them respectively, and of such Examinations or Depositions; and the Prosecutor on the Part of the State, shall not, upon the Trial, be permitted to give Evidence of any *overt* Acts, other than such as shall be charged in such Examinations or Depositions; and the Clerks of the several Courts of Oyer and Terminer, and General Gaol Delivery, and General or Quarter Sessions of the Peace, shall return such Examinations or De-

The Grand Jurors to deliver into Court the Examinations of the Witnesses. Defendants shall have Copies of Indictments and Examinations. On Trial no Evidence to be given of any *overt* Act not charged in the Examinations.

The Clerks of the other Courts to return the Examinations as well as the Indictments, into the Supreme Court.

positions into the Supreme Court, in like Manner as is herein before directed, with Respect to Indictments, taken at the Courts of Oyer and Terminer and General Gaol Delivery, or General or Quarter Sessions of the Peace.

What shall be deemed Evidence of overt Acts of adhering to the Enemies of this State.

IX. *And be it further Enacted by the Authority aforesaid,* That besides the several Matters by the Law of *England,* declared to be Evidence and overt Acts of High Treason, in adhering to the King's Enemies, and which are hereby declared to be Evidence and overt Acts of High Treason, in adhering to the Enemies of the People of this State as Sovereign thereof; the following Matters shall be, and are hereby declared to be Evidence and overt Acts of adhering to the Enemies of the People of this State, whereon and for which Perons may, in Pursuance of this Act, be indicted and convicted for the Offence aforesaid; *that is to say,* Being at any Time since the Ninth Day of *July,* in the Year of our Lord One Thousand Seven Hundred and Seventy-six, (the Day of the Declaration of the Independence of this State within the same) in any Part of the United States, not in the Power or Possession of the Fleets or Armies of the King of *Great-Britain,* and afterwards voluntarily withdrawing to any Place within the Power or Possession of the King of *Great-Britain,* his Fleets or Armies; or being apprehended by order of, or Authority from the Commander in Chief of the Armies of the said United States; or of or from the Provincial Congress, or Conventions or Committees thereof, or Councils of Safety of this State; or the Commissioners above mentioned, appointed for enquiring into, detecting and defeating all Conspiracies which may be formed in this State against the Liberties of *America;* or County, District, or Precinct Committees within this State; or by the Supreme Executive Authority of this State, and confined within certain Limits upon Engagement, by Parole or other wise, not to go beyond such Limits, and breaking such Engagements, and voluntarily escaping to any Place in the Power of the Fleets or Armies of *Great-Britain;* or being so confined as aforesaid, and afterwards permitted by proper Authority, to go to any Place in the Power of the Fleets or Armies of *Great-Britain,* upon Engagement to return within a certain given Time; and not returning within such Time, but afterwards remaining at any Place within the Power or Possession of the Fleets or Armies of *Great-Britain.*

Preamble with Respect to certain Persons within the Power of the Enemy.

X. *And whereas* divers Persons, Inhabitants and well affected Subjects of this State, at the Time of the Declaration of the Independence thereof, who had their fixed Residence in the Southern District of this State, were obliged, on the Invasion of the said District by the Enemy, to fly before their superior Force, into Parts of this, or some other or others of the said United States, and some of them having thereby abandoned all or the greatest Part of their Property, were so reduced as to have been respectively obliged, through absolute Necessity, and the Want of sufficient Habitations, and the necessary Means of Support and Subsistence, to return to their respective Places of Abode; and others of them, for the same Cause, having deserted their Habitations, and fled in Manner aforesaid, have for particular Reasons, been permitted, either by the Commander in Chief of the Armies of the said United States, or other lawful Authority, in the Places to which they respectively fled, so returned within the Power of the Enemy, where they also severally still do reside; *Be it therefore futher Enacted by the Authority aforesaid, and it is hereby provided,* That nothing in this Act contained, shall be construed to extend to or affect the said Persons, severally and respectively, or any or either of them, except such of them as since his, her or their Return to any place or Places within the Power of the Enemy, has or have done any Act or Thing, which in Judgment of Law would be construed, deemed and adjudged an Adherence to the Enemies of this State, and High Treason against the People thereof, had such Person or Persons respectively, voluntarily and freely, and without any such Cause as aforesaid, returned within the Power of the Enemy. In which Case, such Return within the Power of the Enemy, and such Act or Thing as aforesaid, shall in Judgment of Law, be construed, deemed, and is hereby declared to be adjudged an Adherence to the Enemies of the People of this State.

Exemptions in their Behalf.

XI. *And be it futher Enacted by the Arthority aforesaid, and it is hereby provided,* That no Conviction or Attainder, in Pursuance of this Act, shall be construed to exempt any Person or Persons from being apprehended, tried, convicted, attainted and executed for High Treason, according to the ordinary Course of Law.

No Attainder on this Law to exempt from Punishment in ordinary Course.

XII. *And be it further Enacted by the Authority aforesaid,* That all Conveyances and Assignments of any real or personal Estate, made or executed since the Ninth Day of *July,* in the Year of our Lord One Thousand Seven Hundred and Seventy-six, by any or either of the Persons, who are immediately convicted and attainted by this Act; or any or either of the Persons who shall be convicted or attainted in Pursuance of this Act; or any or either of the Persons who shall be convicted or attainted of High Treason, in the ordinary Course of Law, for Offences committed during the present War, shall be presumed to be fraudulent, and to have been made with Intent to prevent a Forfeiture of the Estates, by such Conveyances or Assignments

Conveyances since 9th *July*, 1776, presumed fraudulent.

respectively intended to be conveyed or assigned; and upon every Trial, wherein any such Conveyance or Assignment shall come in Question, the Burthen of the Proof shall lay upon the Person or Persons claiming under such Conveyance or Assignment; that the same was made and executed *bona fide,* for a valuable Consideration, and not with Intent to prevent a Forfeiture as aforesaid.

And Proof of their being otherwise to lay upon the Claimant.

Executory Devises & contingent Remainders, subject to Forfeiture.

XIII. *And be it further Enacted by the Authority aforesaid,* That all Titles, Estates and Interests, by executory Devise or contingent Remainder, claimed by any Person hereby, or by Virtue of this Law to be convicted; shall, on Conviction, be as fully forfeited to all Intents, Constructions and Purposes, in the Law whatsoever, to the People of this State, as any other Titles, Claims, Estates or Interests whatsoever.

And Lands and Rights of the Crown vested in the People of this State, and their Sovereignty and Seignory declared.

XIV. *And be it further Enacted by the Authority aforesaid,* That the absolute Property of all Messuages, Lands, Tenements and Hereditaments, and of all Rents, Royalties, Franchises, Prerogatives, Privileges, Escheats, Forfeitures, Debts, Dues, Duties and Services, by whatsoever Names respectively the same are called and known in the Law; and all Right and Title to the same, which next and immediately before the Ninth Day of *July,* in the Year of our Lord One Thousand Seven Hundred and Seventy-six, did vest in, or belong, or was, or were due to the Crown of *Great-Britain,* be, and the same, and each and every of them, hereby are declared to be, and ever since the said Ninth Day of *July,* in the Year of our Lord One Thousand Seven Hundred and Seventy-six, to have been, and for ever hereafter shall be vested in the People of this State, in whom the Sovereignty and Seignory thereof are and were united and vested, on and from the said Ninth Day of *July,* in the Year of our Lord one Thousand Seven Hundred and Seventy-six.

Commissioners to be appointed for the Sale of forfeited Estates, and how they are to proceed.

Amended and altered, 4th Sess. Ch. 13 and 51. 5th Sess. Ch. 45. 7th Sess. Ch. 64.

XV. *And be it further Enacted by the Authority aforesaid,* That the Person administring the Government of this State for the Time being, shall be, and he is hereby authorised and required, by and with the Advice and Consent of the Council of Appointment, to appoint, during the Pleasure of the said Council and Commission, under the Great Seal of this State, three Commissioners of Forfeitures, for each of the Great Districts of this State. That the said Commissioners, or a Majority of them, shall be, and hereby are authorised and required, from Time to Time, to sell and dispose of all real Estates within their respective Districts, forfeited or to be forfeited to the People of this State, at public Vendue, to the highest Bidder or Bidders; and in such Parcels as they shall from Time to Time think proper, first giving eight Weeks Notice of each Sale, in one or more of the public News-Papers in this State, containing a Description as to the Quantity, by Estimation, of the Lands or Tenements to be sold, the Situation thereof, and the Name or Names of the Person or Persons, by the Conviction and Attainder of whom the said

Lands or Tenements are deemed to have become forfeited; and to make, seal and deliver to the Purchaser or Purchasers respectively, good and sufficient Deeds and Conveyances, in the Law, to vest the same in them respectively, and their respective Heirs and Assigns, upon such Purchaser or Purchasers respectively producing such Receipt from the Treasurer, as is herein after mentioned. That every such Purchaser and Purchasers, shall by Virtue of such Deeds and Conveyances, respectively, be so vested in Title, Seisin and Possession of the Lands and Tenements so purchased, as to have and maintain in his, her or their Name or Names, any Action for Recovery thereof, or Damages relating thereto; any actual Seisin or Possession thereof, in any other Person or Persons, notwithstanding. That every such Deed and Conveyance, shall be deemed to operate as a Warranty from the People of this State, to the Purchaser or Purchasers respectively, and their respective Heirs and Assigns, for the Lands or Tenements thereby respectively, granted and conveyed, against all Claims, Titles and Incumbrances whatsoever; and such Purchaser or Purchasers respectively, and their respective Heirs and Assigns, shall in Case of Eviction, have such Remedy and Relief upon such Warranty, in such Manner as shall be more particularly provided for in such future Act or Acts of the Legislature, as are herein after mentioned. *Provided,* That the said Commissioners shall not be authorised to sell any Lands, in larger Parcels than the Quantity of five Hundred Acres in each Parcel; that no more than one Farm shall be included in one and the same Sale; and that the Sales shall be made in the County where the Lands or Tenements to be sold, respectively lie. *And provided further,* That nothing in this Law contained, shall be construed, deemed, esteemed or adjudged to authorise the Commissioners to be appointed by Virture hereof, to make Sale of any of the Lands, Messuages, Tenements or Hereditaments hereby forfeited, or by Virtue hereof to become forfeited, before or until the first Day of *October* next; and that all such Sales shall be, and the same hereby are wholly prohibited until that Day.

Powers given Commissioners by this Act repealed 7th Sess. Ch. 64. Sec. 54.

No Sales to be made before 1st October, 1780. Altered 3d Session Ch. 51.

XVI. *And whereas* it is impossible at present to form an Estimate of what will be a proper Compensation to the said Commissioners, for their Services and Expences in executing the Business hereby committed to them: *Be it therefore further Enacted by the Authority aforesaid,* That the public Faith of this State shall be, and hereby is pledged to the said Commissioners, for such Allowance and Compensation to them for their Services and Expences (besides the Expences of Surveyors, Clerks, and other incidental Charges) as shall hereafter by the Legislature, be deemed just and reasonable.

The Commissioners to be paid for their Services and Expences.

XVII. *And be it further Enacted by the Authority aforesaid,* That the Treasurer of this state shall be, and he is hereby authorised, out of the Monies which now are, or hereafter may

The Treasurer to advance 2000L. to the Commissioners of each District.

be in the Treasury, to advance to the said Commissioners for each District, a Sum not exceeding Two Thousand Pounds, to defray the Expence of the Business hereby committed to them.

XVIII. *And whereas* in many Instances, Lands, the Reversion or Remainder whereof is, or may become forfeited to this State, are possessed by Tenants who have, at considerable Expence, made or purchased the Improvements on the same, and which Tenants have constantly, uniformly and zealously, since the Commencement of the present War, endeavoured to defend and maintain the Freedom and Independence of the United States; *Be it therefore further Enacted by the Authority aforesaid,* That where Lands, the Reversion or Remainder whereof is hereby, or may become forfeited to the People of this State, shall be possessed by any Tenant of the Character above described, and who or whose Ancestor, Testator or Intestate, shall have made or purchased the Improvements on the same, they shall continue in Possession at their former Rents, and be at Liberty as heretofore, to transfer their Improvements, until the Fee Simple of the said Lands shall be sold, they paying their respective Rents, and the present Arrearages thereof in Money, equal to the current Prices of the Articles of Produce, in which their Rents were heretofore paid, into the Treasury of this State; if such Rents were reserved in Produce or if reserved in Money, then in so much Money, as will be equivalent to the Price of Wheat at Seven Shillings per Bushel; and that when the Fee Simple of the said Lands shall be sold by the Commissioners, to be appointed in Pursuance of this Act, they shall cause such Lands to be appraised by three Appraisers, at what shall be deemed the then present Value thereof, exclusive of the Improvements thereon, at the Time of appraising; That one of the said Appraisers shall be elected by the Commissioners, another by the Tenant claiming the Benefit intended by this Clause, and the third by the said other two Appraisers; That the said Appraisers, previous to the making of such Appraisment, shall each of them take an Oath, and which Oath the said Commissioners are herby authorised to administer, well and truly to appraise the Lands held by such Tenant, at what shall be deemed the then Value thereof, exclusive of the Improvements thereon; and upon Payment into the Treasury by such Tenant, of the Sum at which such Lands shall be so appraised, within three Months after the making of such Appraisment, together with all Arrearages of Rents then due thereon; the Commissioners shall convey the Lands so appraised to such Tenant, in like Manner as if such Lands had been sold at public Vendue, and such Tenant had appeared, and been the highest Bidder for the same; *Provided,* That no Person being a Tenant himself, or of Affinity or Consanguinity to the Tenant, requiring such Appraisement to be made, shall be an Appraiser.

Provision in Favor of Tenants of forfeited Lands.

XIX. AND in Order that the Commissioners may be enabled to determine, who are the proper Objects of the Benefit intended

How Tenants to avail themselves of the above Provision.

by the aforegoing Clause; *Be it further Enacted by the Authority aforesaid,* That no Tenant shall be entitled to such Benefit, unless he or she shall, within one Month after the same shall be required of him or her by the said Commissioners, produce to them a Certificate, to be subscribed by at least twelve reputable Inhabitants of the County, of known and undoubted Attachment to the American Cause, to be approved by the Commissioners, and which Inhabitants shall severally declare upon Oath, the Truth of the Matter by them certified, before a Justice of the Peace of the County, who is hereby authorised to administer such Oath, certifying, that such Tenent, hath constantly and uniformly, since the said ninth Day of *July*, One Thousand Seven Hundred and Seventy-six, demeaned himself or herself, as a Friend to the Freedom and Independence of the United States; and hath, as far forth as his or her Circumstances would admit, taken an active and decisive Part, to maintain and promote the same.

Memorandums in Writing to be made of all Sales.

XX. *And be it further Enacted by the Authority aforesaid,* That whenever the said Commissioners shall within their respective Districts, make Sale of any Lands, either at public Vendue, or upon such Appraisment as aforesaid, and the Commissioners and the Person or Persons to whom such Sale shall be made, have reciprocally subscribed a Memorandum or Note, in Writing, of such Sale; the Commissioners shall immediately thereupon, give to the Person or Persons, to whom such Sale shall be made, a Certificate therof, to contain the Sum for which the Lands purchased by such Person or Persons were sold; and if such Sale was made upon such Appraisment, then also of the Arrearages of Rent due on such Lands. That the said Person or Persons to whom such Cerificates shall be given, shall, within three Months from the Date thereof, pay into the Treasury of this State, the Sums in such Certificates respectively specified; and the Treasurer is hereby required and authorised to receive the same, and to give to the said Person or Perons paying, duplicate Receipts for the Monies by them respectively paid; and the several Persons to whom such Receipts shall be given, shall, upon their respectively producing and lodging with the said Commissioners one of the said Receipts, be entitled to Deeds and Conveyances for the Lands by them respectively purchased.

Commissioners to sue Purchasers for Non-performance of Contracts.

XXI. *And be it further Enacted by the Authority aforesaid,* That the Commissioners for the respective Districts, shall and may, in their own Names, commence and prosecute any Suit upon a Contract, for the Sale of any Estate against any Person or Persons who shall have subscribed such Note or Memorandum in Writing thereof as aforesaid; and all Damages which shall be recovered by the said Commissioners in such Suits, shall be by them paid into the Treasury of this State.

XXII. *And be it further Enacted by the Authority aforesaid,* That all Purchases made at such Vendues by the said Commis-

All Purchases made by, or for Commissioners, declared void.

sioners, or any or either of them, or by any other Person, to or for the Use of them, or any or either of them, shall be null and void; and that each Commissioner, before he enters upon the Execution of his Office, shall appear before one of the Judges of any of the Counties within the District for which such Commissioner shall be appointed, and take and subscribe the following Oath; which such Judge is hereby authorised and required to administer, *viz.*

Each Commissioner to take an Oath.

Form of the Oath.

I A. B. *appointed a Commissioner of Forfeitures, for the District, do solemnly and sincerely swear and declare, in the Presence of Almighty God, that I will faithfully and honestly execute the said Office, in such Manner as I shall conceive most for the Benefit and Advantage of the People of this State, according to the true Intent and Meaning of an Act, entitled,* An *Act* for the Forfeiture and Sale of the Estates of Persons who have adhered to the Enemies of this State, and for declaring the Sovereignty of the People of this State, in Respect of all Property within the same."

No Lands to be sold while in the Power of The Enemy.

XXIII. *And be it further Enacted by the Authority aforesaid, and it is hereby provided,* That the said Commissioners shall not be authorised to sell any Lands which at the Time of the Sale thereof, shall be within the Power of the Enemy, any Thing herein before mentioned notwithstanding.

The Treasurer in his Accounts of Monies arising by Sales to specify to whom the Estates respectively belonged.

XXIV. *And be it further Enacted by the Authority aforesaid,* That the Treasurer of this State shall, in his Accounts of the Monies arising by the Sales of forfeited Estates, specify the Names of the several Persons to whom the several Estates immediately before the Forfeiture thereof were deemed to belong, as the same shall appear from the Certificate of the Commissioners; *To the End,* That when the Legislature shall by future Act or Acts, to be passed for the Purpose, provide for the Payment of the Debts due from the said Persons respectively, the Amount of the Monies arising from the Sales of their respective Estates, may with the greater Ease be ascertained.

Forms of the several Proceedings on this Law.

XXV. *And be it further Enacted by the Authority aforesaid,* That the Forms of the several Proceedings to be had in Pursuance of this Act, and of the Deeds or Conveyances to be executed by the Commissioners to be appointed in Pursuance of this Act, shall be as follows, *that is to say,*

Form of the Notices by the Sheriff.

Form of Sheriff's Notice.

"State of *New-York,* fs. By Esq; Sheriff of the County of

WHEREAS at a Supreme Court of Judicature," *or* "Court of Oyer and Terminer and General Gaol Delivery," *or* "Court of General Sessions of the Peace," *or* "Court of Quarter Sessions of the Peace, (as the Case may be)—*(here insert the*

Name or Names of the Person or Persons indicted, with their respective Additions) was" *or* "were severally (as the Case may be) indicted for adhering to the Enemies of the People of this State. These are therefore to notify the said *(here insert the Name of the Person indicted)* if he" *or* "she (as the Case may be) shall, at the Expiration of the Time for that Purpose herein after limited, be in full Life; and all Persons claiming any Estate or Interest under him" *or* "her, (as the Case may be) if he" *or* "she (as the Case may be) shall, at the Expiration of the said Time be deceased, that unless he" *or* "she (as the Case may be) if in full Life as aforesaid, do personally appear in the Supreme Court of Judicature of this State, within the Time herein after limited, and traverse the said Indictment" *or* "Indictments, (as the Case may be) or if the said *(here insert the Name of the Person indicted)* shall be deceased; that unless some or one of the said several Persons so claiming an Estate or Interest as aforesaid, do personally, or if Feme Coverts, insane, or within Age respectively, do by their several and respective Barons, Guardians, or next Friends, respectively, appear in the said Supreme Court, on or before the fourth Day after the first Day of the second Term next succeeding the Day of the Date of this Notice, and traverse the said Indictment" *or* "Indictments, (as the Case may be) the said *(here insert the Name of the Person indicted)* will be adjudged if in full Life, guilty, or if deceased, to have been at the Time of his" *or* "her (as the Case may be) Death, guilty of the Offence" *or* "Offences (as the Case may be) charged against him" *or* "her (as the Case may be,) and that all and singular the real and personal Estate within this State, held or claimed by him" *or* "her (as the Case may be) if in full Life as aforesaid, or which were held or claimed by him" *or* "her, (as the Case may be) at the Time of his" *or* "her (as the Case may be) Death, (if deceased as aforesaid, will) be forfeited to the People of this State;" *or if more than one Person shall be indicted, then,* "These are therefore to notify such of the said several Persons who shall, at the Expiration of the Time for that Purpose herein after limited, be in full Life; and all Persons claiming any Estate or Interest, under such of the said Persons above named, who shall at the Expiration of the said Time be deceased; that unless they the said several Persons above named, who shall be so in full Life, do personally appear in the Supreme Court of this State, within the Time herein after limited, and traverse the Indictment" *or* "Indictments (as the Case may be) against them respectively; and that unless some or one of them the said several Persons, claiming any Estate or Interest as afore-said, do personally, or if Feme Coverts, insane, or within Age, do by their respective Barons, Guardians or next Friends, appear in the said Supreme Court, on or before the fourth Day after the first Day of the second Term next succeeding the Day of the Date of this Notice, and traverse the Indictment" *or* "Indictments (as the Case may be) against the Persons respectively, under whom they respectively so claim, they the said several Persons above named, will be adjudged, if in full Life, guilty, or if deceased, to have been at the Time of their Death respectively, guilty of the Offence" *or* "Offences (as the Case may be) charged against them respectively; and that all and singular the real and personal Estate within this State, held or claimed by such of the said Persons respectively who shall be in full Life as aforesaid, or which were held or claimed at the Time of their Death respectively, by such of the said Persons as shall be deceased, will be forfeited to the People of this State. Given under my Hand the Day of in the Year of the Independence of the said State, A. B. Sheriff."

The Form of a Record where Judgment shall be entered by Default.

Form of Record of Judgment by Default.

"*New-York,* Supreme Court, ss. Of the Term of *(here insert the Term in which Judgment shall be awarded)* in the Year of the Independence of this State.

BE IT REMEMBERED, That on the *(here insert the Day and Year when the Indictment was preferred into Court)* the Jurors of the People of this State, for the Body of the County of *(here insert the Name of the County where the Indictment was taken)* did upon their Oath present, that *(here insert the Residue of the Indictment, as far as the same shall relate to the Person or Persons against whom Judgment shall be entered)* and the said *(here insert the Name or Names of the Person or Persons charged in the Indictment, and against whom Judgment is to be entered)* having according to the Form, of the Act of the Legislature, entitled, "*An Act for the Forfeiture and Sale of the Estates of Persons who have adhered to the Enemies of this State, and for declaring the Sovereignty of the People of this State, in Respect to all Property within the same,*" been notified to appear and traverse the said Indictment, and not having appeared and traversed within the Time, and in the Manner, in and by the said Act limited and required, it is therefore considered, that the said *(here insert the Name or Names of the Person or Persons charged in the Indictment, and against whom Judgment is to be entered)* do forfeit," *or if more than one Person,* "severally forfeit all and singular the Estate, both real and personal, whether in Possession, Reversion or Remainder, held or claimed by him" *or* "her" *or* "them respectively (as the Case may be) within this State, to the People of this State."

Form of Record on a Trial.

Form of a Record where a Trial shall be had.

"*New-York,* Supreme Court, ss. Of the Term (and so on, as in the Case of a Record where Judgment shall be entered by Default, to the End of the Indictment) and the said *(here insert the Name of the Person who shall appear and traverse)* appearing here in Court in his own proper Person, on the *(here insert the Day of the Month when the Person shall appear in Court and traverse)* in this present Term, *(or if of a preceding Term, then)* in the Term of *(here insert the Term)* in the Year of the Independence of this State. And saith, that he is not guilty of the Offence" *or* "Offences (as the Case may be) in the said Indictment, charged against him" *or* "her, (as the Case may be) and of this he" *or* "she (as the Case may be) puts himself" *or* "herself" (as the Case may be) upon the Country, and who prosecutes for the People of this State in this Behalf, in like Manner, &c." *And so on, as nearly similar as may be, to the Form of a Record of a Trial, at the Bar of the Supreme Court, in a Case of Felony, without Benefit of Clergy.* That the Judgment, in Case of Conviction, shall be the same with the Form contained in the Form of the Record of a Judgment by Default.

Form of a general Verdict.

The Form of a General Verdict.

After the Word *Oath,* "do say that the said *(here insert the Name of the Person charged)* is guilty of the several Offences charged against him" *or* "her (as the Case may be) *or* not guilty of the several Offences charged against him" *or* "her (as the Case may be) *(or if guilty only of certain of the Offences charged in the Indictments, and not guilty of other, or others of them, then)* is not guilty of the Offence" *or* "the several Offences (as the Case may be) charged in the said Indictment to have been committed on *(then insert the Day and Year when the Offence or Offences* (as the Case may be) *is or are charged to have been committed)* but guilty of the Offence" *or* "Offences (as the Case may be) charged to have been committed on the *(here insert the Day and Year when the Offence or Offences* (as the Case may be) *of which the Person charged in the Indictment shall be convicted, were committed.)*

The Form of the Judgment shall be the same with the Form of the Judgment where Judgment shall be entered by Default.

Form of the Conveyance from the Commiffioners.

Form of Conveyance.

"THIS INDENTURE, made the Day of in the Year of the Independence of the State of *New-York,* and in the Year of our Lord between Esquires, Commissioners of Forfeitures, for the District, appointed in Pursuance of an Act of the Legislature of the said State, entitled, *An* Act *for the Forfeiture and Sale of the Estates of Persons who have adhered to the Enemies of this State, and for declaring the Sovereignty of the People of this State, in Respect to all Property within the same,"* of the one Part, and of the other Part; Witnesseth That the said Commissioners, by Virtue of the Power and Authority to them, in and by the said Act granted, and for, and in Consideration of the Sum of by the said paid into the Treasury of the said State, have granted, bargained, sold, enfeoffed and confirmed; and by these Presents do grant, bargain, sell, enfeoff and confirm, unto the said and Heirs and Assigns, all *(here describe the Lands or Tenements to be conveyed)* and all and singular the Estate, Right, Title and Interest, whether in Possession, Reversion, or Remainder of, in or to the said Premises, which, in Consequence of any Conviction or Attainder, is become forfeited, attached, or vested in, or to the People of the said State. TO HAVE AND TO HOLD, all and singular the said Premises, hereby granted, bargained, sold, enfeoffed and confirmed, with the Appurtenances, unto the said and Heirs and Assigns, to the only proper Use and Behoof of the said and Heirs and Assigns forever. In Witness whereof, the said Parties to these Presents have hereunto interchangeably set their Hands and Seals, the Day and Year first above written."

Forms of Proceedings not hereby particularly prescribed, to be similar to those in Cases of Felony, without Benefit of Clergy.

AND that all the Forms of Proceedings in Prosecutions, for the Offence aforesaid, to be had in Pursuance of this Act, other than such as are hereby otherwise specially directed, shall be as nearly as may be, similar to the Forms of the Proceedings in Cases of Felony without Benefit of Clergy, except, that the Word or Words "Offence" *or* "Offences" (as the Case may be) shall be used instead of the Word or Words "Felony" *or* "Felonies;" and that where a Traverse shall be put in by any Person or Persons, claiming any Estate or Interest under a Person deceased as aforesaid, all and singular the Proceedings and Processes, shall, notwithstanding, be of the same Form, as if the respective Persons, charged in the several Indictments, had been severally in full Life, and had in their own respective proper Persons, appeared and traversed; and for Want of such Traverse, as if such Person had made Default in full Life.

On Traverse by the Representatives of Persons deceased, Proceedings shall be the same as if the Person was living.

Representatives on Affidavit of Interest, to be admitted to traverse,

XXVI. *And be it further Enacted by the Authority aforesaid,* That each and every Person or Persons, claiming an Estate or Interest under any Person deceased, shall and may, upon Affidavit of such Claim, and of the Death of the Person, under whom such Claim shall be made, to be read and filed in Court, be admitted to traverse the Indictments against the Persons under whom they so respectively claim. That in every Case of such Traverse as last aforesaid, no Trial shall be had thereon, until after the Expiration of the Time herein before limited for putting in such Traverse. That where two or more Persons shall appear at one and the same Time, and produce such Affidavit, and

And where two or more separately offer to traverse, the Court may compel them to join.

thereupon apply to be admitted to traverse, the Court may compel such Persons to join in the Traverse; and that where any Person or Persons, so claiming as aforesaid, shall have been admitted to traverse, and shall have traversed accordingly, and any other Person or Persons shall afterwards apply to be admitted to traverse, the Person or Persons so afterwards applying, having respectively produced such Affidavit of a Claim as aforesaid, shall upon the Trial of such Traverse, be permitted to employ Counsel, produce Witnesses, sue forth Subpœnas, for the Attendance of Witnesses, cross examine the Witnesses on the Part of the State, and do every other Act and Thing, in and about a Defence, in like Manner, and as fully as the Person or Persons by whom the Traverse shall have been put in.

After Traverse any other Person applying on Affidavit, may be admitted to join in the Defence.

[Source: New York State, *Laws of the State of New York. . .from the First to the Twelfth Sessions* (New York: Printed by Hugh Gaine, according to an act of the legislature, 1789), Vol.1, pp. 39–51. *New York University Law Library*.]

APPENDIX III

Prayer for Relief

A. Oneida Complaint (First Amended Complaint [with addition of inadvertant omissions], *Oneida Indian Nation of N.Y.* v. *State of N.Y.*, 78-CV-104), pp. 131–2:

WHEREFORE, plaintiffs pray that this Court:

1. Order that this action shall be maintained as a class action pursuant to Rule 23 (b) (1) or Rule 23 (b) (3);

2. Declare that plaintiffs are the owners of and have the exclusive right of possession of every portion of the subject lands claimed or held by any defendant or member of the defendant class; or, in the alternative, declare that plaintiffs have a reversionary interest or beneficial interest in that part of the subject lands conveyed to defendant State of New York in 1788 and order defendant State of New York to specifically perform its obligations under its "treaty" of 1788 with the Oneida Nation.

3. Restore plaintiffs to immediate possession of all portions of the subject lands claimed by any defendant or member of the defendant class;

4. Award plaintiffs the fair rental value for each portion of the subject land claimed by any defendant or member of the defendant class for the entire period of plaintiffs' dispossession;

5. Award plaintiffs the costs and disbursements of this action and attorney's fees;

6. Award plaintiffs interest for the entire period of plaintiffs' dispossession on the fair rental value determined for each portion of the subject land claimed by any defendant or member of the defendant class;

7. Award plaintiffs all tolls heretofore collected by the New York State Thruway Authority for passage over Oneida lands, including all tolls collected until judgment is entered herein;

8. Declare plaintiffs' hunting, fishing and other rights under the 1788 transaction, in the event that the Court finds that the 1788 transaction is not void;

9. Award plaintiffs five hundred million dollars as compensatory and punitive damages for the loss of possession of the subject lands in violation of the Constitution and laws of the United States and pursuant to 42 U.S.C. 1983.

10. Award such other and further relief as the court deems just.

Prayer for Relief

B. Sample Version for an Hypothesized Wickham Complaint:

WHEREFORE, plaintiffs pray that this Court:

1. Declare that plaintiffs and the residual heirs of Parker Wickham (d. 1785) are the owners of and have the exclusive right of possession to the subject lands claimed or held by any defendant; or declare that plaintiffs have a beneficial interest in the subject lands;

2. Restore plaintiffs and other qualifying heirs to immediate possession of the subject lands claimed by any defendant;

3. Award plaintiffs their portion of the fair rental value of the subject lands claimed by any defendant for the entire period of plaintiffs' and their lineal predecessors' dispossession;

4. Award plaintiffs the costs and disbursements of this action and attorneys' fees;

5. Award plaintiffs interest for the entire period of plaintiffs' and their lineal predecessors' dispossession on the fair rental value determined for their portion of the subject lands claimed by any defendant;

6. Award plaintiffs ten million dollars as compensatory and punitive damages for the loss of possession of the subject lands in violation of the Constitution and laws of the United States and pursuant to 42 U.S.C. sec. 1983.

7. Award such other and further relief as the Court deems just.

SELECTED BIBLIOGRAPHY

Attainder

PRIMARY SOURCES

Commonwealth of Massachusetts. Massachusetts Acts and Laws. "Act To Confiscate the Estates of Certain Notorious Conspirators." Chap. IX, April 30, 1779.

Great Britain. Statutes at Large. "Acte Whereby Divers Offences Be Made High Treason." 26 Hen. VIII, Chap. 13 (1535).

New-York Historical Society, New York City. "Abstracts of Sales of Forfeited Lands in the Southern District upon Locations."

New York. Laws of New York. "An Act for the Forfeiture and Sale of the Estates of Persons Who Have Adhered to the Enemies of This State. . " 3rd sess. Ch. 25, Oct. 22, 1779.

New York State Archives. Revolutionary Manuscripts, Commissioners of Forfeiture: Southern District.

New York State. *Assembly Journal.*

New York State. *Senate Journal.*

Street, Alfred B. *The Council of Revision of the State of New York.* Albany: William Gould, 1859.

Suffolk County Clerk's Office. "Conveyances in Forfeiture, 1784."

U.S. Congress. "An Act To Suppress Insurrection, To Punish Treason and Rebellion, To Seize and Confiscate the Property of Rebels, and for Other Purposes." 37th Cong., Ch. 195, July 17, 1862; pp. 589–591.

U.S. *Congressional Globe.* 37th Cong., 2d sess., June 23-July 17, 1862. (Appendix, pp. 106–7, 115, 122).

SECONDARY SOURCES

Blackstone, William. *Commentaries on the Laws of England.* 4th edition. Dublin: Printed for John Exshaw. . . , 1771.

Chapin, Bradley. *The American Law of Treason.* Seattle: University of Washington Press, 1964.

———. "The Law of Treason During the American Revolution, 1765-1783." Unpublished Ph.D. dissertation, Cornell University (Olin Library), 1951.

"The Constitutional Prohibition of Bills of Attainder: A Waning Guaranty of Judicial Trial." *Yale Law Journal* (63) 1954, p. 844 *et seq.*

Goebel, Julius, ed. *The Law Practice of Alexander Hamilton.* New York: Columbia University Press, 1964.

Kent, James. *Commentaries on American Law*. 11th edition. Boston: Little, Brown, & Co., 1867.

Story, Joseph. *Commentaries on the Constitution of the United States*. 5th edition. Boston: Little, Brown & Co., 1891.

Wilson, William D. *Attainder of Treason and Confiscation of the Property of Rebels*. Albany: Weed, Parsons & Co., printers, 1863.

CASE LAW

Avery v. *Everett,* 110 N.Y. 326 (1888).

Bigelow v. *Forrest,* 9 Wall. (U.S.) 350 (1869).

Calder v. *Bull,* 3 Dall. (U.S.) 389 (1798).

Catlin v. *Jackson,* 8 Johns. Rep. (N.Y.) 555 (1811).

Cummings v. *Missouri,* 4 Wall. (U.S.) 323 (1870).

Fisher v. *Harnden,* 9 Fed. Cas. No. 4,819 [1 Paine, 55] 129 (1812).

Inglis v. *Trustees of the Sailor's Snug Harbour,* 3 Pet. (28 U.S.) 99 (1830).

Jackson v. *Catlin,* 2 Johns. Rep. (N.Y.) 248 (1807).

Jackson ex dem. St. Croix v. *Sands,* 2 Johns. Rep. (N.Y.) 271 (1801).

Jackson ex dem. Williams et al. v. *Stokes and Thompson,* 3 Johns Rep. (N.Y.) 151 (1808).

McFarran v. *Ward,* Parchment Rolls 147 K8 (1786), New York County, Hall of Records.

M'Ilvane v. *Coxe's Lessee,* 4 Cranch (8 U.S.) 209 (1808).

Platner v. *Sherwood,* 6 Johns. Ch. (N.Y.) 128 (1822).

Republica v. *Gordan,* 1 Dall. (1 U.S.) 233 (1788).

Smith v. *Maryland,* 6 Cranch (U.S.) 297 (1810).

U.S. v. *Lovett,* 328 U.S. 315, 317 (1945).

Wallach et al. v. *Van Riswick,* 92 U.S. 210 (1875).

Estates Tail

PRIMARY SOURCES

Great Britain. Statutes at Large. "De Donis Conditionalibus." Westm. 2, 13 Edw. 1, Ch. 1, sec. 2.

The Memorial of William Pepperell, New York Public Library, MS Div., American Loyalists, Audit Office Transcripts, Calendar of Original Memorials. . . , Vol. 2, p. 525 *et seq*.

SECONDARY SOURCES

American Law Institute. *Restatement of the Law of Property*. St. Paul: American Law Institute, 1936.

Aron, Harold G. *Aron's Digest of New York Real Property Law*. New York: Matthew Bender & Co., 1923.

Chitty, Henry. *A Treatise of the Law of Descents*. London: Joseph Butterworth & Son, 1825.

Foster, Michael. *A Report of Some Proceedings on the Commission for the Trial of the Rebels in the Year 1746, in the County of Surrey and of Other Crown Cases. . .* 2d edition. Dublin: James Moore, 1791.

Plucknett, T.F.T. *Legislation of Edward I.* Oxford: Clarendon Press. 1949.

Powell, Richard R. *The Law of Real Property*. New York: Matthew Bender, 1977.

Tiffany, Herbert Z. *The Law of Real Property*. 2d edition. Chicago: Callaghan and Co., 1920.

Washburn, Emory. *A Treatise on the American Law of Real Property* 3d edition. Boston: Little, Brown, and Co., 1868.

Williams, Joshua. *Principles of the Law of Real Property*. 13th edition. London: H. Sweet, 1880.

Wooddeson, Richard. *A Systematical View of the Laws of England*. London: Printed for Thomas Payne, 1792.

CASE LAW

Borland v. *Dean*, Fed. Cas. No. 1,660; p. 908 [4 Mason, 174] (1826).

Hazzard v. *Hazzard*, 29 Del. 94; 6 Boyce (1916).

Hinchman, Denn v. *Clark*, 1 N.J. Law (Coxe) 360 (1795).

Van Rensselaer v. *Kearney*, 11 How. (U.S.) 314 (1850).

Wendell v. *Crandell*, 1 Comstock (N.Y.) 493 (1848).

Parker Wickham–Suffolk County–Enemy Occupied Territory

PRIMARY SOURCES

Akerly, Lucy D., comp. "Wickham–Paine." *New York Genealogical and Biographical Record.* (32) July, 1901. p. 137.

Clinton, George. *Public Papers of George Clinton, First Governor of New York, 1777–1795, 1801–1804*. Edited by Hugh Hastings and J.A. Holden. 10 vols. New York and Albany: State of New York, 1899-1914.

Connecticut. General Assembly. *Public Records of the State of Connecticut, 1778–80*. Edited by Charles J. Hoadly. Hartford: Press of the Case, Lockwood & Brainard Co., 1895.

Davies, K.G., ed. *Documents of the American Revolution, 1770–1783*. Dublin: Irish Academic Press, c. 1976.

Force, Peter, ed. *American Archives*. 9 vols. Washington, D.C.: Prepared and published under authority of an act of Congress, 1837-53.

Goshen Public Library, Goshen, N.Y. William Wickham Papers.

Griffin, Augustus. *Griffin's Journal*. Orient, L.I., N.Y.: By the author, 1857.

Hall, Charles S. *The Life and Letters of Samuel Holden Parsons*. Binghamton, N.Y.: Otseningo Pub. Co., 1905.

Hamilton, Alexander. *The Papers of Alexander Hamilton*. Edited by Harold C. Syrett. New York: Columbia University Press, 1962.

Harris, Edward D., trans. "Long Island Epitaphs." Vol. 3. New York Genealogical and Biographical Society, N.Y.; 1885. [Bound manuscript.]

Hempstead, Joshua. *Diary of Joshua Hempstead of New London, Connecticut,*

1711-1758. ("Collections of the New London County Historical Society," Vol. 1). New London, Conn.: New London County Historical Society, 1901.

Jay, John. *John Jay, the Making of a Revolutionary: Unpublished Papers 1745-1780*. Edited by Richard B. Morris. New York: Harper & Row, c. 1975.

Jones, Thomas. *History of New York During the Revolutionary War*. Edited by Edward F. DeLancey. 2 vols. New York: New-York Historical Society, 1879.

Lincoln, Charles Z. *The Constitutional History of New York*. Rochester, N.Y.: The Lawyers Cooperative Publishing Co., 1906.

London. Public Record Office. "Journal of H.M. Sloop *Swan*, Captain James Ayscough." Admiralty 51/960, (1921).

Long Island Historical Society, Brooklyn, N.Y. Landon Papers.

Mango, Karin N., comp. *The Long Island Historical Society Calendar of Manuscripts: 1763-1783*. [Brooklyn]: L.I.H.S., c. 1980.

Mather, Frederick G., ed. *New York in the Revolution as Colony and State: Supplement*. Albany: Oliver A. Quayle, 1901.

Maxwell, William Q. *A Portrait of William Floyd, Long Islander*. Setauket, L.I.: Society for the Preservation of Long Island Antiquities, 1956.

Museums at Stony Brook, Stony Brook, L.I. Military Records.

New York. *Calendar of Council Minutes, 1668-1783*. New York State Library, Bulletin 58, History 6. Albany: University of the State of New York, 1902.

———. *Calendar of Historical Manuscripts Relating to the War of the Revolution in the Office of the Secretary of State*. 2 vols. Albany: Weed, Parsons, and Co., 1868.

———. *Journals of the Provincial Congress, Provincial Convention, Committee of Safety, and Council of Safety of the State of New York, 1775-1776-1777*. 2 vols. Albany: Thurlow Weed, 1842.

New York City. *Abstract of Wills on File in the Surrogate's Office, City of New York*. Collections of the New-York Historical Society. 15 vols. New York: 1893-1913.

New York County Surrogate's Court, Hall of Records, Record Department (Room 402), New York City. New York Wills.

New-York Historical Society, New York City. "Declaration of Dependence."

New York Public Library, Annex Division, New York City. Wick-Blachly-Colles Papers.

New York Public Library, Manuscript Division, New York City. American Loyalists. Transcripts of the Manuscript Books and Papers of the Commission of Enquiry into the Losses and Services of the American Loyalists . . . preserved amongst the Audit Office Records in the Public Record Office of England, 1783-1790. 60 vols.

———. British Headquarters Papers, Calendar. Transcript of the Historical Manuscripts Commission, *Report on American Manuscripts in the Royal Institution of Great Britain*. Vol. 4. London: H.M.S.O., 1904.

———. Brookhaven, L.I., Committee of Safety, etc., Minutes 1775-1776. Copy of a manuscript "found in a garret in New Haven in 1898 after the death of the widow of Rev. Smith Dayton, who was a son of Ebenezer Dayton." [Photostat.]

———. Calendar of the Original Memorials, Vouchers, and Other Papers deposited with the Commission of Enquiry into the Losses and Services of the American Loyalists . . . preserved Amongst the Audit Office Records in the Public Record

Office, London, 1783-1790. 6 vols.

New York State Archives, Albany, N.Y. Andrew Elliot Papers.

O'Callaghan, Edmund B. *Calendar of New York Colonial Commissions, 1680-1770.* ("John Divine Jones Fund Series of Histories and Memoirs," Vol. 7.) New York: New-York Historical Society, 1929.

———. *The Documentary History of the State of New York.* Albany: Weed, Parsons & Co., 1850.

O'Callaghan, Edmund B., and Fernow, Berthold, eds. *Documents Relative to the Colonial History of the State of New York.* 15 vols. Albany: Weed, Parsons, and Co., 1853-87.

Ritchie, Carson I.A., ed. "A Diary of the Revolutionary War." In: *Narratives of the Revolution in New York.* (Collections of the New-York Historical Society, the John Watts DePeyster Publication Fund Series, LXXXV.) New York: New-York Historical Society, 1975.

Salmon Records, 1696-1811. Edited by William A. Robbins. New York: New York Genealogical and Biographical Society, 1918.

Schaukirk, Ewald Gustav. *Occupation of New York City by the British.* Reprint from *Pennsylvania Magazine of History and Biography,* Vol. 10, 1886, p. 418. New York: New York Times and Arno Press, c. 1969.

Scott, Kenneth. "Absentee Patriots from British-Occupied Suffolk County, L.I., 1778." *New York Genealogical and Biographical Record* (107), 1976, pp. 73–78.

———. "Suffolk County, Long Island, New York, 1778 Census." *National Genealogical Society Quarterly.* Dec. 1975; pp. 276–282.

Scott, Kenneth, comp. *Rivington's New York Newspaper, Excerpts from a Loyalist Press, 1773-1783.* New York: New-York Historical Society, 1973.

Smith, Josiah. "Diary of Colonel Josiah Smith, from July 23 to September 7, 1776." Long Island Historical Society, Brooklyn, N.Y. ("Copied from the original in possession of Mr. Conklin Havens, East Moriches, Long Island, and contributed to the MAGAZINE by Mr. W.T. Avery.") [Typewritten.]

Smith, William. *Historical Memoirs . . . of William Smith, Historian of the Province of New York. . .* [March 16, 1763-July 25, 1778]. Edited by William H.W. Sabine. 2 vols. New York: Colburn and Tegg, 1956-58.

Smithtown Historical Society, Smithtown, L.I. "Inhabitants of Smithtown v. King George III. Blydenburgh Manuscript." Copy of original described as being an old manuscript account book owned by Vail Blydenburgh.

Society for the Preservation of Long Island Antiquities, Setauket, L.I. Richard Floyd Papers.

Southampton, L.I. *Minutes of the Board of Trustees, Town of Southampton.*

———. *Southampton Town Records.*

Southold, L.I. *Southold Town Records.*

Stevens, Benjamin Franklin. *Facsimiles of Manuscripts in European Archives Relating to America, 1773-1783.* 24 vols. Reprinted from the edition of 1898, London. Wilmington, Del.: Mellifont Press, [1970].

Suffolk County Clerk's Office, Riverhead, L.I. Common Pleas Minutes.

———. General Sessions Minutes.

Tallmadge, Benjamin. *Memoir of Colonel Benjamin Tallmadge.* Edited by Henry Phelps Johnston. New York: Gillies Press, 1904.

U.S. Congress. *Journals of the Continental Congress, 1774-1789.* Edited by Worthington C. Ford from original records in the Library of Congress. 34 vols. Washington, D.C.: U.S. Government Printing Office, 1904-37.

U.S. House of Representatives. *The Revolutionary Diplomatic Correspondence of the United States*. Edited by Francis Wharton. Washington, D.C.: Government Printing Office, 1889.

Washington, George, Pres. U.S. *George Washington Papers*. Presidential Papers Microfilm. Washington, D.C.: Library of Congress, 1961.

———. *The Writings of George Washington from the Original Manuscript Sources, 1745-1799*. Edited by John C. Fitzpatrick. 39 vols. Washington, D.C.: U.S. Government Printing Office, 1931-44.

Webb, J. Watson. *Reminiscences of Gen'l Samuel B. Webb*. New York: Globe Stationery & Printing Co., 1852.

Wickham, J. Parker. Parker Wickham Papers.

William Floyd Estate, Mastic Beach, L.I. Fiske Papers. (Photostats of originals.)

———. William Floyd Papers.

NEWSPAPERS

Connecticut Gazette; and the Universal Intelligencer
New-York Gazette and the Weekly Mercury (Gaines)
New-York Journal, and the General Advertiser (Holt)
New-York Packet (Loudon)
Royal Gazette (Rivington)

SECONDARY SOURCES

Bailey, Paul, ed. *Long Island, a History of Two Great Counties: Nassau and Suffolk*. New York: Lewis Historical Publishing Co., 1949.

Countryman, Edward. *A People in Revolution: The American Revolution and Political Society in New York, 1760-1790*. ("The Johns Hopkins University Studies in Historical and Political Science," Ninety-ninth Series, 1981) Baltimore: The Johns Hopkins University Press, c. 1981.

Craven, Charles E. *History of Mattituck, Long Island, N.Y.* Mattituck, N.Y.: By the author, 1906.

Flick, Alexander Clarence. *Loyalism in New York During the American Revolution*. New York: Columbia University Press, 1901.

Frost, Josephine C., comp. *Ancestors of James Wickham and His Wife Cora Prudence Billard*. Brooklyn, N.Y.: Privately printed, 1935.

Holbrook, Dwight. "Reconstructing the River Head." New York, [1982]. (Typewritten.)

Jefferson, Wayland. *Cutchogue, Southold's First Colony*. New York: 1940.

Jensen, Merrill. *The New Nation: A History of the United States During the Confederation, 1781-1789*. New York: Alfred Knopf, 1967.

Koke, Richard J. *Accomplice in Treason: Joshua Hett Smith and the Arnold Conspiracy*. New York: New-York Historical Society, 1973. (The John Divine Jones Fund Series of Histories and Memoirs, XIV.)

Maggee, J. Francis. "Fanning History on Tombstone." *Long Island Forum* (9) Dec., 1946; p. 241.

———. "The Formative Years of Riverhead." *Riverhead News*. March 19, 1948, p. 9; Arpil 2, 1948, p. 4.

Mather, Frederic Gregory. *Refugees of 1776 from Long Island to Connecticut*. Albany, N.Y.: J.B. Lyon Co., printers, 1913.

Onderdonk, Henry, Jr. *Revolutionary Incidents of Suffolk and Kings Counties*. New York: Leavitt & Co., 1849.

Osborne, Chester G. "Thomas Fanning of Bellport." *Long Island Forum* (May 1966), p. 50.

Overton, Albert G. *Plunderers from Across the Sound*. Florissant, Mo.: Micro-Records Publishing Co., c. 1980.

Peckham, Howard H., ed. *The Toll of Independence*. Chicago, Ill.: University of Chicago Press, c. 1974.

Pelletreau, William. *A History of Long Island*. New York: Lewis Publishing Co., 1903.

Pennypacker, Morton. *General Washington's Spies on Long Island and in New York*. Brooklyn: Long Island Historical Society, 1939.

Reilly, John Thomas. "The Confiscation and Sale of the Loyalist Estates and Its Effect upon the Democratization of Landholding in New York State." (University Microfilms 74-25, 123) (1974).

Ritcheson, Charles R. *Aftermath of Revolution: British Policy Toward the United States, 1783-1795*. Dallas, Texas: Southern Methodist University Press, c. 1969.

Sabine, Lorenzo. *Biographical Sketches of Loyalists of the American Revolution with an Historical Essay*. 2 vols. Port Washington, N.Y., 1966.

Sabine, William H.W. *Murder, 1776 and Washington's Policy of Silence*. New York: Theo Gaus' Sons, Inc., 1973.

Snow, Freeman. *International Law*. 2d edition. Washington, D.C.: G.P.O., 1898.

Stokes, I.N. Phelps. *The Iconography of Manhattan Island, 1498-1909*. 6 vols. New York: Robert H. Dodd, 1915-28.

Story, Joseph. *Commentaries on the Conflict of Laws*. 5th edition. Boston: Little, Brown & Co., 1857.

Vail, R.W.G. "Loyalist Declaration of Dependence." *New-York Historical Society Quarterly*. (31, no. 2) April 1947; p. 68.

Van Tyne, Claude H. *The Loyalists in the American Revolution*. New York: MacMillan Co., 1902.

Wheaton, Henry. *Elements of International Law*. 8th edition. Boston: Little, Brown & Co., 1866.

Wines, Virginia. *West from Canoe Place*. Riverhead, N.Y.: Suffolk County Historical Society, 1979.

Yoshpe, Harry B. *The Disposition of Loyalist Estates in the Southern District of New York*. New York: AMS Press, 1967.

CASE LAW

The Amy Warwick, 1 Fed. Cas. No. 342 [2 Spr. 143; 24 Law Rep. 494] 808 (1862).

Davis v. *Police Jury of Concordia*, 9 How. (50 U.S.) 280 (1850).

De Lima v. *Bidwell*, 182 U.S. 1 (1900).

The Fama, Great Brit., High Court of Admiralty, 1804 (5 C. Rob. 106).

Jackson v. *White*, 20 Johns. Rep. 313 (N.Y.) (1822).

Pennoyer v. *Neff*, 95 U.S. 714 (1877).

Respublica v. *Chapman,* 1 Dall. (U.S.) 53 (1781).
Shanks v. *Dupont,* 3 Pet. (28 U.S.) 242 (1830).
U.S. v. *Rice,* 17 Wheat. (U.S.) 254 (1819).

Treaties

PRIMARY SOURCES

Bevans, Charles I. *Treaties and Other International Agreements of the United States of America, 1776-1949.* Washington, D.C.: Government Printing Office, 1974. (Dept. of State Pub. 8761.)

Great Britain. Parliament. *Parliamentary Register.* Vol. 26 (1782-1783), pp. 228-367.

Miller, Hunter, ed. *Treaties and Other International Acts of the United States of America.* (Vol. 2: 1776-1818). Washington, D.C.: U.S. Government Printing Office, 1931. (Pub. of Dept. of State, No. 175.)

New York Public Library, Manuscript Division, New York City. Bancroft transcripts of: Great Britain, Peace Commissioners, Correspondence. (Lansdowne MSS)

U.S. Congress. *American State Papers. Documents, Legislative and Executive, of the Congress of the United States, from the 1st Sess. of the First to the 3rd Sess. of the 13th Congress (1789-1815).* Washington, D.C.: Gales & Seaton, 1832.

———. *Papers of the Continental Congress, 1774-1789.* ("National Archives Microfilm Publications.") Washington, D.C.: National Archives *et al.,* 1958-1959.

SECONDARY SOURCES

Coxe, Brinton. *An Essay on Judicial Power and Unconstitutional Legislation.* Philadelphia, Pa.: Kay and Brother, 1893.

Crandall, Samuel B. *Treaties: Their Making and Enforcement.* 2d edition. Washington, D.C.: John Byrne & Co., 1916.

Haskins, George, and Johnson, Herbert A. *Foundations of Power: John Marshall, 1801-1815.* Vol. 2 of *History of the Supreme Court of the United States.* New York: Macmillan, c. 1981.

Kettner, James H. *The Development of American Citizenship, 1608-1870.* Chapel Hill, N.C.: University of North Carolina Press, c. 1978.

———. "Subjects or Citizens? A Note on British Views Respecting the Legal Effects of American Independence." *Virginia Law Review,* (LXII) 1976; pp. 945-967.

Moore, John Bassett, ed. *Arbitration of Claims for Compensation for Losses and Damages Resulting from Lawful Impediments to the Recovery of Pre-War Debts.* Vol. 3 (Mod. Ser.) of *International Adjudications, Ancient and Modern.* Edited by John Bassett Moore. New York: Oxford University Press, 1931.

Morris, Richard B. *The Peacemakers.* New York: Harper & Row, c. 1965.

Vattel, M. De. *The Law of Nations or, the Principles of the Law of Nature Applied to the Conduct and Affairs of Nations and Sovereigns.* Dublin: Luke White, 1792.

CASE LAW

Board of County Commissioners . . . v. *U.S., 308 U.S. 343 (1939).*
Clark v. *Allen,* 331 U.S. 503 (1946).
De Tenorio v. *McGowan,* 510 F.2d 92 (1975).
Fairfax v. *Hunter,* 7 Cranch (U.S.) 604 (1812).
Gordon v. *Holiday,* Fed. Cas. No. 5,610 [1 Wash. C.C. 285] (1805), 10 Fed. Cas., pp. 799-800.
Har[n]den v. *Fisher,* 1 Wheat. (U.S.) 301 (1816).
Hauenstein v. *Lynham,* 100 U.S. 483 (1879).
Henfield's Case, 11 Fed. Cas. No. 6,360 [Whart. St. Tr. 49] 1099 (1793).
Higginson v. *Mein,* 4 Cranch (U.S.) 416 (1808).
Karnuth v. *U.S.,* 279 U.S. 229 (1928).
Oneida County, N.Y. v. *Oneida Indian etc.,* 105 S. Ct. 1245 (1985).
Oneida Indian Nation of N.Y. v. *State of N.Y.,* 691 F. 2d 1070 (1982).
Orr v. *Hodgson,* 4 Wheat. (17 U.S.) 453 (1819).
Owings v. *Norwood's Lessee,* 5 Cranch (9 U.S.) 344 (1809).
Palila v. *Hawaii Dept. of Land & Natural Resources,* 471 F. Supp. 985 (1979).
Rutgers v. *Waddington,* Mayor's Court Minutes (August 17, 1784) 170, New York Co., Hall of Records.
Society for the Propagation of the Gospel v *Town of New-Haven,* 8 Wheat. (21 U.S.) 464 (1823).
Strother v. *Lucas,* 12 Pet. (37 U.S.) 410 (1838).
Ware v. *Hylton,* 3 Dall. (U.S.) 237 (1796).

INDEX

This Indenture

in the Ninth Year of the Independence of the State of New-York, and in the Year of Our

Esquires, Commissioners of Forfeitures for the Southern District of the said State, appointed in Pur

Estates within this State, and for other Purposes therein mentioned," passed the Twelfth Day of M

Suffolk County

of the other Part, **WITNESSETH** That the said *Isaac Stoutenburgh* and *Philip Van Cortla*

and in Consideration of the Sum of Nine hundred pounds lawful money

to them in Hand paid by the said Nathanel Norton

Enfeoffed and Confirmed, and by these Presents **DO** Grant, Bargain, Sell, Enfeoff and Confirm

and to his Heirs and Assigns, **ALL** that Farm of Land and Meadow

of New York in seperate pieces on the North and South

by the Lands of Jonathan Jennings, Silas Moore and

Nathan Goldsmith and Southerly by the said Highway

The Lands Southerly of the Highway is Bounded Easterly by

Creek Southerly by the Bay Westerly by the Lands of Daniel

Thomas Wickham and said Highway Containing about

of this State by Parker Wickham.

And all and singular the Estate, Right, Title and Interest, whether in Possession, Reversion or Remai

to, or vested in the People of the said State, **To HAVE and to HOLD** all and singular the said P

Nathanel Norton and to his Heirs an

and his Heirs and Assigns forever. **In Witness whereof,**

Sealed and Delivered in the Presence of us

Be it Remembered, *That on the* Day

personally came and appeared before me

the above-named Isaac Stoutenburgh *and* Philip Van C

had executed the above Indenture by sealing and deliverin

therein mentioned; and I having examined the said Inden

DEED TO WICKHAM'S NECK AND THE NORTH SIDE
issued by the New York State
Commissioners of Forfeiture in 1784
Cutchogue-New Suffolk Historical Council
Photograph by Harvey Weber